AF529233

SCHOOL EDUCATION MANAGEMENT

SCHOOL EDUCATION MANAGEMENT

Edited by
Vijaya Kumari Kaushik
S.R. Sharma

S.D. INSTITUTE OF RURAL TECHNOLOGY
SCIENCE AND CULTURE, NEW DELHI

&

ANMOL PUBLICATIONS PVT. LTD.
NEW DELHI - 110 002 (INDIA)

ANMOL PUBLICATIONS PVT. LTD.
4374/4B, Ansari Road, Daryaganj
New Delhi - 110 002
Ph.: 23261597, 23278000
Visit us at: www.anmolpublications.com

School Education Management

© Reserved, 2004

ISBN 81-7488-515-3

[All rights reserved. No part of this publication may be reproduced, stored in a retrieval system or transmitted, in any form or by any means, mechanical, photocopying, recording or otherwise, without prior written permission of the publisher.]

PRINTED IN INDIA

Published by J.L. Kumar for Anmol Publications Pvt. Ltd., New Delhi - 110 002 and Printed at Mehra Offset Press, Delhi.

Contents

	Preface	vii
1.	Introduction	1
2.	Problems of School Management	8
3.	Management of Funds	22
4.	Managing Quality Processes	33
5.	Audit of Funds	60
6.	Sponsored Programmes	72
7.	Customer Satisfaction in Schools	88
8.	Cost Analysis of School Education	105
9.	Capital Costs	129
10.	Economies of Scale	156
11.	Making Decisions	178
12.	Models for Thinking	201
13.	Educational Law and School Management	208
14.	Teaching and Bureaucratic—Professional Dichotomy	220
15.	Educational Administration	232
16.	Students As Active Learners	246

1

Introduction

Perhaps the most fundamental domestic problem of latter twentieth-century America is the persistence of gross inequalities in the life opportunities of youth from different social classes and racial groups. A critical component of the problem is the failure of most poor children to master the basic knowledge and skills that are necessary for assimilation into a highly technical and industrialized economy. The scholastic achievement gap that separates pupils in the slums from those in affluent neighborhoods remains tragically wide. This was shown in a recent nationwide survey conducted by James Coleman and others (1966) for the United States Office of Education. In every region of the country about 85 percent of Negro elementary and high school students scored below white averages on objective tests of scholastic ability and achievement.

Identifying the causes of academic failure in depressed-area schools is an issue of intense controversy among school officials, political leaders, spokesmen for minority group parents, and other interested groups. Even the views of social scientists concerned with the problem are widely divergent—ranging from Kenneth Clark's (1965) telling criticism of black ghetto schools to Bruno Bettelheim's (1964) psychoanalytically inspired contention that lower-class homes inflict irreversible damage upon the personalities of children even before they enter kindergarten or first grade. Unfortunately, in the current national debate over the causes of unequal opportunity, basic assumptions about class and race differences in psychological development continue to rest more upon conjecture and subjective impressions than upon the findings of scientific research.

Accordingly, it is altogether fitting that the Society for the Psychological Study of Social Issues, an affiliate of the American Psychological Association, should sponsor a book which seeks to clarify the present state of knowledge about social and biological influences on intellectual development. Most of the chapters that follow were written specifically for this volume; the rest are more or less extensive revisions of significant papers that were first published elsewhere. Each of them makes a unique contribution to an understanding of the larger subject.

Part One on "Biogenetic Perspectives" offers an objective exposition of research dealing with the traditional nature-nurture problem, particularly as it impinges on the issues of social-class and racial differences in intelligence. As Arthur Jensen observes in his introduction, many of the polemics in the field have issued from misconceptions about genetics and failure to think in terms of interactive effects of heredity and environment. "When the wrong questions are posed," he remarks, "the answers tend to be sought in the realm of argument rather than in scientific research, which by its very nature does not lend itself to answering ill-framed questions."

It is hoped that the discussion of genetics will indicate to social scientists and educators both the legitimacy and importance of this topic, and the need for greater theoretical and methodological sophistication in research on biological factors in class and ethnic characteristics.

Until the 1960's very little scientific research was done on the causes and types of intellectual impairment of children coming from low-income homes, and most of it was narrowly concerned with the description of group differences in IQ. There has recently developed in American psychology a trend toward studies of the processes that underlie children's intellectual growth.

In Part Two, three chapters dealing with the topic of "Basic Processes in Intellectual Development" delineate various specific processes whereby the home environment influences psychological development. The discussions reflect recent efforts by behavioral scientists to move beyond simple correlational studies of indicators of socioeconomic status, on the one hand, and such global characteristics as general intelligence and academic achievement, on the other. In the past, most of the social-class variables examined, such as income, occupation, and physical condition of the home, were essentially nonpsychological in nature and thus did little to expose the causal factors underlying observed differences in the measured intelligence of poor and affluent children.

One of the chapters in this part analyzes recent theory and research on the developmental aspects of perceptual functions, the role of experience in their formation, and their relation to reading and problem-solving skills. Another contribution reports early findings from an extensive survey of linguistic skills, intelligence test scores, and social background factors in a balanced sample of Negro and white boys of both middle-class and lower-class status. The study concentrates on those aspects of environment which are most likely to be causally linked to language ability and mental proficiency, that is, on qualities of the parent-child interaction and the family constellation. An empirically derived "Deprivation Index" predicts more of the variance in educationally relevant traits than do the usual indices of socioeconomic status. Current thinking gives language a central place in problem solving and in cognitive processes generally. Bernstein's work in England highlighted a general relationship between language structure and particular social milieus. The third paper in this part employs a wealth of data from verbal learning experiments to suggest numerous ways in which social-class variations in language usage, hence in the early verbal stimulation of children, inexorably shape children's later intellectual ability.

Social factors that influence the disadvantaged pupil's will to learn are emphasized in Part Three, titled "Social and Psychological Perspectives." Certain characteristic deficiencies in the academic motivation of minority group children are glaringly obvious to anyone who observes typical fourth- or fifth-grade classrooms in urban ghetto schools. At the same time, it is equally clear that there are gross inadequacies in the educational services offered in nearly all these schools. Elsewhere, one of the present authors (Deutsch, 1960) has reported observations made in predominantly Negro public schools in Harlem which revealed that 50 to 80 percent of all classroom time was devoted to disciplinary and other essentially nonacademic tasks, as compared with only 30 percent of classroom time given to such activities in schools attended mainly by white children of roughly similar economic status. What the comparison conveys about the behavior and attitudes of socially disadvantaged students is poignantly elaborated in a recent article by a young, Harvard-trained teacher in a Negro ghetto school (Levy, 1966). She writes:

> What impressed me most was the fact that my children (9–10 years old) are already cynical and disillusioned about school, themselves, and life-in-general. They are hostile, rebellious, and bitter.... They are hyperactive and are constantly in motion. In many ways they can be compared with wild horses that are suddenly fenced in (pp. 430–431).

A common theme of the chapters in this part is that discrimination tends to create in its victims those very traits of "inferiority" that are mentioned to rationalize its practice. Even in the absence of the more blatant forms of discrimination, traditional stereotypes about the low ability and apathy of Negroes and other ethnic minorities can operate as self-fulfilling prophecies. Thus the belief that Negroes are intellectually incompetent can cause both whites and Negroes to behave in such manner as to yield confirmatory evidence.

The ways in which expectancies about others and about oneself develop, and their relation to academic performance, are explored from various perspectives. There is a review of studies dealing with the general topic of Negro self-concepts. Another contribution reports a series of intriguing experiments on human and animal subjects which support the hypothesis that the expectations of power figures, regarding the behavior of those whom they control, importantly influence the latter's behavior. The main experiment utilized an entire elementary school as a natural laboratory for a full academic year. Pupils from whom teachers were arbitrarily led to expect strong intellectual growth (the teachers were given fictitiously high intelligence test scores for the children involved) actually showed such growth during the ensuing year.

The primary thrust of the third paper on "Social and Psychological Perspectives" is toward motivational factors that favorably or adversely influence the achievement behavior of minority group children in biracial classrooms. Drawing upon evidence from a wide range of studies on the effects of stress and isolation, as well as from several experiments on Negro adolescents, the author suggests a model for predicting Negro performance in desegregated schools. The reactions—both real and anticipated—of white peers and teachers, and the Negro child's expectancies of success or failure on particular scholastic tasks, figure prominently in the conceptual scheme that is outlined. It is proposed that the racially mixed environment has greater potentiality both for academic success and failure than does the all-Negro environment. Whether the outcome for the individual pupil will be favorable or detrimental depends in large measure upon the specific social conditions that prevail in the classroom.

Part Four, the final section of the book, "On the Education of the Disadvantaged," describes the recent contributions of psychology to educational theory and practice, contributions that have been stimulated in part by the overturning of the concept of fixed intelligence and the concomitant rediscovery of the importance of experiential factors in cognitive development. The opening chapter elaborates the notion of intrinsic motivation, conceived as an autonomous urge toward novel experiences, and toward the exploration and manipulation of the physical environment. Presumably intrinsic motivation, which is essential for cognitive growth, requires for its own development variety of stimulation in early life. As Piaget has put it, "the more a child has seen and heard, the more he wants to see and hear." The obverse of this—that monotonous and restricted environments produce apathy—appears also to be true, though systematic evidence as yet is scarce. It is suggested that by the third year of life the physical and social conditions of low-income homes—with their crowding, dearth of manipulable objects, and restricted adult language patterns—are no longer adequate for the proper growth of intrinsic motivation. Hence, early enrichment of the disadvantaged child's environment is essential for satisfactory cognitive growth.

All the chapters in thc final part discuss new or recently rediscovered approaches to the education of the disadvantaged. In a few instances the methods and rationales of particular enrichment programs—for example, those of Montessori and Bereiter—are discussed in some detail. In addition, fairly comprehensive surveys of compensatory projects for children of different ages are presented. Regrettably, few of the efforts that have been instituted above the preschool level have been genuinely innovative with respect either to instructional methods or curriculum content. Nor have these efforts usually been based upon well-established pedagogical principles. Moreover, very few of the programs have had evaluations of sufficient scope and objectivity to establish whether they were really effective over the long run.

While each chapter in this book has a specific focus, and each was written independently of the others, several themes emerge from the book as a whole. One such theme is the complexity and multiplicity of factors that influence psychological traits and govern their development. While emphasis is mostly on social and interpersonal influences, biological factors are not neglected. But those factors related to negative living conditions receive the most emphasis. In one way or another, all the chapters of the book are concerned with the deleterious effects of poverty on children's development. Another major theme is the search for psychological variables which mediate between the child's social background and his intellectual and school performance. One might begin with race or class as a kind of encompassing description of a social milieu, and one might end with academic competence as a criterion measure. But unless the intervening processes are specified, so that cause-and-effect relationship can be understood, sound bases for social and educational action programs will not result.

This book illustrates the current involvement of behavioral scientists with important social problems, especially in the field of education. Its contents show that, contrary to the tenets of some psychological systems which were influential in the past, research on urgent practical problems can also have basic scientific value, by providing effective tests of existing theories and by generating new ones. The editors hope that the volume will provide a useful assessment of what is known, and what still needs to be known—from the standpoint of providing equal educational opportunities—about the biological, psychological, and social factors governing the achievement of students from different types of home background.

2

Problems of School Management

The labelling of some programs as "non-traditional" explicitly conveys that our institutions are tradition based and have tended to be change resistant. But this is no longer as true as it once was.

During the past half century we have witnesses technological advances (perhaps more dramatic and far reaching than the industrial revolution), major demographic changes, changes in the family structure, a greatly heightened social consciousness, and an increased emphasis on access to higher education for the economically and educationally disadvantaged.

An institution such as Higher Education could not survive in a society undergoing such radical changes unless it succeeded in adapting to those changes while striving to maintain its traditional values. Within this context, it is important that those concerned with the management of our educational enterprise have some appreciation of the specific ways in which societal changes are affecting higher education so that they may be in a position to better judge the effectiveness with which the specific institutions that are the subject of their concern are adapting to these changes.

The trends that will be briefly highlighted here are: Loss of Public Confidence in the Value and Utility of Higher Education;

Changing Enrolment Patterns; Competition Among and Between Institutions and Sectors; The Rising Cost of Education to the Consumer and the Taxpayer; The Growth of the Community Colleges; Increasing Concern about Effective Management in Educational Institutions; and Erosion of Collegiality. These trends have been apparent over the last decade and appear likely to continue and, perhaps, accelerate in the next decade.

Loss of Public Confidence in The Value and Utility of Higher Education

This loss has been attributed to such factors as: campus unrest in the '60s; the perceived lowering of standards and requirements for admission and success in college; the proliferation of programs; the loss of uniqueness in holding a BA degree because of the large number of individuals attending college; the seemingly large number of individuals who have been disappointed in the quality of their educational experience; the exposure to the public of college graduates who are lacking in the basic skills that, it is believed, should have been acquired at the secondary level (but certainly at the collegiate level); the sense that teaching is just a job and nothing more; and the absence of a sufficient number of educational statesmen, leaders, innovators. beyond these factors, there is a recognition that the social and economic argument that has often been blatantly or subtly advanced for going to college—you'll get a better job, have doors opened for you, lead a better life, meet good friends who will help you later in life—may not be totally or even partially accurate. At the very least, recent studies suggest that the gap between lifetime earnings of college graduates in contrast to non-college graduates appears to have narrowed considerably.

One recent study, in particular, suggests that we may have to re-examine some of our expectations in regard to higher education as an agency for social reform. The thrust of "open admissions" policies has been to open the doors of higher education to those who have historically been economically and educationally disadvantaged (generally members of minority groups), and to attempt through remedial courses, tutorial programs, special counselling and enlarged student financial aid, to ensure that the open admissions student is given every opportunity and encouragement to succeed and to achieve a degree.

For many of these disadvantaged students, despite attempts to ease their path to collegiate success, the handicap of inadequate academic preparation at the secondary school level is a most difficult one to overcome.

Moreover, there is a severe financial hardship involved for the economically disadvantaged to gain a higher education, despite the availability of financial aid. That they have been induced to pursue higher education under these circumstances is largely attributable to the fact that higher education is one of society's status symbols and that for some time there has been an impression that higher education represents the only sure path to upward economic and social mobility. This belief has been so widespread that in some instances students have been motivated to continue their education despite the handicap of low academic ability, as well as poor academic preparation. A recent study of Larry Leslie and Lowell Crary of the University of Arizona Center for the Study of Higher Education suggests that we may have done a great disservice to these students in creating false expectations.

The study suggests that many low-income or disadvantaged students who do not perform well in high school might be hurting themselves financially if they forego four years of earned income for a college degree of increasingly questionable economic value. Those who are likely to see the greatest financial return on their college education, the study asserts, are high ability students who may recoup "two or three times or more" the financial return that low-ability students can expect.

The study, which used data from the National Longitudinal Study of the High School Class of 1972, based ability on students' high school grade averages or class rank. Study findings indicate that whether or not these are appropriate indices of true academic ability, they are reliable predictors of financial success. An alternative conclusion that this may support is that an educational thrust aimed at the disadvantaged must begin at a much earlier stage than college to be effective (a conclusion already reached by many governmental and educational leaders). The adequacy of the sample may also be called into question. But taken at face value, the study leads to the conclusion that while *some* post-secondary educational training may have a financial payoff for low-income, low-ability students, extended study may not. To the extent that such a conclusion has validity, social concern for the disadvantaged might well also focus on removing the stigma associated with the lack of a degree and on fostering career opportunities for financial success that do not necessarily require advanced education. Stated differently, the sense of social justice and obligation that impels us to strive for equality of opportunity for the disadvantaged would seem to require that even more than the average student, the disadvantaged student should be provided with meaningful, realistic information on career opportunities, and their relationship to a post-secondary education.

Observes differ in the importance that they attach to each of the various factors presumed to have an influence on current attitudes toward education. Yet it is hard to dispute that the economics of today's environment—as reflected in both the diminishing number of promising career opportunities in proportion to the number of college graduates and in the rising cost of education—has aggravated the dichotomy between the concept of the liberal arts education as necessary to the full development of the individual and the career oriented concept of education.

Among the ingredients in today's environment that must be recognized as bearing on this dichotomy, two are perhaps the most critical. The exponential expansion of knowledge has meant that the well-educated individual will, under the best of circumstances, not be as comparatively well educated as his counterpart of fifty or even twenty-five years ago because the body of knowledge to be mastered is simply too large. A second point is that we cannot fail to recognize that the communications media (television in particular, despite the major defects in programming) constitute a major source of informal education.

The strong liberal arts institutions today continue to stress the traditional values of college and shy away from espousing and often attack the vocationalism and pre-professionalism approach that many admissions brochures stress. But, in fact, many institutions are stressing the job related aspects of the curriculum and the placement services available, in order to attract students. Even in fields of traditional study that have in the past attracted a large number of student majors, there is now an evident tendency toward building a coalition or joint major and minor with subject matter that appears to be more career oriented in order to maintain enrolments. Thus, as an example, we see less emphasis on political science and more on public administration and pre-law; English now involves a stress on communications and business writing; economics is more closely geared to management and business; philosophy geared to the policy-making sciences and public policy; and languages are geared to translation and business. Many colleges and graduate schools of arts and sciences seek various incentives such as scholarships, assistantships, combined, shortened, or accelerated programs in order to compete with the professional-school programs such as those in business, law, medicine, nursing, or social work. Striking an appropriate balance between the concepts of education as life preparation and education as career preparation is critical to our society. But it is, perhaps, even more critical to the mission assessment and survival or individual institutions.

Changing Enrolment Patterns

Enrolment changes have occurred in the shift to career related departments and schools, and, in response to apparent changes in employment opportunities, such as from elementary education teaching preparation to special education. Recent publicity on the surplus of teachers has also resulted in fewer students being attracted to schools of education. Further, as is well recognized, due to the slowing down of the United States birthrate, there will be fewer 17–21 year olds than in the great expansionary period of the '60s until sometime in the 1990s. Thus, most institutions have experienced or will experience declining enrolments from among new high school graduates. This has increased competition among institutions and induced many institutions to modify their approaches (such as by adoption of more community oriented and "mid-life" programs) and marketing. The term marketing validly describes the increasingly aggressive efforts of respectable institutions to recruit new students. Declining enrolments have also resulted in lowering of standards of admission at some institutions and led to unemployment and underemployment of PhDs. Enrolment declines have also created concerns about tenure, promotion, and job security and led to excess space, particularly dormitory space. Projections of educational statistics published by the National Center for Educational Statistics reflect a total of 2,679,000 high school graduates in 1966–67 peaking to 3,149,000 ten years later and declining to 2,740,000 in 1986–87. Total college and university enrolments were at a level of 6,390,000 in 1966 and showed a steady but declining rate of increase projected to yield total enrolments of 12,903,000 in 1986. In this period, two year institutions are projected to increase from an enrolment level of 1,326,000 in 1966 and 3,883,000 in 1976 to 5,979,000 in 1986. Enrolments of four year institutions were 5,064,000 in 1966, 7,219,9000 in 1976 and projected to decline to 6,924,000 in 1986. Graduate enrolments which were at 768,000 in 1966 and 1,333,000 in 1976 are projected to increase to 1,532,000 in1986.

These statistics appear to reflect that, at least in the view of those compiling the projections, very substantial numbers of high school graduates are expected to attend post secondary institutions, despite the current state of disillusionment regarding job prospects for college graduates. But the statistical projections reflect two other interesting points. First, they suggest that the relative proportions of students enrolling at two years colleges and four year colleges are showing a marked trend towards two year institutions. This reflects a response by students to the apparent plethora of college graduates and emphasizes their inclination toward the career oriented and paraprofessional programs. This is also a response to the increased cost of education since two-year institutions are less costly; particularly since they are generally close to home.

The second point of interest is that the proportionate number of graduate students in relation to four year institution enrolments is expected to increase dramatically over 1966 levels by 1986. One interpretation of this statistic suggests that those who attend four year institutions tend, preponderantly, to be preparing for graduate and professional work recognizing that the bachelor's degree is, to an increasing extent, insufficient for career preparation. This statistic has particular meaning to the extent that four year institutions engage in mission reassessment and consider the possibility of specialization.

Competition among and between Institutions and Sectors

Loss of public confidence and changing enrolments have created circumstances in which institutions have felt constrained to become increasingly competitive in order to maintain quality, provide salary increases meet inflationary costs, replace or refurbish aging facilities and undertake new programs.

This competition has been between and among public and independent institutions; between the four year institutions and the universities; between four year institutions and community colleges; and between the various colleges and universities and the various proprietary "trade" or "vocational" schools, some of which are now authorized to grant associate degrees. Within a particular institution there is competition for students and resources among departments and schools and between traditional schools and non-traditional colleges for adults or evening students often with the latter more flexible e.g., granting life learning credits. A number of business firms provide very satisfactory technical and broad training programs that are of direct value to employees and, in total can be accepted for college credits.

It should be understood that competition, when used in the context of this discussion, does not connote the same kind of aggressive actions that characterizes competitior in the commercial marketplace. In the education sector competition still carries the more limited connotation of offering the same kinds of educational services as one or more institutions drawing from the same marketplace (this takes into consideration geographic location, the size of the institution, the range and quality of programs and tuition and fee levels, among other things.)

Although it is fair to say that most institutional administrators and their faculty have long maintained an awareness of "who the competitions is," it is equally fair to say in general that they have not found it appropriate or necessary to make any particular use of this knowledge. In this connection, it might also be noted that too frequently the admissions office, which is ultimately concerned with marketing the institution to prospective students, is too remote from, rather than integrated with, the essential activities that relate to the mission and identity of the institution—as is development, the other marketing activity.

But signs of change are emerging. Increasing fiscal pressures and the heightened competition for students and funds are leading to a truer competition in which institutions are beginning to examine the reasons for the apparent success of their competitors, not necessarily with a view toward becoming more like them, but more broadly, in the interests of improving their own competitive position. This has not yet become a very sophisticated process. But, as an increasing number of institutions begin to approach competition more independently and aggressively, we can look to the model which combines market analysis with rigorous self-analysis, to be replicated.

Rising Price of Education to Consumers and Taxpayers

At many independent institutions the total cost of one year at college for the freshman entering in 1979 is approximately equal to about three or four years of college for the freshman entering in 1959. Depending upon the time frame chosen, a tremendous increase in prices charged can be demonstrated, although a more sophisticated analysis might show that the percentage increase has not significantly or may not at all have outpaced the rise in middle class income. There can be further comparisons between disposable income at two points in time, in relation to college costs or the net cost to a family of tuition after significantly expanded scholarship and loan programs have been developed and implemented. These programs have a more favorable impact on lower income families. There are also reasonable arguments to be made that, with the expansion of lower cost community college and public institutions, college is more accessible to more people at a lower average cost.

In the congressional debates of 1977–78 on tuition tax credit bills, it was claimed by the Congressional Budget Office that family income increased during 1967–76 at a faster rate (78.6% in the aggregate) than total student charges (76.7% in the aggregate.) However, research performed by the Congressional Research Service of the Library of Congress disclosed that during that nine year period federal income tax, Social Security Tax, and state and local taxes more than doubled. As a result, disposable family income experienced an aggregate growth during the period of only 66.8%. Within the same time the consumer price index increased by 70.5%. Thus, rising student charges competed with the rising costs of other consumer expenses for disposable dollars that were increasing at a less rapid rate.

Clearly, the debate about college costs is more complex than the general figures on the considerable increases in tuition and fees, room and board costs would seem to reflect. It is, in any event, reasonably evident that for families with incomes in the $20,000 to $50,000 range (an income level still regarded as quite comfortable and which would make the children ineligible for *most* forms of student financial aid or eligible for only minimal amounts other than loans) the cost of sending children to independent institutions and even, in some cases, to public four year institutions, can constitute a very serious drain on savings, or cause a large debt burden on the family or the student. The problem becomes even worse when two or more children are in school at the same time.

Until recently, it has generally been the case that the variety of scholarship programs including no-need scholarships have had very little applicability to the family in the income range cited. (It is perhaps worth noting, in this connection, that nearly 17% of students from families with incomes of less than $12,000 were denied basic grants in 1978–79 because of "high family assets." In that same year dependent students from families earning less than $6000 annually got BEOG awards averaging $1,562 and totaling 29.9% of their college costs. Students from families with incomes below $12,000 comprise approximately 23% of the total number of private college students and in 1978–79 total financial aid awards (not merely BEOG) provided 70.9% of college expenses for students from families with income in the $6,000 to $12,000 category. For students in the category of under $6,000 family income this percentage increased slightly to 72.4%.) As discussed in the section on Student Financial Aid, two major federal programs. Basic Education Opportunity Grant

(BEOG) and National Defense Student Loan (NDSL) have until recently been oriented primarily to families with incomes below $15,000 a year. Even in those cases, work and loans have often been part of the student package and the out-of-pocket costs may still be very burden-some. It is not uncommon for students to graduate from independent institutions with family or personal debts ranging from $5000 to $10,000 or more to cover the costs of education.

It can be reasonably argued that this is a very sound investment on the part of the student or family and a rate of return might even be calculated. A further argument is that the debt is paid off in inflated dollars. But for a 21 year old, the idea of starting graduate school or a job (which may be difficult to find) with a debt of $5,000 to $10,000 or more can be staggering. If one shares the view that the incurrence of a huge debt is not a desirable way to finance education (witness the large number of bankruptcies to avoid repayment of student loans until this was prohibited by law), the lifting of the income ceiling on eligibility for guaranteed student loans in late 1978 may be viewed as something less than a panacea. At the same time the taxpayer sees his taxes rising to support community colleges—the portion of the tax increase attributable to community colleges can be determined with relative ease and is often announced by county officials—support for public and independent institutions, in addition to other governmental services also creates a rising tax burden. One manifestation of this unrest has been the voting down of school budgets.

Growth of the Community College

The most rapid growth sector in higher education has been the community college which, at its best, offers proximity, lower cost, emphasis on teaching (as contrasted with research and other activities not directly student related), and flexible approaches adapted to the needs demands and desires of the community. At its worst, the community college can be a vocational high school wih low academic standards, offering no more than the illusion of post secondary education. But the growth of the community college and its ability in a buyer's market to attract good faculty and, at least in the past, to provide modern facilities, has posed a significant challenge to four year colleges and universities.

In order to gain students, these institutions have tried to attract transfer students from the community colleges, but more directly, they have tried to compete for freshmen. Tension have been created within the four year colleges because some view the recruitment of community college students as a dilution of academic standards. One could probably generalize that the academic standards at community colleges are not high for a variety of reasons, but many students with high scholastic ability attend community colleges simply because they and their parents cannot afford the cost of other institutions, including the cost of living away from home.

With all institutions concerned about enrolment and the effects of an enrolment decline, it now appears that the competition between community colleges, universities, and four year institutions will intensify. Bodies such as State Post Secondary Coordinating Commissions are beginning to deliberate on whether such competition ought to be encouraged or whether appropriate allocation of resources would call for some greater degree of mission delineation.

Increasing Concern about Effective Management in Educational Institutions

There has emerged what has become known as the "Proposition 13 mentality." In its most aggravated form, this thinking is in the nature of a taxpayer revolt in which the taxpayer, responding to the general financial pressures to which he is subject, seeks substantial redress from his tax burden and, in so doing, questions the worth of the services which the tax dollars support. As this manifests itself in regard to higher education, it focuses in part on the quality of education, but even more pervasively on higher education management.

The traditional image of the higher education administrator is not unlike the conventionally unfavorable portrayal of civil service employees, i.e., people who are secure in their positions, isolated from reality, slothful in their work habits, and who generally "could not make it elsewhere." This uninformed view, in addition to its other inaccuracies, ignores the substantial and significant efforts to heighten the professionalism associated with higher education management by such organizations as the American Council on Education and the National Association of College and University Business Officers, among others.

One of the significant results of this attitude is that it has contributed to a trend toward recruiting for educational managers from outside the educational system, e.g., Financial and Business Affairs Vice Presidents have been recruited from banking, insurance, and other segments of the profit sector. This effort has met with mixed success. Some of the recruits have brought a fresh and valuable perspective to higher education management. Other, accustomed to a more structured and disciplined environment, find themselves unable or unwilling to cope with the dynamics of university governance. In any event, we can expect to see a continued emphasis on higher education management and on the training and development of educational administrators.

Erosion of Collegiality

It has been traditional at colleges and universities to have a sense of acting within a community with shared information, considerable consultation, decision-making among administration, faculty, and trustees, and in some institutions, a sense of the primacy of the faculty in all major decisions not only in strict academic matters, but also in terms of budgeting, construction, advertising, selection of administrative officers, and so on. In addition, there has been a sense of collegiality among and between institutions for sharing of information and ideas.

In recent years, however, there have been considerable external and internal pressures creating tensions which indisputably have weakened the concept of collegiality. Two of the major forces affecting collegiality, which we discuss in the following separate sections, are collective bargaining and the patterns and practices associated with federally sponsored research. Among the external and internal pressures the following are particularly important:

1. Enrolment changes at the institution and in its schools and departments caused by the changing population pool, and by economic and employment conditions;

2. Financial strains caused by the above and by the impact of governmental funding, impact of foundation and individual gifts, and by escalation of costs in all areas, including salary costs;
3. Collective bargaining pressures such as costs, emphasis on legalities, and, given the adversarial nature of the collective bargaining process, changes in the basic relationships;
4. More active role of trustees and governmental bodies; and
5. Resource allocation decisions at the institutions as a result of 1–4, causing more conscious and more difficult choices to be made in regard to size of faculty and staff and allocations of space, equipment, supplies, research and travel funds. For example, if there are staff reductions to be made, how will they be accomplished?

There appears to be a trend toward potential conflict, competition, and controversy in the various relationships that previously were thought to be collegial. It is to be expected that a heightened atmosphere of insecurity and more restricted availability of resources to support the range of educational activities produces tensions and competition among the various segments of the institution. The competition would seem to be in the categories indicated below, and often at one institution several competitive pairings and various combinations and permutations are taking place at the same time. These categories are:

1. Faculty versus administrations;
2. One or more colleges or schools versus other colleges or schools;
3. Liberal arts versus professional school;
4. Graduate versus undergraduate teaching or departments;
5. Teaching versus research;
6. Department versus department;
7. Tenured versus non-tenured faculty;
8. Sciences departments versus humanities departments;
9. Minorities and women versus white males;
10. Junior versus senior faculty;

11. Required subjects or core curriculum versus non-required subjects;
12. Students versus faculty/students versus administration;
13. Faculty versus Board of Trustees;
14. Administration versus trustees;
15. Trustees or administration versus State Education Department or regents or governor's office or legislature.

The effects of the decline of collegiality can also be listed:

> A. Impact on the atmosphere on campus, cooperation, joint proposals interdisciplinary approaches, and impact on the sense of community; and
>
> B. In regard to cooperation with other institutions, there is some evidence of a tendency toward a diminution in the exchange of ideas, information, consortia approaches, joint research proposals, and referral of students and organizations to another institution (although many of these still take place). There is increased competition in recruitment for students, and thus increased costs attributable to advertising, publicity, and scholarship competition, particularly in the area of no-need scholarships. There is also increased competition among institutions (and even within institutions) for faculty, contacts with business, industry, foundations, government, individual donors. There is inherent in this competition the possibility and the reality of duplication of program, seminars, and community service approaches.

The above are just a few of the trends affecting higher education today. It is important to note that there continue to be significant variations among institutions in the degree to which there tensions or competitive conflicts. exists. Nonetheless because they add an important dimension of complexity to policy-making deliberations and, indeed, day to day administration, those associated with higher education management need to be alert to the potential for these competitive conflicts and sensitive to their implications and nuances.

3

Management of Funds

At the end of 1977 higher education institutions had an aggregate endowment of $16.3 billion. Various surveys of endowment funds and their use have disclosed wide variations in the extent to which institutions depend on endowment fund income to support current operations ranging from three percent to fifty-three percent. This wide variations suggests that the critical first question to be asked to any institution is "What is the function of the endowment at our institution?" It is only within the context of that question that an intelligent and explicit policy for endowment fund management can be formulated.

As suggested in the chapter on Development Activity, endowment fund management begins with the fund raising process. Appealing to the special interests of donors, while avoiding restrictions on donations, to the fullest extent possible, is part of the art of fund raising. It is also to be noted in this connection that a surprising number of restrictions are self-imposed; i.e., imposed not by the donor but by the trustees or even by the administration.

There are three basic classifications for endowment funds. "True" endowments involve restrictions on the purpose for which income is to be used or on the manner of use. Endowment fund income may also be unrestricted as to use and finally, there is the category of funds functioning as endowment. This latter classification applies to gifts or other funds, with respect to which a decision has been made, generally by the trustees, but on occasion, by the administration, to set them aside as part of the endowment because they are not needed for current purposes.

There should be a periodic examination to verify that funds included in the endowment are properly classified. This examination should also be the occasion for determining whether funds functioning as endowment should continue to be so treated. The occasion may arise when special circumstances create the need for additional funds to meet current expenditure requirements. Under such circumstances the potential utilization of some portion of the funds functioning as endowment would be one of the alternatives to consider.

The circumstances referred to above would not only be special, but generally unpredictable. One operating definition of a true endowment fund is that it is a perpetual pool of capital with no *predictable* need to utilize principal. This understanding of the nature of a true endowment fund has significant implications in regard to endowment fund management. The absence of any predictable likelihood that capital will be utilized, means that factors such as liquidity and volatility become irrelevant. It should perhaps be stated, at this early juncture, that although many discussions on endowment fund management assume an investment in securities, there are a range of other opportunities for securing a return on invested capital; e.g., real estate, oil and gas properties, going business, etc., none of which are ignored by the imaginative and aggressive endowment fund manager.

However well conceived and articulated, endowment fund policy, as it relates to the need for current income, should be re-examined periodically, not only within the context of changing internal conditions, but also giving consideration to the external economic environment and its impact on investment opportunities.

In 1967, the Ford Foundation commissioned a study on problems in endowment management. A primary point of emphasis in the report, resulting from that study, was that by unduly stressing current income and failing to establish the clear-cut objective of maximum long-term total return, institutions and their endowment fund managers had failed to insulate their endowment funds against the inroads of inflation and a shrinking dollar.

Among the major recommendations contained in the report were that:

- Trustees should not themselves attempt to manage their endowment portfolios, but should instead utilize professional managers;
- All funds that may have to be converted to cash within the near future (a period up to five years) should be removed from the endowment portfolio and invested separately in prime short-term obligations; and
- A plan should be adopted in which, each year, transfers are made from endowment to operating funds in an aggregate amount equal to five percent of the three-year moving average market value of the fund, whether or not that amount is provided by interest or dividends.

Concurrent with the report mentioned above, the Ford Foundation sponsored another report entitled. "The Law and the Lore of Endowment Funds" which has intended to support the total return concept advocated in the first report. The thrust of this report was to indicate that, generally, there is no legal impediment to utilizing a prudent portion of the appreciation on endowment funds. Many states passed the Uniform Management of Institutional Funds Act, which made such use possible. But there continues to be some variation in governing state laws.

These studies had a profound impact on college and university endowment fund management. Institutions hastened to adopt the "total return" concept, without necessarily giving full consideration to its applicability or lack of applicability to their circumstances, the external circumstances which provided a context for the Ford study recommendations and, most particularly, to what was required for effective implementation.

The experience of one institution in illustrative. A "total return" philosophy was adopted and the portfolio oriented heavily to industry leader, low yielding growth stocks. Unrestricted endowment fund principal was being utilized annually to produce the difference between the 6% return on the endowment needed to support the operating budget and the 2.6% return the interest and dividends actually being generated in current income by the endowment.

Unfortunately, the unrestricted endowment fund was being rapidly depleted by these drawdowns which did not represent amounts attributable to realized appreciation. Quite the contrary. The institution had not been *realizing* any gains, only losses. The growth oriented stocks were retained indefinitely in the portfolio, fluctuating widely in price over the years, but never liquidated. Securities would be sold only when the institution found itself in need of cash (and this never coincided with a high in the market) or when the investment manager lost confidence in a security whose value had plummeted.

The above scenario does not suggest that the total return concept is faulty or even that it was inappropriate for the particular institution whose experience was described. What it does suggest is the absence of a sufficient understanding of endowment fund management concepts and an ineffective implementation of investment goals.

As suggested earlier, every institution should carefully assess, and periodically reassess, the extent to which endowment fund income must be relied upon as a source of current revenue. This need will be balanced against the desire to preserve endowment fund capital in real dollar terms. There may also be the desire or the need to set aside funds to provide for some specifically identified future requirements.

This balancing of present and future needs is the basis for establishing endowment fund management policy. There are alternative investment policies that can be pursued to effectuate the endowment fund management policy. The investment policies relied upon should reflect a current assessment of the state of the economy and the nature of investment opportunities.

For example, an institution might conclude that a six percent annual income from the endowment fund is needed to support current operating expenditures. Its endowment fund management policy might, consequently, encompass a targeted objective of nine percent annual return and the three percent difference between the targeted return and the six percent would be an addition to endowment fund capital to offset inflationary erosion.

At a time when short-term yields, e.g. Treasury bills, are ten percent or higher, an appropriate alternative might be to temporarily maintain a portfolio that is highly income oriented. The increment of income above six percent would not be used, but would be transferred to do endowment capital and invested.

A second viable alternative might be a long-term appreciation oriented approach which would be likely to involve the necessity to augment current income by liquidating securities and utilizing a portion of endowment fund capital to meet the need for six percent in current income.

Either approach can effect the same endowment management objective, if effectively implemented. But in the first illustration, use of the entire amount of endowment income earned for current needs would effectively result in a long-term depletion of the endowment. In the second illustration, long-term endowment depletion will also occur unless the portfolio, despite cyclical fluctuations, does in fact experience a long-term appreciation consistent with the targeted nine percent return.

In a 1976 study, statistics on about 150 college and university endowment funds reflected that portfolio were invested about 60% in common stocks, 30% in bonds, and ten percent in short-term investments. This suggests a thoughtful attempt to balance risks, current income yield, and long-term growth.

The preceding discussion raises an important question about the kind of information trustees need about the endowment fund in order to exercise prudence in making investment decisions or in support of decisions to utilize fund income, capital gains, or endowment principal. It has been suggested that the income account of the fund should reflect: interest received; dividends received; appreciation or loss in investments realized; appreciation gain or loss on investments during the period not realized; *and* and inflation loss factor to be deducted to maintain fund principal intact.

The inclusion of this last factor suggests a philosophy which says that the endowment fund must yield in current income and capital gains, an amount greater than that which is needed to support the current operating budget as a means of insulating the endowment fund from inflation. The alternative is to insure that development activity will produce a rate of growth in the endowment sufficient to offset the rate of inflation.

On several occasions in this discussion, emphasis has been placed on the *realization* of capital gains. Bearing in mind the illustrative scenario cited earlier, one can question whether a policy of investing in growth stocks is meaningful unless it encompasses an intent to liquidate the stock when a major portion of the growth potential is deemed to have been achieved with a concomitant substitution of a stock which is in an earlier growth stage.

These are not easy judgment to make, and this is one of the reasons that institutions engage outside investment managers. Utilization of outside managers is not necessarily the answer for every institutions. But few institutions possess the necessary staff skills and informational resources and even the largest among the institutions make some use of outside professional investment managers to augment their internal skills.

If the trustees elect to use outside management for their endowment, they should consider the possibility of using more than one manager, so that explicit performance comparisons can be made. They should examine performance records in making their selection and seek to determine whether the investment manager has a particular investment philosophy and if so,whether it is one which is in consonance with their own.

The general principles that apply to the selection and utilization of consultants as discussed in the chapter on the Use of Consultants are applicable to the utilization of outside investment managers. Any outside expert must be afforded that degree of latitude which is necessary to effectively utilize his expertise. There is little point in paying for specialized expertise and then exerting a degree of control that unduly limits the discretion of the investment manager.

This means, for example, the trustees should eschew the practice of approving day-to-day transaction decisions. Beyond this, it also means that they should consider carefully the restrictions they seek to impose on the investment manager. On the other hand, it is essential that they establish an investment policy which makes clear to the investment manager the objectives to be achieved, secures his commitment to those objectives and measures his performance against them. In this latter connection, statistical performance measurement service, such as the A.G. Becker studies, are generally useful in investment management, but particularly valuable in assessing performance of outside managers.

Among the opportunities for enhancing endowment income, two which relate to securities should be considered: (1) lending of securities and (2) selling of options. Lending of securities is a transaction in which an institution temporarily gives up physical possession of securities in its portfolio in exchange for collateral which can produce short-term income. Typically, the lending institution causes the securities to be delivered to a broker who utilizes them to make delivery in completed transactions. The borrowing broker is required to return the securities upon notice and deposits with the lending institutions collateral equal to or greater than the value of the borrowed securities. Ownership continues to reside in the lending institution and the institution. is consequently, entitled to any interest or dividends earned during the loan period.

Some firms specialize in serving as brokers between borrowers and lenders of securities. Smaller instituations with limited portfolios may find the net income derived from such a program, after broker fees and related expenses, to be insufficient to justify the administrative burdens. But many of the larger institutions have had such a program for years as a segment of their cash management program, and continue to find it profitable.

The selling of options is gaining more general acceptance as a hedging, rather than a speculative, technique and represents a legitimate opportunity for institutions to increase investment return. The growth of the options market has greatly facilitated options trading. At the same time, the process has become more complex, transaction costs can be high, and the opportunities for gain less spectacular. The institution that contemplates the use of this technique should not do so casually and should expect to utilize professional advice.

In considering these and other techniques, those charged with administration should be mindful of the issue of "unrelated income." Congress in 1950 imposed a tax on "operations of businesses which are clearly unrelated to the primary function" of tax exempt institutions or organizations. Where extensive activity involving "unrelated business" income is engaged in (as noted in the earlier discussion on other revenue generating activities), there is the risk not only that the unrelated income will be taxed, but also that institution may lose its tax exempt status. The two techniques referred to above have been explicitly found to be outside the definition of unrelated business income.

The subject of endowment fund management cannot fully be discussed without dealing with social responsibility as an aspect of investment policy. The various constituencies of colleges and universities, but most particularly students and faculties, have expressed the strong view that, although the primary purpose of endowment fund management is to secure the most favorable return to the university, institutions cannot ignore the uses to which such invested funds are put. It is wrong, they contend, to use university funds to support activities not in consonance with university policies and values.

Taken to its extreme, such an argument would preclude an investment in government securities when federal policies are considered by some to be particularly onerous. But it is not the purpose here to engage in a discussion as to the appropriateness of actively voting proxies or of avoiding investments in the shares of certain companies at a certain time because such companies are insufficiently mindful of ecology or support repressive foreign governments directly or indirectly, or give other evidence of not being socially responsible.

They key point is that the issue of social responsibility as a facet of investment policy did not disappear when the activism of the '60s receded. It continues to be a matter of widespread concern and cannot be ignored by trustees and administrators. Consequently, it is incumbent upon the institution that does not now have one, to adopt an explicit policy on social responsibility in investment.

Such a policy should clearly state the institution's posture on the extent to which social responsibility issues will or will not influence purchase and sale of securities and the mechanism to be used in giving effect to that influence. The voting of proxies should be similarly dealt with. If the trustees have established an endowment subcommittee, that body would be the appropriate one to initiate a policy on social responsibility in investment. As an aspect of the broader considerations involved in governance, it might be appropriate to recognize this as one of the areas of university activity that has special meaning for faculty and students and both ought, consequently, to be given an opportunity to make suggestions in regard to the policy that is to be established.

As noted earlier, there are wide variations among the practices of institutions in managing their endowment funds and pursuing appropriate investment policies. They vary in the extent and manner in which they utilize outside investment counsel, they vary in their emphasis on short-term or long-term considerations, they vary in the diversity of their investments and they vary in the nature of their investments.

But there is a discernible trend in the direction of making more widespread use of investment vehicles which at one time might have been considered quite unorthodox by college and university officials. A striking illustration is provided by a small institution that has departed from endowment fund management norms with enormous success. The example is even more dramatic because the institution is not one of the major universities, but rather a small college with an enrolment of considerably less than 2000.

From 1973 to 1978 this college has doubled to book value of its endowment to $37.5 million (a valuation at market would reflect a value closer to $60 million with new contributions during that period accounting for only $5.4 million of the increase.) Stated in its most conservative terms, there has been an average investment return during the period of 16.2% annually. By contrast, the median total return for 150 endowment funds charted by the A. G. Becker Company during that period was 1.7% annually.

The trustees departed from the conventional wisdom in a number of ways. As noted earlier, the highly influential study sponsored by the Ford Foundations contained as one of its major recommendations the statement that trustees should not attempt to manage the endowment fund themselves. At this college that caveat was ignored and the Finance Committee retained total control without relinquishing any aspect of day-to-day control of the endowment either to a bank, outside portfolio manager, or even a professional in-house manager.

The conventional wisdom also calls for diversity in investments. An examination of the formal investment policies adopted by institutions would disclose that one of the most common features is a limitation on the concentration in any one security, as well as in any one form of investment. This accords with the age-old maxim regarding placing all of one's eggs in one basket. The college in this illustration have very deliberately departed from this policy and, in fact, has concentrated its investments in a very few highly successful vehicles.

A key tenet of the college's investment policy is to seek out an undervalued company and invest in it heavily. The departure from tradition also manifests itself in the selection of investment vehicles as exemplified by the purchase from the AVCO Corporation of its WDTN television station in Dayton. It might be noted, relative to the issue of unrelated business income, that a separate company formed to run the TV station and that company pays taxes on earnings.

Other institutions both large and small, have also exhibited a tendency to depart from some of the more cherished traditions of conservative endowment fund management. One major university, with a very substantial endowment engages profitably in arbitrage opportunities. A medium-size college, with an endowment of $11.2 million has pursued at least one aspect of the approach described above, ferreting out undervalued companies among second tier stocks, and has succeeded in achieving a total return averaging nine percent annually over a 10-year period. Another large institution has effectively used a small portion of its endowment funds (about four percent) for both venture capital and commodities. Still another institution counts a shopping center among its diversified investments.

A key ingredient in all of the illustrations cited is not that the institutions adopted approaches that were non-traditional or unorthodox, but rather that they adopted thoughtfully conceived approaches that were deemed appropriate for *their* circumstances. The bold approach adopted by the college in the first illustrations might well have spelled disaster for another institution whose trustees were less astute investment managers *or* could not devote the necessary time and attention to the affairs of their institution.

Endowment fund management is an area that presents one of the more significant opportunities for trustees to utilize their business acumen in making a contribution to managing the financial affairs of the institution. But it demands a thoughtful assessment of their own capabilities, as well as all of the other factors discussed which bear on the development of specific policies and practices related to the needs and circumstances of the particular institution. There is both a moral imperative and a legal consideration in terms of the fiduciary responsibilities of trustees.

In legal terms, it is unquestionably true that for many years the "prudent man" test would be deemed to have been satisfied when trustees pursued a highly conservative policy aimed at avoiding risk of loss. Such an attitude is still likely to be found in many of the courts today. But one can speculate that the time is not far off when a court will define prudence in different terms and will question the stewardship of the trustee who fails to take reasonable business risks to generate an improved return on the endowment when the institution is starved for income.

Quite aside from legalities, the example of the college, which has been able to increase the proportion of the operating budget funded by the endowment from 11% to 20% is compellingly attractive to the concerned trustee. The trustee who is not content with a passive role, will have to give serious consideration to whether a departure from orthodox methods is appropriate when endowment fund management is considered within the context of that institution's overall financial circumstances.

4

Managing Quality Processes

Quality organisations are obsessed with measurement. Every aspect of every process is measured and one of the first signs of trusting the work force is to delegate the responsibility for statistical processes to operative level. Measurement is used to ensure conformity to standards, to identify the cost of deviation and to monitor the impact of improvements. Very limited changes in vocabulary are necessary to find paraellels in schools—the use of registers, marking and assessment, reading ages and setting are all forms of quantification used in the management of children's learning. This chapter argues that a similar approach is necessary in the management of all school processes. Three main issues are discussed.

- understanding process in schools;
- the cost of quality;
- techniques for improving work processes.

The key purpose of improving work processes is to add value, to make the process and thereby its product closer to customer requirements and so of higher quality. Adding value is a matter of listening to customers and making modifications in the light of their feedback. Each improvement, each development makes it more likely that the product or process will conform to customer expectations and so retain their loyalty. Adding value is not a matter of embellishment or increasing complexity but getting ever closer to customer specification. In schools, for example, this does not necessarily mean more resources, it means meetings that solve problems, lessons that are understood, INSET days that can be applied in practical terms.

- If the letter is sent out incomplete then time would be wasted in answering queries.
- Incorrect information might result in a limited response so causing the trip to be cancelled.

The financial cost of reissuing such a letter might be £ 50 (£ 12 for teacher time, £ 8 secretarial time, £ 5 copying × 2) and this is avoidable waste. Few teachers would throw away £ 25 worth of stock but many will lose much more in wasted time because of a failure to prevent errors. This direct waste is, at least, matched by the frustration, loss of credibility, opportunity cost and poor reputation for efficiency arising from such an incident.

It is comparatively easy to assign a cash value to a range of examples: a senior management team meeting that fails to reach a solution to a problem and has to reconvene could be costed at £ 100; the social cost is significantly higher. A primary school staff meeting where a circular is read to the staff for 30 minutes probably costs £ 40 in terms of salary but far more in resentment and a sense of powerlessness.

In order to ensure the optimum use of resources the emphasis in managing has to be on prevention—one of the cornerstones of TQM. In the example described above the costs resulting from an incorrect letter were discovered by inspection, i.e. after the event and therefore had to be corrected; the additional costs arose from inspection and could have been negated by a policy of prevention, i.e. finding out needs and working to established procedures. Prevention has to be built into working procedures through a variety of techniques. This is where BS 5750 is of particular importance and help.

Prevention in an industrial context is very much concerned with establishing a range of highly detailed statistical process control techniques. It is difficult, if not impossible to translate these into an educational environment. However, there is a model in the use of testing in the classroom—if that test is used to modify teaching strategies rather than simply recorded, and used as a measure of ignorance rather than as feedback on teaching methods. Some possible applications of these techniques to management processes are outlined in section 3 of this chapter.

Prevention is directly linked to knowledge; it is a central responsibility of management to ensure that requirements and standards are public, explicit and understood. Failure to articulate requirements makes conformity impossible. It is therefore necessary to implement a range of strategies which make quality intrinsic to every operation.

Quality Policy

This is driven by the school's mission; it is a declaration of hope, aspiration and ambition and it spells out what quality means. The components of a quality policy might include:

- a definition of quality for the school;
- the systems to be applied;
- customer orientation;
- respect for the individual;
- the significance of training and development;
- management commitment;
- responsibility for quality.

Operating Procedures

Many of the problems that occur in schools are due to a breakdown in working procedures. This is the fault of managers whose responsibility it is to ensure that operating procedures are clear, understood and capable of implementation. The failure of a process says more about the system and its designer than the people who operated it. Schools often have published procedures for basic processes, e.g. marking registers—however, if a process is significant (and if it is not, why continue it?) then it requires an operating procedure. The best examples of operating procedures in schools are syllabuses and schemes of work.

Operating procedures are appropriate for:

- marking, recording and assessment;

- managing pastoral care issues;
- relationships with external bodies—police, social services etc.;
- health and safety issues;
- record keeping;
- consultative procedures;
- homework;
- stock control;
- applying for courses;
- disciplinary matters;
- parents' evenings;
- option arrangements;
- handling finance;
- planning trips;
- transfer to secondary school, post-compulsory education.

There is obviously a danger that itemising procedures in detail could become a bureaucratic nightmare and if such documents are just issued then they will probably be ignored. However, if the development of these procedures is managed as a quality process in itself then they are likely to pervade all aspects of school life. In order to achieve this, procedures need to be developed and improved by the teams that will implement then and they must be written in response to customer requirements. In some instances there will be legal obligations on teachers but in many cases writing the procedures will be a first step towards customer satisfaction. Producing the procedures is a classic example of delegation and trust in action and those who write them will need training.

Once produced the procedures should be an essential component of working life, constantly referred to, used in meetings and as a standard reference point. This means that they should be well produced, meeting teachers' and non-teachers' needs in terms of language, design and organisation. They might well take the form of a handbook which includes the mission statement, quality policy and job descriptions of *all* those employed in the school.

The handbook will thus become an essential component of induction, appraisal and development and will provide support for teachers, managers and governors in a wide range of personnel procedures.

Quality Criteria

These may well form part of operating procedures; they are necessary to identify exactly the standard of work required—in essence procedures will identify who? and when? and the quality criteria will indicate how?. For example the National Curriculum will specify the content, sequencing and level of a topic, a school's quality criteria will identify the resources to be used, the strategies to be employed, the subject and methods of assessment. The concern here is with consistency of practice and ensuring that every process is delivered to the optimum quality.

One of the most important applications of quality criteria is in the appraisal and staff development policy of a school. Criteria are essential components of the self-review, classroom and task observation and target setting processes. There are two central issues here: firstly the appraisal and development process is designed to recognize and reinforce the successes of the teacher and identify development needs. Those needs must be met in accordance with the mission and development plan of the school which are expressed in the quality criteria. Secondly the management of the appraisal and professional development processes must, of themselves, be quality processes, i.e. quality can only be achieved by delivering quality. The medium is the message.

The implementation of the School Appraisal Regulations will necessitate the development of criteria for appraisal; it is suggested that the following areas need to be covered:

- relationships with children;
- lesson planning and preparation;
- organisation of the classroom and resources;
- classroom management;
- assessment and monitoring of pupils' progress;
- subject knowledge;

- pastoral care;
- departmental management;
- leadership.

The detailed components of each of these areas need to take into account DES, LEA and diocesan requirements, the provisions of the Education Acts and the community in which the school works.

Monitoring and Review

It is important to distinguish between monitoring and inspection in the context of TQM and inspection in the LEA/school context. A TQM organisation strives to eliminate inspection as manifested in quality control. HMI and LEAs have a statutory responsibility to inspect schools. In some senses the notion of external inspection is alien to a quality management approach unless advisers and HMI are seen as clients/customers who have rights and duties which the school has to meet.

Therefore it is not inspection in the sense of *post-facto* fault finding but rather a process of obtaining feedback and advice from two major customers (DES and LEA) on the extent to which requirements are being met. Within the school, monitoring and review are implicit to every school process, e.g. appraisal team meetings, budget planning, school development plans etc. The important thing is that the process of monitoring and review should be carried out by those actually responsible for the process and that it should become implicit to the way of working. A number of review techniques are outlined in section 3 of this chapter. As far as possible the review process should be specific and focus on the question, 'To what extent have customer requirements been met?' Monitoring should be a regular component of all processes which in time can contribute to a review, i.e. an overview of how they are contributing to the achievement of the school's mission statement.

THE COST OF QUALITY

One of the great myths surrounding traditional views of quality is that it costs more. This is understandable if quality is viewed as 'goodness'—as an intangible which has to be struggled for. If goodness is the top of the mountain then it is obvious that the greater the energy expended the better the chance of getting to the top. However, an analysis of the map might reveal a better route, planning and preparation will maximise the distance covered—appropriate equipment will ease the journey—a greater distance can be covered with less output of energy. Even with the right equipment a wrong turning means wasted effort, having to retrace the journey and start again. Getting it right first time means the objective is achieved at minimum cost.

It takes time, money, effort, skill and knowledge to produce defective services. No manager or teacher in a school will deliberately waste resources, yet a great deal of time will be spent 'reworking', checking and inspecting, all of which are symptomatic of waste. No amount of additional expenditure will improve a faulty system or process, the process itself has to be modified in response to client needs. Figure 4.1 provides a basis for analysing the extent to which non-conformance to customer specifications is responsible for wasted resources of time, skills etc. Every positive response indicates waste. The greater the total the higher the waste and the lower the level of customer satisfaction.

It is not appropriate to blame the person involved, the chances are that they did not conform to requirements because the process was not understood, was inappropriate or badly designed in the first place. The best way to overcome this problem is to redesign the process to ensure that it is driven by customer requirements. This will in turn ensure a higher probability of conformity and thus the delivery of quality.

The traditional approach is demonstrated in Figure 4.2 (A); quality is perceived as costing more in proportion to the reducing number of defects. There is therefore an optimum point after which improving quality means increased costs to customers and thus reduced demand. This approach is symptomatic of many western companies and explains their decline relative to their Japanese competitors. It might also help to indicate why two schools with the same budget, serving similar communities achieve remarkably different outcomes. In essence it is delivering more for the same input.

Select a short time-scene a week or a fortnight and identify the number of times you have had to do each activity.

Activity	
Doing the same job twice	
Having work retyped	
Postpone a meeting	
Ask for clarification of a document	
Reset deadlines	
Provide 'on the spot' training	
Seek more information	
Modify printed material	
Ask for an agenda	
Clarify the purpose of a task	
Ask for work to be repeated	
Seek confirmation of a verbal agreement	
Explain documentation	
Ask for more time	
Find spare accommodation	
Confirm an order	
Change a timetable	
Duplicate information	
Get equipment repaired	
Leave a job half-finished	
Take over a delegated task	
Redefine specifications	
Return wrongly ordered goods	
'Cut corners'	
Abandon agreed procedures	

Fig. 4.1 Understanding the Cost of Non-Conformance

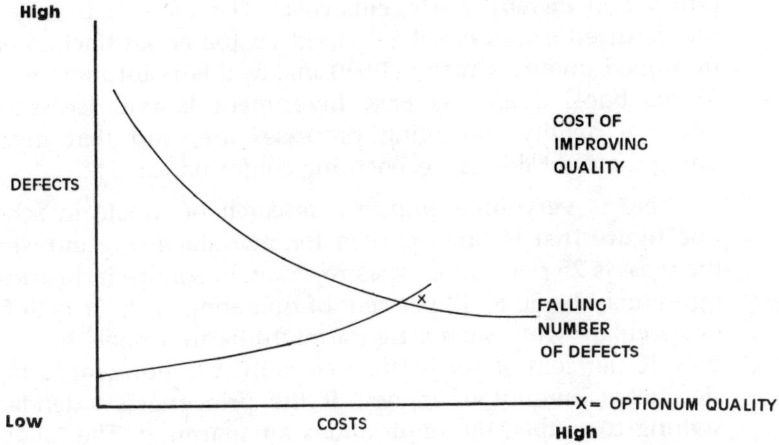

A Traditional View of the Cost of quality

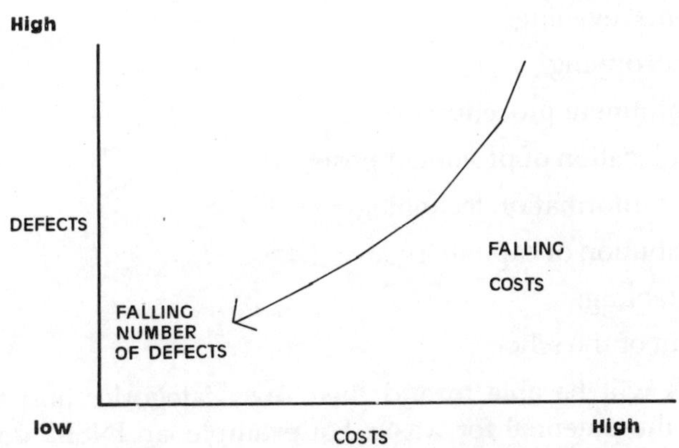

B the Real Cost of Quality

Fig. 4.2 Views of the cost of quality (MacDonald and Piggott, 1990)

The actual cost of quality is shown in Figure 4.2 (B); reducing errors, and thereby waste, cuts costs. The formula is very simple, reduced errors equal increased customer satisfaction equal improved quality. Crosby (1979) makes this point most forcibly in his book *Quality is Free*. Investment is not necessary to improve quality, managing processes are, and that involves doing the right things, i.e. ensuring conformance.

There is very little empirical research on waste in schools. The figure that is often quoted for manufacturing industry in the west is 25 per cent of sales revenue. In service industries the figure may be 30 to 40 per cent of operating costs. It is difficult to speculate what such a figure might be in schools but if it is only 10 per cent of non-staffing costs then it represents a highly significant amount of money. If the principle is extended to staffing costs then the implications are alarming. The following are possible areas for investigating waste:

- all meetings;
- INSET days, short and award bearing courses;
- inappropriate textbooks;
- underutilised equipment;
- the stationery store;
- parents' evenings;
- photocopying;
- appointment procedures;
- the allocation of promoted posts;
- use of information technology;
- distribution of capitation;
- timetabling;
- layout of the school.

Readers will be able to add their own categories and then reflect on the potential for waste. For example: an INSET day is a waste unless it leads to change, the stationery store may be full of stock that will not be used for six months—that is a waste of the potential of that money. Photocopying is necessary but teacher time spent copying is wasted. Is capitation allocated on the basis of the School Development Plan and the attainment of learning objectives or on a spurious notion of fairness? Do teachers spend hours writing out lesson notes in longhand and then have them word processed doubling the time needed to produce them?

These examples will doubtless be recognised by many and dismissed as 'that's the way schools are'. However, confirmation is not vindication. The cost of teacher time spent photocopying would probably amount to far more than the cost of employing a copier operator, thus releasing professional 'quality' time.

It may take many years to see the results of working to eliminate waste especially in the intangibles of the education process. However, there are many areas where direct benefits will be almost immediate, not least in enhanced customer satisfaction and increased commitment from those involved in the process. The next section in this chapter describes techniques for measuring and improving work processes.

TECHNIQUES FOR IMPROVING WORK PROCESSES

In this section a variety of techniques are described which are designed to help measured and structure techniques to improve work processes. Some are quantitative, others are structured in such a way as to facilitate analysis of complex situations. None of these techniques are new to schools, all have been used, if not always in the manner described. In the context of quality management they are not so much techniques to be employed as ways of working. It is important to place them in the context of effective team functioning, to see them as skills and tools which facilitate a team approach. All of these approaches require practice and review in order to work effectively.

The techniques described are:

1. Benchmarking.
2. Brainstorming.
3. Cause and effect diagram.
4. Five 'hows', five 'whys'.
5. Force field analysis.

6. Measurement charts.
7. Pareto analysis.
8. Problem solving techniques.
9. Readiness and capability.

Benchmarking

This is one of the most widely used techniques in TQM organisations and is essentially an exercise in comparative analysis. In the commercial sector it is examining a competitor's product to establish in what ways they are better, or worse, test the quality and examine customer satisfaction.

Benchmarking already takes place in education—it is one of the principal reasons for attending courses and conferences and reading the educational press. In essence it is about finding good ideas and ways to improve existing practice. However, it may be more appropriate to adapt a more systematic and detailed approach. This process works best with a specialist team although it may well draw on the experience and expertise of a range of teams.

Aim: To improve on best practice.

Step 1 Review

- Identify the process or product to be improved.
- Identify those who 'do it better'.
- Gather hard data to inform analysis.

Step 2 Analysis

- What factors contribute to their success?
- Is their product/approach right for us?
- What are the implications of adopting their approach?

Step 3 Planning

- What can we achieve?
- How are we going to achieve these outcomes?

Step 4 Action

- Implement specific actions.
- Monitor progress against norms.
- Go back to the original and review.
- Consider ways of extending improvement.

This process can be carried out on the basis of good practice in different schools. However, it is likely to be more effective within a school. What happens in other teams, departments and classrooms is likely to be a powerful source of improvement. Internal benchmarking has the additional advantage of helping and supporting review and development processes.

Brainstorming

This is a technique used to generate the maximum number of insights and involve all members of the work team on equal terms. It is particularly powerful in generating solutions to apparently intractable problems and in situations where creativity is at a premium. Brainstorming optimises the range of possible solutions and produces lists of ideas that can be evaluated, prioritised and rank ordered. The technique can be used several times in succession, e.g. (1) problem identification, (2) solution generation, (3) implementation strategy.

Brainstorming works best in groups of 5–10. The process should be managed by a facilitator (not necessarily the team leader) and each session should last from 10–20 minutes.

Step 1

- The problem or issue being reviewed is written on a flip chart or black board.
- Each member of the team suggests ideas which are written up without alteration or comment.
- The facilitator encourages each member of the team to contribute as many ideas as possible.
- The following 'rules' are applied at this stage:
    1. No criticisms or judgements.
    2. No evaluation.

3. No discussion.
4. No problem solving.
5. Anything goes! All ideas are valid.
6. Everybody is asked for one more idea.

Step 2

The facilitator takes each suggestion in turn and checks with all members of the team to ensure understanding and accuracy of recording.

Step 3

The ideas generated are reviewed for duplication, trivia, the impracticable and inappropriate. Team consensus is needed before any factor is abandoned.

The ideas that are left are now subject to evaluation by applying criteria to them. Criteria might include cost (e.g. a specified limit), staff availabiiity, training required, feasibility, consistency with agreed strategies. Again the team's view on the 'best fit' should prevail.

Step 4

The outcomes that meet all the criteria are potential solutions which may be self-selecting or require further discussion in order to produce a rank-order.

Cause and Effect Diagram

This technique is also known as fishboning or an Ishikawa diagram after the Japanese management writer who developed it (see Figure 4.3). It is one of the most widely used techniques in quality circles and one of the most powerful diagnostic and team development activities. In some respects it resembles brainstorming but is more structured and focused.

The process can be used to identify the causes of a problem by structuring and displaying them in relation to each other; analysing a process by reviewing factors which may be problematic. The systematic application of a cause and effect diagram can:

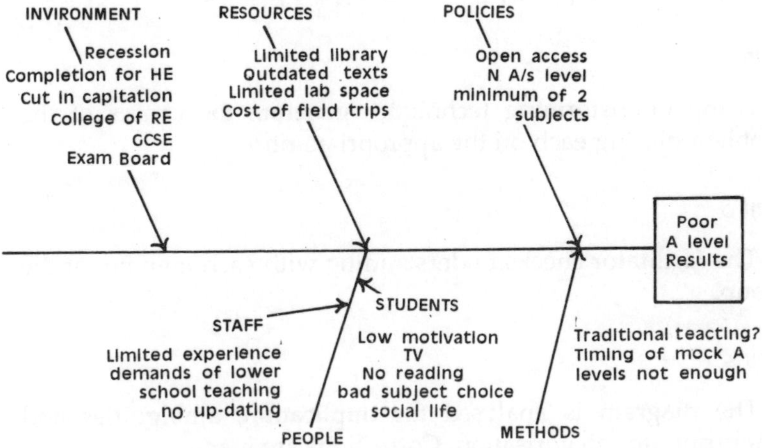

Fig. 4.3 Cause and effect diagram.

- identify *all* the causes of a problem;
- distinguish causes from symptoms;
- analyse the relative significance of related causes;
- provide data for use with other techniques.

The cause and effect approach works best with an established work team led by a facilitator. A maximum of one hour should be spent on the process.

Step 1

Display the diagram (Figure 4.3) on a flip chart, OHP transparency or black/white board. State the problem briefly at the 'head' of the fish. Decide what the characteristics of the 'ribs' should be. It may be helpful to select the most relevant from the list below:

- methods, procedures and stages in the process;
- materials, resources used directly or indirectly;
- people, skills and knowledge;
- measurement, the availability of appropriate data;
- environment, factors influencing the process;

- policies, the principles informing the process.

Step 2

Using brainstorming techniques generate the causes of the problem placing each on the appropriate rib.

Step 3

The facilitator checks understanding with each member of the group.

Step 4

The diagram is analysed for duplication, ambiguities and inappropriate categorisation. Corrections are made.

Step 5

Team members are asked to identify those factors which they perceived to be least significant. Depending on the total number generated 2, 3, 4 or 5 low priorities might be asked for. Those that receive the most 'votes' are deleted.

Step 6

Team members are asked to select the most significant factor (number to be determined by the total available) and to prioritise them. 'Votes' are again collected and the outcome recorded on the diagram.

The process has thus identified possible causes, categorised them, reviewed their relative significance and produced a prioritised list of causes.

Note, For some issues, and for large groups, the diagram can be physically constricting. In this case Step 1 could take the following form:

> Members of the group are asked to note down their contributions and the facilitator then goes round the group recording each contribution on flip chart paper and numbering it. The process is continued until all contributions have been recorded. The sheets

of paper are displayed and Steps 3–6 above are used in the same way.

This approach can also be used to generate and prioritise solutions to a problem, i.e. it is a more sophisticated form of brainstorming. The topic is the problem to be solved and the team are asked to generate possible solutions which are in turn prioritised and reviewed.

This approach is a version of nominal group technique.

Five 'Hows', Five 'Whys'

These are the same techniques with a different focus. In both cases the idea is to explore a problem or solution until it is expressed in the simplest, most basic terms. In essence a team, with facilitator, examines 'how?' or 'why?' and each proposal is then subjected to further questioning until the root cause is felt to have been reached.

This technique can be exasperating and needs skilled facilitating but it is a powerful tool to overcome superficial responses.

Example

We need to extend the working life of textbooks.

How?

By encouraging children to take better care of them.

How?

By making them personally responsible for them.

How?

By introducing a better monitoring scheme.

How?

By designating someone as being responsible.

How?

By HOD reviewing job descriptions and negotiating the new responsibility.

Each stage of the process can generate a number of alternatives, each is followed through to the point where an individual accepts responsibility to act to produce a specific outcome within a specified time scale.

Force Field Analysis

Force field analysis helps a team to understand the context in which it is operating and to target those factors which are working in a favour and those which are opposing change. FFA is derived from the premise that any change is subject to *driving forces* which will move it forward and *restraining forces* which will hinder. The technique can be used to analyse the existing situation, identify and build on strengths, identify and minimise restraints, FFA often centres around perceptions and feelings. However, as these are often the most important factors influencing behaviour in organisations they should be given high significance.

Step 1

The facilitator agrees with the group the topic to be analysed—this might be generated by brainstorming or the cause and effect process.

Step 2

Each member of the team is asked to work individually using the FFA sheet (Figure 4.4).

Step 3

The facilitator manages the process of identifying, agreeing prioritising and recording the team's perceptions. Several drafts of the team diagram may be necessary. Perceptions of the relative strength and significance of each topic can be indicated by the relative size of arrows, placed on the continuum or listed according to priority.

IMPLEMENTING TEACHER APPRAISAL

Driving Forces	*Restraining Forces*
1. Legal requirement	Union concerns
2. Better inset	No time
3. Implementing development plan	Low skills
4. Better quality teaching	Time for training
5. Positive climate	Poor relationships
6. Recognition of success	Confidentiality
7. Career Management	Not needed
8. Better Management	Not my job

Fig. 4.4 Force Field Analysis.

Step 4

The team agrees on the driving forces to be reinforced and the restraining forces to be overcome. The two elements can often be correlated and a readiness and capability chart (see below) used to target specific actions.

Measurement Charts

This is a method of giving graphic representation to trends to facilitate analysis, identify nonconformance, create common understanding and measure change over time. This process can be used for a variety of purposes and helps to maximise the possibility of subjective analysis. The process should not be seen as an attempt to quantify for its own sake but rather to help the process of measurement.

The first step is to identify an individual to be responsible for managing the process. According to the process to be measured, the criteria to be applied, the unit of measurement and the timescale to be used should all be agreed. In many school processes attaching numerical values may be problematic but in fact teachers are experts at translating children's work into grades and there is considerable experience in the evaluation of INSET courses!

Example

It has been decided to review senior management team meetings over a half-term period. The key components of a successful meeting are agreed and each team member completes the review sheet (kept simple) at the end of each meeting. The scores are aggregated and recorded and the reasons used as the basis for review, analysis and implementation of changes.

Senior management team meeting—review

Please rate each category below for this meeting. 1 = poor unsatisfactory; 10 = excellent.

1.	Agenda received in advance	1	2	3	4	5	6	7	8	9	10
2.	Meeting kept to time	1	2	3	4	5	6	7	8	9	10
3.	Documentation/data available	1	2	3	4	5	6	7	8	9	10
4.	Decisions taken	1	2	3	4	5	6	7	8	9	10
5.	Actions agreed	1	2	3	4	5	6	7	8	9	10
6.	Full participation	1	2	3	4	5	6	7	8	9	10
7.	Appropriate leadership	1	2	3	4	5	6	7	8	9	10
8.	Planning and review sessions	1	2	3	4	5	6	7	8	9	10

A crucial decision is to establish a goal-line—a standard which is regarded as the optimum to be achieved. For some processes this may be arbitrary but experience will identify proper levels.

The measurement chart for the team meeting could appear as in Figure 4.5. The chart displays relative satisfaction and provides a focus for analysis. Individual scores may be displayed as a means of generating discussion and involving all team members in the analysis of the factors leading to dissatisfaction.

This technique has the advantage of being simple and immediate, the discussion generated is more significant than the statistical validity of the method.

Pareto Analysis

This technique helps to establish the vital elements of a problem from the relatively trivial. The approach is derived from the work of the Italian economist Pareto who put forward the '80/20' hypothesis, i.e. 80 per cent of the problems are caused by 20 per cent of the process. Pareto analysis is a means of iden-

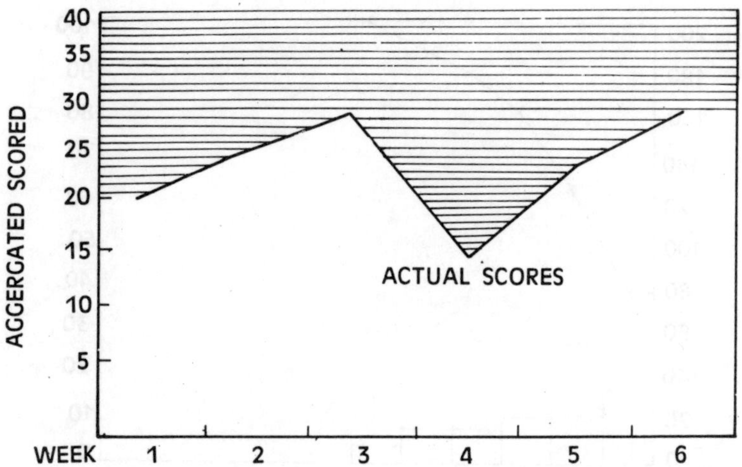

The disparity between the actual score and the possible score is the cost of non-conformance. The objective to reduce that cost.

Fig. 4.5 Measurement Chart SMT Meetings.

tifying the *real* cause of the problem so that it can be addressed directly.

Step 1

Identify the problems to be compared by brainstorming or cause and effect analysis. Identify an appropriate unit of measurement and specify a time period for getting data.

Step 2

Gather results and display them using a histogram. Re-order the histogram so that it displays declining frequency from left to right.

Step 3

Label the right-hand vertical axis to show the cumulative percentage of the total distribution as in Figure 4.6.

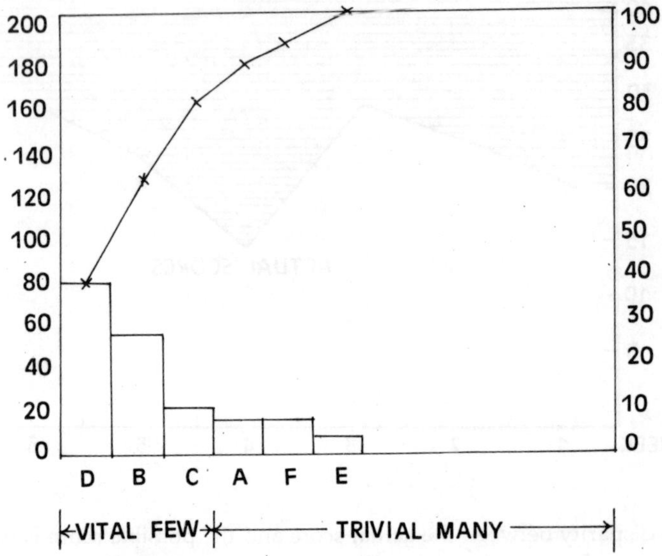

REPORTED PROBLEMS
A—Corrections/spelling mistakes
B—Not completed on time
C—Incomplete comments
D—No envelopes
E—Inappropriate comments
F—Shortage of forms.

Pareto analysis of the factors resulting in reports being sent outlate.

Fig. 4.6 Pareto Analysis.

In the example shown in Figure 4.6 two factors account for two thirds of the late reports. It is therefore possible to identify appropriate remedial activity which is specifically targeted. It also becomes possible to analyse the extent to which the problem has been overcome on future occasions. Although the result might be guessed intuitively the Pareto analysis ensures that the response meets the real need and provides evidence to ensure that future monitoring is effective. It also allows for a further stage of analysis to examine the factors causing the 'vital few' problems.

8. Problem Solving Techniques

A rational, methodical approach to problem solving increases the probability that the problem will be solved with the most appropriate solution. A diagnostic approach is more likely to result in high quality outcomes. It is important to see problem solving as a skill to be developed rather than depend on intuition.

The intuitive response starts from the recognition of the problem, tries to identify causes and then proposes solutions. The outcomes of this approach will include:

- solving the symptoms but not the problem;
- solving the problem but at high cost;
- solving the problem but creating others;
- not solving the problem or the symptoms but learning to live with both.

In a quality environment none of these outcomes is acceptable. The real problem must be solved (thereby removing the symptoms); the solution must not increase costs and must be capable of full implementation.

The components of a rational approach to problem solving are shown in Figure 4.7.

- Identification: This stage involves identifying the actual problem to be solved, i.e. not the symptoms but the core cause. In order to do this it is necessary to specify as many different aspects and components as possible. Techniques such as brainstorming, Pareto analysis, 'five whys' and cause and effect are appropriate at this stage.
- Once the problem has been identified it needs to be 'unpacked', i.e. to be further defined by distinguishing cause and effect; Pareto analysis and 'five whys' are appropriate here.
- Diagnosis: Having identified the actual problem to be solved then systematic analysis of the causes is possible. Brainstorming and cause and effect analysis are appropriate. Once hypotheses have been developed they can be tested using measurement charts, Pareto analysis or active experimenta-

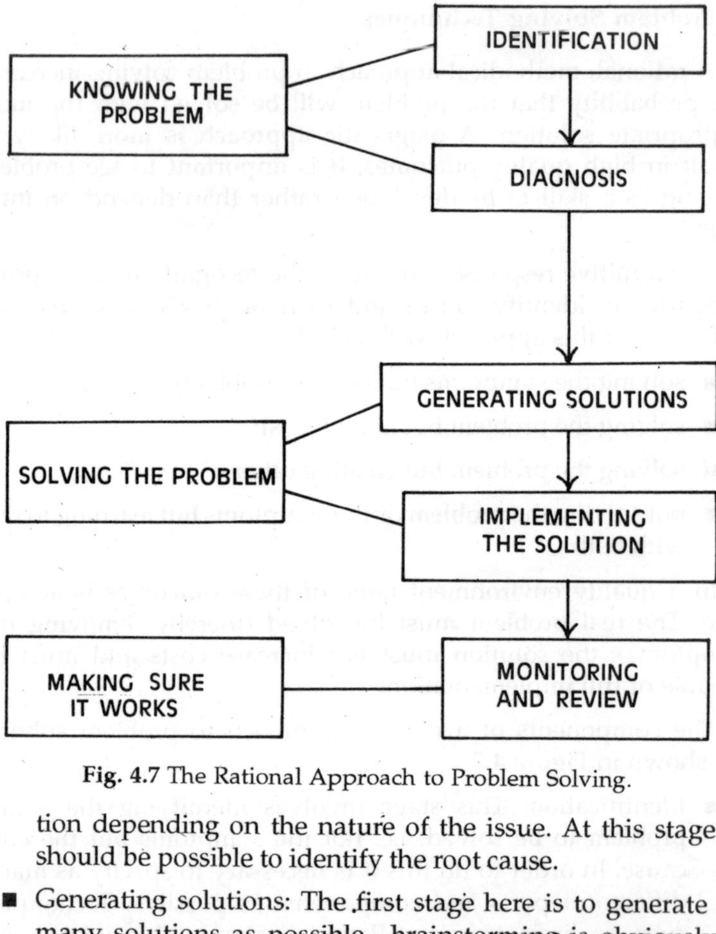

Fig. 4.7 The Rational Approach to Problem Solving.

tion depending on the nature of the issue. At this stage it should be possible to identify the root cause.

- Generating solutions: The first stage here is to generate as many solutions as possible—brainstorming is obviously a powerful technique in this context or nominal group techniques could be used, the 'five hows' may well be most appropriate. Once the options have been identified then it is appropriate to employ team based consensus decision making techniques.
- Implementation: Once the optimum solution has been identified then it is vital to move to implementation. Force field analysis and readiness and capability are appropriate prerequisites to action. The actual solution should be expressed in terms similar to those concerned with delegation and

effective teams—most importantly setting targets specific to named individuals in a clear time scale with appropriate resources and authority.

- Monitoring and review: Monitoring is necessary to ensure that the chosen solution is actually working. Immediate feedback will be obtained by using the same techniques that originally defined the problem. More specifically measurement charts can be employed to allow comparative data to be generated, interviewing those involved can also provide instant feedback. Longer term review is required for two reasons; firstly to ensure that the solution is institutionalised, i.e. it becomes part of the way of working. Secondly it is important to review the problem solving process itself to ensure that it was cost effective and enhanced team skills.

Readiness and Capability

The purpose of this activity is to analyse and increase understanding of the individuals involved in a process in terms of their:

- readiness, i.e. their motivation, capability commitment and willingness to be involved;
- capability, i.e. their knowledge, skills, influence and potential positive or negative power.

This is an individual activity but can usually be carried out by a small team.

The individuals likely to be significant in a particular process are identified and their readiness and capability are then plotted (see Figure 4.8). On the basis of an individual's location on the grid it is possible to identify a range of strategies.

On the basis of the analysis shown in Figure 4.8 AW is clearly a significant person and should be fully involved from the outset. Those with high readiness and low capability clearly need support, development and training. Those with low readiness and high capability need to be involved and motivated to ensure that they do not become negative forces. The potential weakness of this approach (high subjectivity) can be overcome by sharing perceptions, e.g. by each member of the team completing the grid in respect of the other members and pooling

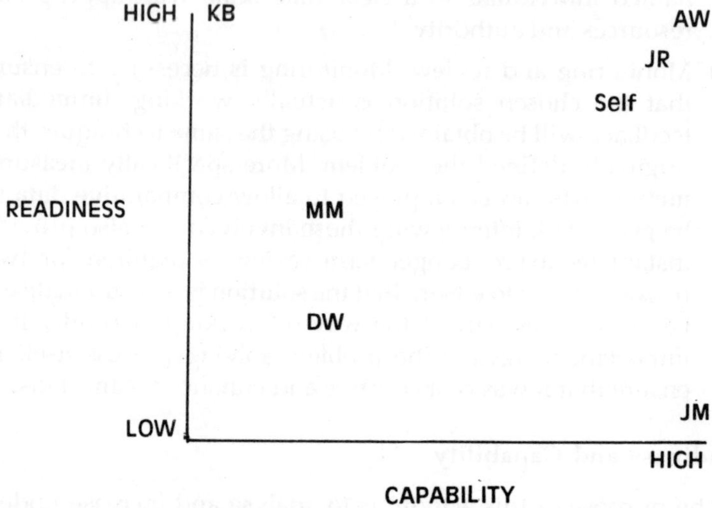

Readiness and Capability chart for introducing a new appraoch to science teaching. (initials refer to teachers involved)

Fig. 4.8 Readiness and Capability.

and sharing perceptions. This will often facilitate openness about attitudes and can be a powerful team development activity.

SUMMARY

- Managing quality is about measurement.
- All work is a process.
- Managing processes is about adding value.
- School processes can be measured.
- Prevention is better then inspection.
- Prevention is achieved through operating procedures.
- Improving quality means reducing costs.
- Quality is free.
- Techniques for improving processes are readily available.

ACTION

- Start calculating the cost of non-conformance.
- Analyse work processes in school and identify ways improving them.
- Identify examples of waste, calculate the cost and improve the process.
- Start using the techniques for improving work processes.
- Analyse your behaviour in terms of:
  - the clarity of the specifications you give;
  - the amount of 'hassle' in your life;
  - the amount of time spent reworking;
  - the amount of time spent dealing with problems, complaints and grievances.

5

Audit of Funds

There is a growing tendency among colleges and universities, public as well as private, to utilize both internal auditors and public accounting firms. In the case of the public institution, the state auditor normally serves the function that would otherwise be performed by a public accounting firm. But in an increasing number of cases the state auditor is contracting with a public accounting firm or authorizing the university to do so.

Internal auditing is a staff function that serves management by reviewing the accounting, financial, and other operations of the institution. Organizationally, this function has traditionally been the responsibility of the chief financial officer. But some institutions have assigned reporting responsibility for this function to the office of the Executive Vice President, the President, or the trustees in order to enhance independence.

College and University Business Administration, the fundamental guide to business administrative procedures governing higher education, published by the National Association of College and University Business Officers, explains that that the activities of the internal auditor should be directed toward:

1. Determining that the system of internal control is adequate and functioning;
2. Ensuring that institutional policies and procedures are being followed;

3. Verifying the existence of assets shown on the books of account, and ensuring the maintenance of proper safeguards for their protection;
4. Preventing or discovering dishonesty; and
5. Determining the reliability and adequacy of the accounting and reporting system and procedures.

To accomplish the internal audit functions in a fully effective manner, a formal written program for the internal auditing operations should be prepared to define the extent and frequency of the review of the financial and business operations of the institution. The program should include, but not necessarily be limited to, provisions for examination of cash receipts, cash disbursements, payrolls, construction accounts, maintenance activities, inventories, and investments.

On the issue of independence, *College and University Business Administration* does not call for a reporting relationship outside the financial management organizational structure. In fact, it recommends that this function should be the responsibility of the chief business officer. But it further states that the internal auditor should not be assigned line responsibilities and should not engage in any activities that he normally would be expected to review and appraise. *College and University Business Administration* also states that the governing board should "require" an audit by independent certified public accountants who are qualified by training and experience to audit the accounts of educational institutions. The function of the independent auditor is defined to include an examination of the financial statements, as well as bringing to the business office assistance, expert advice, and an independent point of view on accounting and fiscal problems.

The American Institute of Certified Public Accountants has outlined four standards of reporting, all of which are applicable to colleges and universities. These are:

1. The report shall state whether the financial statements are presented in accordance with generally accepted accounting principles;

2. The report shall state whether such principles have been consistently observed in the current period in relation to the preceding period;

3. Informative disclosures in the financial statements are to be regarded as reasonably adequate unless otherwise stated in the report; and

4. The report shall contain either an expression of opinion regarding the financial statements, taken as a whole, or an assertion to the effect that an opinion cannot be expressed.

In essence, the "attest" function, which is still fundamental to the role of the auditor, involves a certification that the manner in which financial transactions are processed and recorded accords with generally accepted accounting principles, and that the financial statements fairly present the financial condition of the institution. There are growing pressures to make such statements more meaningful and informative, and the trustees should particularly focus on whether the financial statements and supplementary reports provided to them yield a sufficiently clear picture as to the condition of the institution. With growth in automation, auditors must have the skills to audit computerized records. Public accounting firms are continuing to expand their skills in this area.

Beyond the "attest" function, an extremely important ingredient has been added to the role of the auditors. The growing concerns about the stewardship of the institution and whether its resources are being properly managed, has given special impetus to expansion of the normal scope of audit to include an operational audit. The operational audit is directed toward the broad objective of assisting in the improvement of financial management. This is accomplished by alerting institutional administrators to the breakdown of operational controls, by pinpointing areas for cost reduction, suggesting potential operating improvements, and by pointing out where deficiencies or lapses in the implementation of functional responsibilities in various areas have significantly affected these areas.

A product of this expanded audit is the management letter. This letter should address the effectiveness of internal systems for the budgeting, allocation, and management of resources and make recommendations for the correction of perceived weaknesses or deficiencies.

The broad experience that public accounting firms possess in performing audits of such diverse entities as banks, insurance companies, hospitals, and industrial concerns, as well as a variety of educational institutions, creates a frame of reference in respect to varying financial and operating conditions that permits the firms to bring a highly useful perspective to the audit and to their management recommendations. The quality of the management letter is one key measure of the audit services the institution is receiving.

Issues of disclosure and confidentiality, as they relate to audit reports and management letters, are highly sensitive and complex and need to receive the thoughtful consideration of trustees. These issues have been brought into even sharper focus in the so-called "sunshine" states which have mandated that the affairs of public entities be conducted with full disclosure to the public.

It is fair to say that even in the non-public sector there is a heightened awareness of necessity for adequately informing all constituents and the public in general.

The responsibility that this imposes in regard to audit reports and management letters in particular is to adopt thoughtfully conceived procedures that permit institutional management to be fully informed by auditors on all matters that should properly come to the attention of management, while also adhering to the spirit of full disclosure in respect to the public.

This may well mean that some matters formerly treated with confidentiality because of their sensitivity and complexity may now be subject to broader disclosure. The wider and more diverse audience will require that these matters be treated much more expansively in order to reduce the likelihood that they will be taken out of context, misinterpreted, or misunderstood.

Concurrent with the trend toward and increasing improvement of operational audits has been the growth in management consulting divisions among the major public accounting firms. This is not mere coincidence. The major public accounting firms have found that they serve their audit clients most effectively when they function as full service organizations. As colleges and universities have become more complex and diverse and as the tools and techniques utilized to manage their operations have become more sophisticated, the range of functional specializations and the role of the functional specialist have expanded. In this context the consultant facilitates the audit in two ways.

First, the consultant can provide specialized expertise that will assist in providing analytic and meaningful management letter comments and recommendations. Second, the consultant provides a resource to which the institution can turn for specialized assistance in implementing recommended improvements.

As noted in the chapter on the Use of Consultants, there has been considerable discussion on the issue as to whether public accounting firms can provide consulting services without impairing their independence. Without question, both the accounting profession itself and these institutions and organizations which it services must be alert and highly sensitive to any circumstances, creating a potential conflict of interest or otherwise threatening to diminish the integrity of the audit. But the profession believes, as do other professions such as the medical and legal profession, that the primary means of insuring integrity is through the self-policing mechanisms employed by the profession.

There are some very demonstrable values associated with the provision of consulting services to institutional audit clients by public accounting firms. The specialized knowledge and pragmatic experience of consultants, coupled with the awareness that they may be called upon to assist in implementing management letter recommendations, makes it more likely that these recommendations will be meaningful and realistic. Too often in the past auditors have been criticized by their clients for making recommendations that were "text book" in nature and not realistic or readily implementable.

The consultant who serves an audit client is also likely to be far more effective and cost efficient because he can draw upon the auditor's knowledge of the institution, its operations, *and* its personnel. Additionally, and perhaps most significantly, the continuity of the ongoing audit relationship tends to lend an element of responsibility and responsiveness to the consulting relationship. The consultant who serves an audit client is not apt to "write and run."

As in most aspects of college and university administration, the procedures utilized in selection of public accounting firms for the performance of audits vary widely among institutions.

Among the factors that should normally be considered in the selection of an auditor, is whether the firm being considered has experience in auditing institutions of similar size, nature, and complexity. If such expertise is not available in the local office, the institution should assure itself as to whether it will be provided by transfer of a partner or senior staff member from another office, who has the requisite experience, or through other means. The availability of specialized skills that can provide a convenient and reliable source of support should be another consideration. The institution will want to have the principal staff members who will participate in the audit identified in advance, since the element of personal chemistry is always an ingredient where professional services are involved.

There is an observable distinction in the practices of public and independent institutions although, as in all other areas, a generality as to a practice that is characteristic of a particular category of institutions suggests that the practice is widespread, but not universal. Subject to that qualification, independent institutions tend, more generally, to feel that they have the latitude to select the firm best suited to their needs, even if that firm has not submitted the lowest fee quotation. Their selection procedures will reflect this emphasis. Through the attention they pay to other factors.

By contrast, fee will probably be a predominate criterion in the public sector. The emphasis on fee in the public sector is not confined to audit services, but is more broadly reflective of a general approach to contracting for personal services. It is a manifestation, not so much of the absence of latitude to make a selection on grounds other than fee, as it is the perceived inability to make a meaningful distinction among bidders on other grounds.

Accounting firms, in common with other professional, do not believe that all firms are alike, and indeed it is clear that they are not. Self-policing mechanisms such as the recently introduced peer review procedures, which involve reviews of one public accounting firm by another, unquestionably tend to insure a certain consistency in quality and professionalism. But individual firms nonetheless have unique characteristics and special qualifications that are particularly suited to the specific needs of particular institutions.

Perhaps accounting firms have no alternative but to respond to a market, or one segment of a market, that seeks to treat them as all alike. But they must bear some responsibility as a profession for submitting to a competition on such terms.

Many institutions that engage public accounting firms as auditors have a trustees audit committee. In other instances, selection of an audit firm and interaction with it is a function of the Finance Committee and sometimes of the full Board. The method of handling this is not necessarily based on the size of the institution, but is more likely to be influenced by the size of the Board and whether the trustees are generally organized to conduct their affairs through the committee mechanism.

There is a growing appreciation of the value of an audit committee as an instrument of control as well as a mean of enhancing the quality and acceptability of financial reporting practices. While audit committee practices will necessarily continue to vary significantly from institution to institution, certain issues of policy and procedures are universal:

- What relationship should the committee establish with the independent auditors?
- What kind of information should the committee seek from independent auditors?
- What information should the committee seek from the internal auditors?
- How intensive should the committee's investigations be
- What staff and facilities can audit committees use to accomplish their purposes and how should operations be organized?
- What functions can audit committees perform aside from reviewing the annual independent audit? For example, should they be involved in the budgeting process?

Among the functions of audit committees, the following appear to be gaining the most widespread acceptance:

1. Review of outside auditor's management letter;
2. Meeting with independent auditor;
   (a) to discuss the scope of the audit;
   (b) to review financial statements;
3. Meeting with the chief financial officer:
   (a) to discuss implementing the independent auditor's recommendations;
   (b) to discuss internal controls, procedures, etc.;
   (c) to review alternative accounting policies;
4. Meeting with the internal auditor:
   (a) to discuss adequacy of the internal audit program;
   (b) to review findings of internal audit investigations;
   (c) to discuss adequacy of staff;
5. Discussion of recent American Institute of Certified Public Accountants (AICPA) and other regulatory agency pronouncements and their impact on institutional accounting practices;
6. Discussion of performance and staffing of accounting and financial departments;
7. Appointment or nomination of the independent auditor;
8. Participation in the establishment of fees.

Periodic rotation of auditors has been viewed by some as a means of ensuring independence—by avoiding the development of overly close auditor-management relationship—also of preserving a fresh auditor viewpoint. Countering these advantages are certain significant drawbacks. A newly appointed audit firm must necessarily incur extra audit expenses to accumulate the historical information needed to become familiar with operations, organization, personnel, and special institutional characteristics.

Furthermore, rotation can sometimes lead to a loss of continuity and a lack of familiarity with accounting principles used in prior periods. There is also a cost borne by the institution as a result of the rotation—related to the time of key administrators and expense involved in familiarizing the new auditors with the institution and its procedures.

Those who advocate rotation of auditors believe that the change:

- Reinforces the objectivity of the audit; and
- Reduces the likelihood that the auditors will fail to detect crucial items because they have not recognized a change in conditions.

But it may be possible for a client to preserve the advantages of rotation without forfeiting the advantages of continuity if the auditing firm's internal policies permit this. Thus an audit committee can explore the recurring auditors' attitude toward:

- Rotation of all personnel involved in audit activities; and
- Revision of audit programs to keep auditing relevant to current conditions.

Rotation of auditors can often be the result not of a philosophic conviction as to its desirability, but rather a dissatisfaction with the quality and responsiveness of the existing audit firm's performance. When a change of auditors occurs, it is important that the audit committee meet with both the administration and the existing auditors to obtain their views on the change. In that way, the committee can determine that there are no unstated differences that could have an impact on future relationship and gain insights that may be useful in avoiding future difficulties.

Since institutions receive their support from a number of funding sources, they have traditionally been required to account separately to these various funding sources and have, consequently, been subject to multiple audits. This is particularly true of institutions that receive federal support, whether in connection with campus based student financial aid programs or federally sponsored activity such as research.

The Federal Office of Management and Budget in its *Circular A-110* establishes uniform administrative requirements for grants and other agreements with institutions of higher education, hospitals, and other nonprofit organizations. These include the requirement that institutional recipients maintain financial management systems which, among other things, provide for examinations in the form of external audits or internal audits. Where internal audits are performed, they must meet the independence criteria established by the United States General Accounting Office publication, *Standards for Audit of Governmental Organizations, Programs, Activities and Functions.*

It is further specified that these examinations should be conducted on an organization wide basis to test the fiscal integrity of financial transactions, as well as compliance with the terms and conditions of the federal grants and other agreements. They should be conducted at scheduled intervals no less frequently than every two years. Finally, it is stated that these examinations do not relieve federal agencies of their audit responsibilities, but may affect the frequency and scope of such audits.

It is within the context of this last provision, and in recognition of the limited availability of their own audit resources, that some federal agencies are encouraging the use of public accounting firms to audit federally sponsored activities as an extension of their regular audits.

This applies particularly to the area of student financial aid which has been a source of major concern. Federal agencies can view their own audit responsibilities as being fulfilled by relying on these audits, provided that they can satisfy themselves as to be completeness and effectiveness of the audit program and test the quality of the audit through review of the workpapers.

In one particular respect, public accounting firms can utilize their unique position to provide and effective service both to their clients and to federal sponsoring agencies. Resolution of audit disallowances and "set aside" has been an especially thorny source of conflict between institutions and federal granting agencies. When federal auditors encounter a circumstance in which cost are inadequately documented or supported, their normal practice has been to set the entire amount of such costs aside.

What these set aside cost connote is not that the auditors consider such costs to be improper charges to federal grants and contracts, but rather that the inadequacy of documentation precludes the auditors from determining with any reliability the extent to which such costs may or may not be valid charges to federally sponsored projects. The set asides may be quite substantial in amount, amounting to millions of dollars in the area of faculty compensation, as an illustration. (See discussion on Sponsored Activity.) This will be further exacerbated when, because of limited resources, federal auditors are unable to perform audits annually or even biannually and, hence, are frequently applying their findings retroactively over several years.

As a consequence of the "set aside" there is left to the mechanism of "audit resolution" the establishment of the extent to which the inadequacy of documentation reflects improper charges which should result in refunds from institutional grantees to the federal government. Although this process has often involved extended fact finding beyond that engaged in by auditors, it has generally fallen short of validating or invalidating charges with any degree of conclusiveness. The resolution thus ultimately results in a negotiation which has produced refunds of hundreds of thousands of dollars by individual institutions. These refunds were frequently not acknowledged by the institutions as appropriate, but utilized as a means of terminating the process. Thus the process has been a source of considerable tension, with federal officials upset at the failure of institutions to provide them with satisfactory information on a timely basis and believing the institutions to be recalcitrant and institutions believing that they are being harassed with excessive and unreasonable demands. (HEW's Office of the Inspector General has issued an internal directive requiring federal auditors to extend their audits when confronted with documentation deficiencies. They are expected to make reasonable efforts to avoid set asides. Since it is likely that this resources will continue to be limited, it does not seem likely that directive will do much to solve the problem referred to.)

Interestingly, the General Accounting Office (GAO) has been as critical of the audit resolution process as have institutions. It has been the contention of the GAO that the refunds negotiated were arbitrary and inadequate in relation to the size of the set aside.

Because the accounting firm that serves as auditor for the institution enjoys a position of trust and confidence with the institution and also with the federal government, and because of its professional independence, it is possible for it to serve both parties and to effectively deal with the problem of audit resolution by extending its audit to encompass federally sponsored activity. It accomplishes this by establishing with the institution an acceptable method for validating charges when adequate documentation is not available. The methodology deemed acceptable will be one that the federal authorities will be equally willing to accept. Institutional staff can then perform the validation techniques with test checks performed by the accounting firm to insure the integrity and proper application of the validation process. This involves many complex issues. But as in many other situations, the intrusion of a third party perceived by both parties to be fair and objective, can make a constructive contribution to the process.

6

Sponsored Programmes

Sponsored programmes, as defined in the federal cost principles for educational institutions contained in the Office of Management and Budget (OMB Circular A-21) encompasses organized research, which is sponsored by federal and non-federal agencies and organizations, as well as projects financed by external sources, which involve performance of work other than organized research and instruction. Illustrative projects or programs would include health service projects, community service programs, and agricultural extension services. Although for many years sponsored activity was of significance only to those approximately 200 major institutions that engaged in extensive organized research, the growth of community service programs has enlarged this group of institutions.

The emergence of the federal government as a major source of funding for university research activity can be traced to the accelerated demands of World War II, with increased impetus provided by the launching of the first Russian satellite, Sputnik, in 1957. The 20 year period commencing in 1946 saw the passage of the Public Service Act of 1946, which encouraged support of research investigations at scientific institutions; the authorization of the Office of Naval Research; the formation of the National Science Foundation and the growth of the extramural programs of the National Institutes of Health, culminating in 1967 in a level of federal R & D funding approximating $ 16 billion.

To those concerned with the financial and general well being of the educational enterprise, the increased reliance of the federal government on institutions of higher education as a resource for research and assistance in the implementation of national goals must be regarded as a mixed blessing. Unquestionably, federal funding has provided a stimulus to expanded research programs which have enriched the academic environment. Sponsored projects have also provided an important source of institutional support, funding the acquisition of hundreds of millions of dollars of scientific equipment, providing for substantial assistance in construction of new facilities, funding additional expenditures such as faculty travel and secretarial support and, through funding of research assistants, providing an important source of student financial aid.

However, the degree of reliance on federally funded projects as a source of support for faculty salaries (particularly at many medical schools) has contributed to the erosion of faculty collegiality and to the transfer of loyalties from the institution to the funding sources.

When the faculty member perceives future career advancement as related principally to publications and other externally oriented activities, when needed support services come primarily from federal agencies and federal program officers deal directly with faculty, it is small wonder that faculty members cease to identify with their institutions. The ready availability of federal funding has also induced institutions to take on activities which are not necessarily in full consonance with institutional goals and priorities. This tendency can be exacerbated when long-term commitments are made to programs or activities which are temporarily financed by external "seed money," but for which no long-term source of institutional funding has been identified.

Institutions have become increasingly aware that with federal funds comes federal regulation and the desire to use federal funding to implement public policy goals carrying with it a heavy administration burden and substantial cost. Additionally, and most importantly, there is the "accountability" requirement. Promoted in part by the pressures of the General Accounting Office, the House Government Operations Committee and other "watch dog" groups, federal agencies have moved increasingly to impose on institutional recipients of federal funding a degree of precision in accounting for and documenting costs far beyond that which has governed their internal activities. In fairness, it should be noted that there is a growing perception of need for greater accounting and costing precision for internal purposes.

Accountability must be understood within the context of the special stewardship requirements associated with the expenditure of public funds. Over the years numerous "horror cases" have arisen, involving the improper use of federal funds. At one point, there was a rash of cases in which costs were transferred from one project to another, either to avoid a cost overrun on the former, or to avoid having to return unexpended funds on the latter.

Although institutions have generally been guilty of loose practices, rather than of deliberate malfeasance, the general public, stimulated by sensationalism in news reporting, tends rarely to differentiate the two circumstances. The dilemma for those charged with management of the institution is that federal program officials deal primarily with their faculty counterparts, fostering the impression that the locus of the research is insignificant in relation to the question as to who is performing the research. However, grant and contract awards are made officially to the institution and it is the institution that is charged with insuring compliance with federal requirements.

Because faculty members see university administrators as having no meaningful role in securing federal grant and contract support, they perceive them as exclusively involved in enforcing onerous compliance requirements which "get in the way of research." This makes it particularly difficult for administrators to satisfy accountability requirements. The most controversial of the accountability requirements has been the requirement for "faculty effort reporting" or "personnel activity reporting" to support salary charges to federal grants and contracts.

Federal cost principles establish documentation requirements for costs associated with salaries and wages of faculty or professional personnel that are charged to sponsored agreements, either as a direct project charge or as part of one of the indirect supporting activities, the cost of which is partially allocated to sponsored projects. Those charges must be supported or documented either through a system of monitored workloads or a system of personnel activity reports.

The monitored workload system calls for the distribution of salaries and wages, based on budgeted or assigned workload, revised periodically as required, to reflect any significant changes in work load distribution. Some of the principal categories of significant change would be: a material modification in teaching load, unanticipated addition or removal of administrative assignments, sabbatical leave, or beginning or ending work on a government agreement.

Personel activity reports are intended to reflect an after-the-fact reporting at the end of each academic period, of the percentage of effort devoted by each employee to the various activities in which that employee was engaged. Under either of these two alternatives there is a requirement to account for 100% of the activities on behalf of the institution, whether direct or indirect.

These requirements have undergone modification on several occasions over the years. The most recent major modification was introduced in march 1979 after almost three years of extensive and heated debate. But, despite the extensive time devoted to developing the most recent cost principle revision and, in particular, to the provisions regarding salary support, this area remains a source of tension between the institutions and the federal agencies and within the institution between faculty and administrators. The problem is a major one because salary support is by far the largest component of the costs of sponsored activity. It has involved cost disallowances or cost set asides ranging up to $27 million and more by federal auditors and has provoked bitter and emotional disagreements. The controversy stems from reasons that are practical, emotional, and philosophic.

A very practical consideration that rarely surfaces in the arguments concerning faculty effort reporting is that institutions rely on a number of different sources of funding support for their budgets. In the case of some major institutions, and particularly their medical schools, federally sponsored activity has been a significant source of support for faculty salaries. Consequently, a change in the budgeted activity on which federal salary support was based (i.e., a circumstance where the faculty member ultimately devotes less effort to a sponsored project than had been planned) could have a detrimental financial impact on the institution by causing a reduction in an important source of funding.

An aspect of the faculty salary support problem related to, but separate from, the question of documentation is that many institutions, both public and private, have had a policy or a practice of declining to charge salaries; sometimes medical school faculty will be charged while arts and sciences will not be. This difference reflects that there are more substantive differences among different departments within universities resulting from both internal and external factors than many outside the university environment realize.

There are a variety of reason for the practice of declining to charge faculty salaries to grants and contracts. Faculty members prefer not to have their salaries related to "soft money;" they also feel that if their salaries are not charged to federally sponsored projects, they need not be influenced by federal priorities in the pursuit of their own research interests. This is hardly a valid assumption if they must depend on federal support for other project related expenses. Finally, some institutions adhere to the philosophic belief that it is improper to charge the salaries of tenured faculty to federally sponsored projects.

But whatever the reasons for this practice, it is now being reassessed by most of the institutions that have engaged in it. An appropriate reason for reassessment would have been the recognition that the institution can no longer afford to voluntarily relinquish substantial sums of potential revenue. But the reassessment has been stimulated by another circumstance.

Revision to the federal cost principles in March 1979 have made explicit that the base of organized research to be used in distributing indirect costs must include all costs associated with organized research including salary costs voluntarily absorbed by the institution. Federal agency officials are interpreting this to mean first, that although the institutions formerly did not consider it necessary to document the amount of effort the tenured faculty devoted to sponsored projects, that is now required. Second, it is asserted that the institution must not only absorb the salary costs but must also absorb the related indirect costs.

These interpretations are being contested. But they tend to illustrate what can occur when, in the formulation of policy, government officials fail to give adequate consideration to the incentives created by their policies. Institutions that were formerly inclined to absorb costs that they could legitimately have charged to the government are penalized by being required to absorb even more costs than they intended. The result is that many of them may elect to change their practice and pass the costs on to the government. Government costs will thus have increased with no substantive improvement in research or in the stewardship of federal funds.

The controversy over documentation requirements, particularly as related to salary support, most frequently centers on the differences between the normal practices of most institutions and what federal officials think they ought to be. There are some genuine difficulties in budgeting in advance for some activities, such as committee assignments, as required by the monitored workload system. More generally, colleges and universities have traditionally been more loose in their contractual relations with their professional employees than many other enterprises. Consequently, the articulation of faculty responsibilities at the outset of the academic year in a very explicit and reasonably detailed manner, would represent a radical departure from the normal practices of most institutions. Ironically, the strongest influence on articulating faculty assignments and responsibilities with greater explicitness seems to come from the activities of faculty unions.

An important consideration is that, although other professionals, such as accountants and attorneys, are accustomed to the discipline of accounting for their time, faculty members, who for many years have functioned with a very substantial degree of latitude and flexibility, are not accustomed to account for their time and are highly resistant to such an accounting. (This is a generality that applies with varying intensity to different disciplines; e.g., university spokesmen have pointed out that engineering faculty have far less difficulty in accommodating to effort reporting than do arts and sciences faculty.)

They make the philosophic argument that the interrelatedness of their activities makes it impractical and unrealistic to attempt to allocate or apportion their efforts. The classic case cited is that of the senior faculty member at a teaching hospital who, in treating a research patient, while observed by interns, is simultaneously engaged in teaching, research, and patient care.

Institutional administrators, frustrated by government compliance efforts on the one hand and faculty resistance on the other, have at times contended that documentation for faculty salary charges to federal grants and contracts in unnecessary. The ultimate test, they say, is "did the government get what it paid for—i.e., was the research or other activity for which the granting agency provided support effectively accomplished?"

Such a contention begs the question. The predominant form of support for federally sponsored activity, whether the grant or contract instrument is used, is a cost reimbursement arrangement. So long as this continues to be the major approach to support, federal granting agencies, in the fulfilment of the stewardship requirements associated with spending of federal funds, must take reasonable steps to assure themselves that the costs that have been reimbursed were actually incurred and are properly attributable to the project to which they were charged.

As taxpayers we can accept no less. There have undeniably been instances of genuine abuse in which substantial amounts of money were improperly paid. While these amounts constitute only a minor fraction of the total sums awarded to colleges and universities, they can be viewed within the proper perspective of exceptions only when institutions can effectively demonstrate that they have established adequate systems of control.

What appears to be principally needed is a careful and unemotional reassessment of whether present instruments, methods, and procedures for supporting research and other federally sponsored activities at institutions are appropriate. The significant changes that such a reassessment is likely to produce will not come quickly. But there are some hopeful signs. One of the sources of difficulty is that faculty members engaged in major projects will receive support from several funding sources, each desiring to account for its funds in a discrete way, while the faculty member tends to treat all the funds as one pool of fungible money. At this writing the National Science Foundation is experimenting with an approach that seeks to at least partly ameliorate this circumstance.

In the interim, until some solutions are found, both federal officials and university officials need to adopt a broader, more objective perspective than either party has evidenced in this highly emotional controversy. Federal officials need to recognize that in providing support for activities conducted at colleges and universities, they must avoid the imposition of requirements aimed explicitly or implicitly at changing the character of the institution. Institutional officials must in turn make an objective reassessment of the manner in which the institution conducts its affairs in the context of the major changes that have taken place. Both parties should find a common meeting ground in the identification of reasonable procedures and controls which are necessary for effective internal management and, hence, should be capable of satisfying external requirements.

Another important and highly controversial component of federally sponsored activity is the reimbursement of indirect costs. In accounting terms, the concept of indirect costs is a relatively simple one. Those costs which can be directly attributed to a particular project or activity, such as travel, salary, or fringe benefits of an individual who serves the project on a full time basis, are classified as direct. Those costs associated with services which benefit a number of activities, such as the services of the purchasing department, are classified as indirect. The key to whether a cost is classified as direct or indirect is the ease with which that cost can be identified with activities which it benefits and the amount of trouble and expense the institution is willing to incur to make such identification. In theory, all costs could be treated as direct.

Recovery of indirect costs has been a source of tension between faculty and university administrators. One principal reason for this is that as funding sources utilize the fixed price contract or program officials seek to stretch their funds, the impression is conveyed to the faculty that any increase in indirect costs will diminish the funds available to support the direct costs associated with their projects. Additionally, faculty members who believe their support services to be inadequate, such as those who are dissatisfied with the office space allocated to them and how it is maintained, unhappy with their secretarial support, or irritated by the time and difficulty involved in processing purchase requisitions, view the reimbursement by the federal government of the costs associated with those services to be more akin to a profit.

Concerns by faculty members and others who question indirect cost reimbursement have led to invidious comparisons; with those institutions having lower indirect cost rates being held forth as shining examples of efficiency. More often than not a comparatively low rate signifies under-recovery either through neglect or as a matter of deliberate policy, rather than efficiency in operations.

But comparisons of rates among institutions, though frequently made, should be avoided because they are apt to be misleading. There are some major variations in indirect cost calculation procedures, which make for a high degree of non-comparability. These include:

- Differences in whether given activities are charged directly to projects or treated as indirect costs;
- Variations in the base used to distribute research indirect costs to organized research projects;
- Determinations as to whether specific activities are to be assigned to one indirect cost pool or another. Because the various pools are distributed differently, this determination can significantly influence the rate and cost recovery;
- Selection of the appropriate unit of measure or base for allocating indirect cost pools to research;
- Results of audit and negotiation; and
- Variations in the way institutions organize activities.

In order to promote greater comparability, as an additional tool to assist them in evaluating the "reasonableness" of indirect cost rates, federal officials have been striving to impose requirements for greater uniformity in costing practices among institutions. These efforts are not likely to be fully successful. Significant variations in the way institutions organize their activities and in the precision with which they account for the costs of those activities, will continue to justify differences which make indirect cost rates among institutions non-comparable.

Indirect costs are recovered from the federal government by establishing a rate which is then applied to grants and other agreements with federal agencies. The rate is a ratio, expressed as a percentage, between indirect costs and a direct cost base—historically either direct salaries and wages or total direct costs excluding capital expenditures.

The rate is established through negotiation with a single cognizant federal agency that has been designated to act on behalf of all federal agencies in this capacity, generally because it provides more support to a particular institution than any other agency. Institutions are required to submit an indirect cost proposal annually to support the establishment of an indirect cost rate. The proposal and its supporting documentation may be subject to review by an auditor, a negotiator, or both, depending on the procedures employed by the cognizant federal agency.

Those institutions with relatively modest amounts of federal support for research and educational service (the current figure is $ 3 million or less) may use the so-called simplified method for submitting an indirect cost proposal. This method, which involves a formula approach, is far less burdensome to the institution, but has traditionally produced significantly less cost recovery.

The alternative to the abbreviated procedure is the so-called long form, which *must* be used by institutions with federal support in excess of $ 3 million, and may be used by institutions with less support. This requires the use of sound cost finding techniques involving an analysis of the research, instructional, and other activities conducted by an institution to determine the type and level of administrative and other services supporting them and the most appropriate unit(s) of measure for allocating the costs of these supporting services to the benefiting activities in reasonable proportion to the services rendered to them. The cost of the supporting is then distributed by the use of work sheets to those activities serviced.

Indirect cost rate calculation and negotiation is a rather sophisticated process requiring skilled personnel who are familiar with the subtleties of federal procedures. It is fair to say that most institutions under-recover the cost associated with support of research and other sponsored activity. The under-recovery takes place at three levels.

The most readily perceived level of under-recovery results from an explicit waiver. This occurs when an institution deliberately accept an indirect cost rate less than that which has been officially established on a particular grant or agreement. There are cogent and valid reasons for such a waiver in some instances, particularly when the project in question is deemed to be of special value to the institution. But more often than not, such waivers are not adequately controlled and not subject to critical scrutiny.

A second level of under-recovery occurs when an indirect cost rate is negotiated which is appreciably lower than the rate that had been calculated. This is generally attributed to "hard nosed" federal auditors and negotiators. It is indeed inevitable that among the multitude of federal personnel involved in this process, some will be intractable and unreasonable. But, success in negotiation a rate equal to or closely approximating the rate that had been calculated, is largely in the hands of the institution. It depends primarily on the cost finding techniques employed by the institution and the adequacy with which the institution supports or documents its costs.

Institutions have all too frequently negotiated rates that represent less than full recovery of allowable costs, reflecting their sensitivity to faculty concerns about "high" rates. Under such circumstances the institution makes a blanket waiver of revenue without ever fully determining how much income is being given up or why. A more prudent approach would regard the rate establishment process as a vehicle for establishing the institution's full entitlement. Waiver of reimbursement could then be handled on a case-by-case in the course of which the income relinquished can be weighed against the benefits to be obtained and the necessity for waiver for indirect costs can be verified.

The most subtle form of under-recovery results from the variations in permissible rate calculation procedures. The failure to utilize legitimate techniques which will have the effect of more accurately and equitably assigning costs appropriately attributable to sponsored activity contributes significantly to under-recovery of costs. However, this form of under-recovery is not likely to be detected by institutional management except by those skilled in the techniques of rate calculation.

Another important aspect of the indirect cost rate process that bears significantly on the extent to which cost are recovered is the manner in which rates are established. Indirect cost rates may be established either provisional, final, predetermined, or fixed with a carry forward provision.

A provisional rate is a temporary rate, used by awarding agencies as a basis for estimating and funding the amount of indirect costs applicable to a grant or other agreement until actual indirect costs are determined and a final indirect cost rate established. Two major difficulties with this procedure are first, that when the final rate is established, a substantial amount of administrative effort may be entailed in adjusting the rate on each project.

Even more significant is the fact that the final rate may call for a refund on the part of the institution, if it is lower than the provisional rate. On the other hand, if the final actual rate is higher than the provisional rate—and this is more likely to be the case—the institution must seek to collect the difference from each supporting federal agency. Frequently, the funds to reimburse this difference may not be available, particularly since there may be an interval of two years or more between the establishment of the provisional rate and the determination of the final rate.

A second alternative is predetermined fixed rate negotiated and agreed to for a specific future period. Since this rate is not subject to adjustment, it is appropriate for use only when there is reasonable assurance that the rate agreed to will approximate the institution's actual rate. This requires a degree of economic stability that has not been present in recent years and is not foreseeable in the predictable future. For example, energy costs impact materially on the indirect cost rate. Given the potential for fluctuations in these costs, it would be highly risky for institutional representatives to fix a rate based on an existing level of cost.

Because of the palpable shortcomings in both of the alternatives outlined above, a third alternative was developed and referred to as the fixed rate with carry forward. Under this procedure a rate is computed and fixed, for a specified future period, based on an estimate of that future period's level of operations. When the actual costs of that period are known, the difference between the estimated costs and the actual costs is carried forward as an adjustment to a subsequent period for which a rate is established.

This latter procedure is the *only* procedure that will insure full recovery of costs *based on the rate that has been established.* Nonetheless, because of the interval between the fixing of a rate for a period and the determination of the actual rate experienced, in an inflationary period, the cost difference may create a balloon of such significant impact on the rate that some institutions have waived a portion of the "carry forward" to avoid too large a rate increase.

This is an uncalled for relinquishment of funds which the institution is legitimately entitled to recover. The procedures contemplate, whether or not they are sufficiently explicit on this point, that the rate will be adjusted whenever a material fluctuation can be demonstrated. This will minimize the "balloon." The length of the interval between the close of the year and the establishment of the final rate is due to the workload of federal auditors and negotiators and their consequent inability to keep current. For additional discussion on this point.

A surprising number of institutions continue to utilize the second alternative, namely the fixed predetermined rate. Since federal negotiators will be reluctant to agree to this alternative, unless they are reasonably certain that the actual rate will be equal to *or lower than* the predetermined rate, one may be assured, prima facie, that this procedure results in under-recovery. The majority of institutions utilizing this procedure are public institution. Hence, this is additional evidence that unenlightened policies on the part of states in sharing indirect cost recoveries with public institutions, results in under-recovery of indirect costs to the detriment of both parties.

Public institutions encounter a special problem associated with indirect cost recoveries since technically the state, which funds all of the indirect costs which are being reimbursed, is entitled to the full recovery of such costs. In practice, states vary in their treatment of this source of revenue and the varying state policies bear a direct relationship to the aggressiveness of public institutions in seeking full recovery of indirect costs. Some states permit the institution to retain all recoveries. Others insist that all such recoveries be remitted to the state or be treated as a budgeted source of revenue to supplement the state appropriation.

In many instances this revenue is shared between the state and the institution, based on the recognition by state officials that such sharing can stimulate research and, hence, the growth of sponsored activity which will result in the financing of many costs which would otherwise be borne by the state and will also result in the growth of indirect cost revenues. The recognition of the benefits that can result from sharing a portion of indirect cost recoveries to be used as seed money to stimulate research has also prompted many private institutions to distribute a portion of recoveries to academic departments in proportion to the indirect costs which they generate.

Federal grant programs have, for many years, been governed by a cost sharing requirement, which is congressionally mandated. The congressional intent has never been clearly established, except that it is evident that the institution must bear *some* share of the costs associated with federally supported projects. Institutions must, consequently, be wary of attempts by federal agencies to impose a degree of cost sharing that is unwarranted. The implications of specific agency policies must also be examined with care. For example, where agency policies specify that costs shared by the institution must also bear their proportionate share of indirect costs, the institution might well look to share in another element of cost, perhaps indirect costs. many institutions cost share to a much greater degree than is legally required. For example, institutions that, as a matter of policy, do not charge the salaries of tenured faculty to federal grants are cost sharing those salaries. Nonetheless, some institutions in this category also engage in additional cost sharing.

Although, as noted, federal agencies will vary in their implementation of the cost sharing requirement despite continuing efforts to achieve greater consistency in this and other areas of federal grant administration policy, there is a tendency to look to historical patterns of institutional cost sharing—formal and informal—and to seek to establish those patterns as a level for continued cost sharing. But institution cannot afford, in today's changed financial circumstances, to sustain historical levels of cost sharing and, consequently, should be actively engaged in an assessment of the costs they can and should bear.

The special requirements associated with federally sponsored activities have caused many research oriented institutions to set up special units to administer grants and contracts. At times, these units also act as information sources and assist faculty in identifying opportunities for outside funding. Public institutions have, in many instances, established these units as separate corporate entities, often called Research foundations. This has been a device for avoiding the application of state regulations (e.g., in regard to purchasing) which may inhibit effective support of research activities. The important considerations to be balanced are the necessity for creating mechanisms which facilitate research activity, while avoiding a loss of institutional control.

As a postscript to the foregoing, reference has been made several times to the fact that in March 1979 OMB Circular A-21, the cost principles governing reimbursement under federal grants and contracts, was significantly revised. This event warrants more than a passing reference.

The specific impetus for the modification was the testimony of the Office of Management and Budget (OMB) officials in an appropriation hearing. At that hearing, in which imposition of a statutory ceiling on indirect cost reimbursement was being considered, OMB officials, in arguing against the imposition of the ceiling, committed to "tighten" the cost principles.

The cost principles revision is of significant importance to sponsored project administration, in part because of its salutary effect in stimulating improved accountability; and in part because of its adverse effect in increasing the burdens and the costs of sponsored project administration.

But possibly of even greater significance is the nature of the process in which the cost principle changes were promulgated and the climate that governed those change. The changes were developed over a period of almost three years during which there was much heated and rancorous discussion among university and government representatives. This is reflective of pervasive and highly disturbing change in the federal/university relationship.

For many years, commencing in 1946, as referred to in the introductory portion of this chapter, the federal/university relationship in the pursuit of research and related activities was conceived of by both parties as one of mutuality. A contribution to sustaining our institutions of higher learning as a vital national asset was explicitly recognized as an objective of federal policy. The essential research role of our institutions in helping to expand the frontiers of knowledge was also recognized.

By contrast, this past decade has been marked by a pronounced deterioration in this relationship. The former partners have taken on the appearances of adversaries, with neither exhibiting a willingness to understand the imperatives and constraints that govern the behavior of the other. It will take a high degree of statesmanship on the part of both parties to restore the relationship to its former healthy state.

7

Customer Satisfaction in Schools

The quality organisation exists for its customers, it has no other purpose other than providing products and services which satisfy customer needs. The commercial organisation which fails to meet its customers' requirements will rapidly go out of business. The rest of this book is devoted to principles and processes to help ensure a focus on the customer. This chapter is concerned with explaining the issues involved in the concept of customer. There are many problems associated with using the term 'customer' in an educational context; there is no cash transaction, education is a statutory requirement, in many parts of the country there is no choice of school available so the notion of customer choice is spurious. More significant is the objection that education is a professional relationship so the term 'client is more appropriate and the role of schools is not to perpetuate existing social norms but rather to enhance society, to pass on moral, intellectual and social skills to children.

This view presupposes a unique body of knowledge to which access is restricted, teachers are the custodians of that knowledge and transmit it according to best professional practice. The customer can't know best because the customer doesn't know. A quality approach denies the validity of this approach. The 1988 Education Reform Act has done much to challenge this view by giving parents the potential power to choose. Many trends in schools have highlighted the issue of responsiveness to children, community and the full range of stake-holders in education.

The purpose of this chapter is to examine the components of customer satisfaction through a variety of issues:

- Defining the customer.
- The nature of quality customer service.
- Ensuring customer satisfaction.z

DEFINING THE CUSTOMER

Figure 7.1 A caricatures the traditional customer relationship in education—passive recipients of a professional service rather like patients in a hospital bed being talked about rather than listened to. It is easy to parody this situation—'no parents past this point'; 'generally satisfactory work and progress'; the options booklet that assumes training in deductive logic; the school prospectus written by teachers for teachers; the exclusion of non-teachers from the staff room; home work instructions so cryptic that the allocated time is spent deciphering them. These are all minor irritants or symptomatic of a failure to perceive customer needs and expectations.

The academic debate about who is the customer in education is capable of metaphysical convolutions; working on permutations of professionality, professionalism, accountability, answerability a wide range of answers are possible. The TQM response is quite simple and central to this book:

A CUSTOMER IS ANYONE TO WHOM A PRODUCT OR SERVICE IS PROVIDED

A customer is therefore defined in terms of relationships and processes rather than relative status, role or function. Customers are internal and external. The quality approach to customers is shown in Figure 3.1B.

The implications of this model are:

- Everyone is a supplier and a customer.

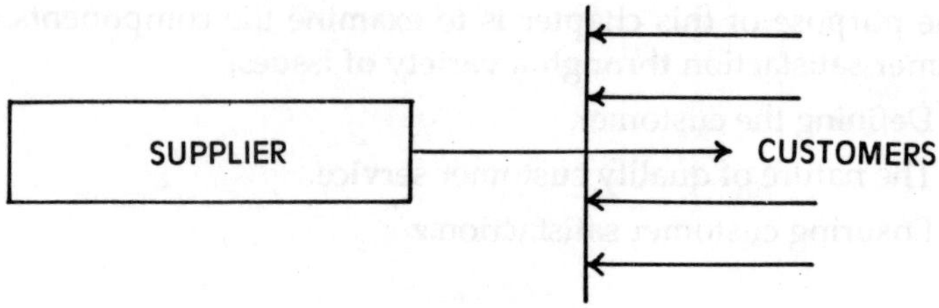

A The Traditional Supplier-Customer Relationship

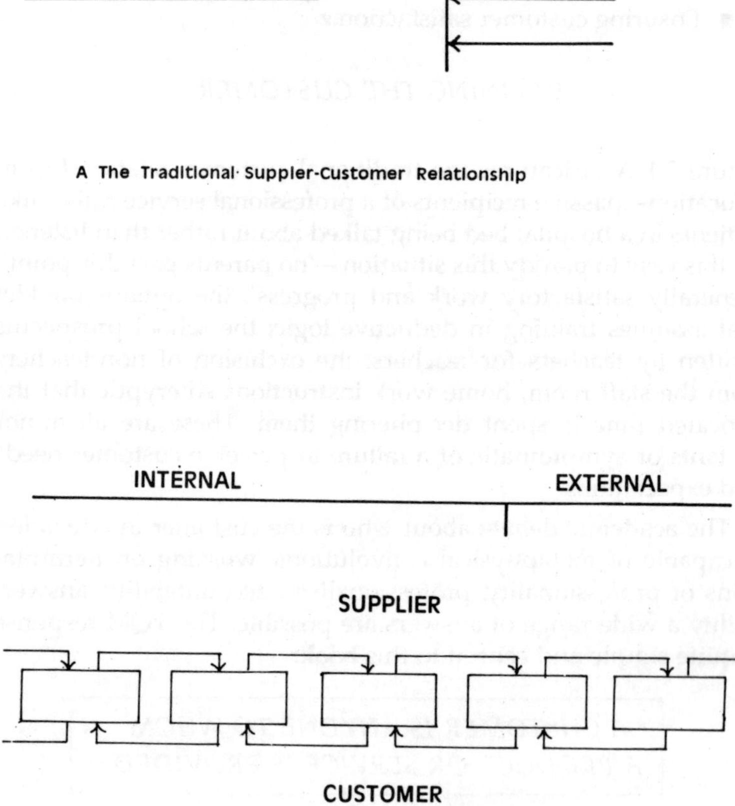

B. Quality Supplier-Customer Relationship

Fig. 7.1 Supplier—Customer Relationships.

- There are equal responsibilities on suppliers and customers.
- Work processes have to be defined in terms of customers and suppliers.
- It may be helpful to differentiate between internal and external customers and suppliers but not to discriminate in levels of service.
- Supplier-customer 'chains' may be of variable length but this cannot be used as an excuse to compromise the process.

In order to ensure the integrity of the chain a significant amount of analysis is required to establish who exactly is involved—unless this first step is taken then quality will be problematic.

Figure 7.2 shows the supplier-customer relationship involved in organising a class trip to a museum. Unless all the participants are identified then it will be impossible to identify requirements and so impossible to provide quality service.

If one component is missed then the information flow will be incomplete and the trip will probably not taken place. There may be associated processes, the teacher liaising with the head teacher, with the bus company etc. Each link in the chain has to be of equal strength; the information from the museum has to be complete opening times, eating facilities, educational support services, prices etc. However, this will be to no avail if the letter is not typed and copied in time, if children do not deliver it and if parents do not have a date by which to return it. At each stage requirements have to be stated so that customers and suppliers are aware of their interdependence.

In this example parents might be regarded as the 'final' customer and their needs therefore determine the whole process. In order to make the process a quality one the needs of the final customer have to be clearly understood and expressed in such a way as to inform the design and delivery of the process. This involves defining the customer and then developing mechanisms to ensure monitoring and feedback. These mechanisms are discussed in the third section of this chapter, 'Ensuring customer satisfaction'; defining the customer involves understanding a complex range of factors, as shown in Figure 7.3.

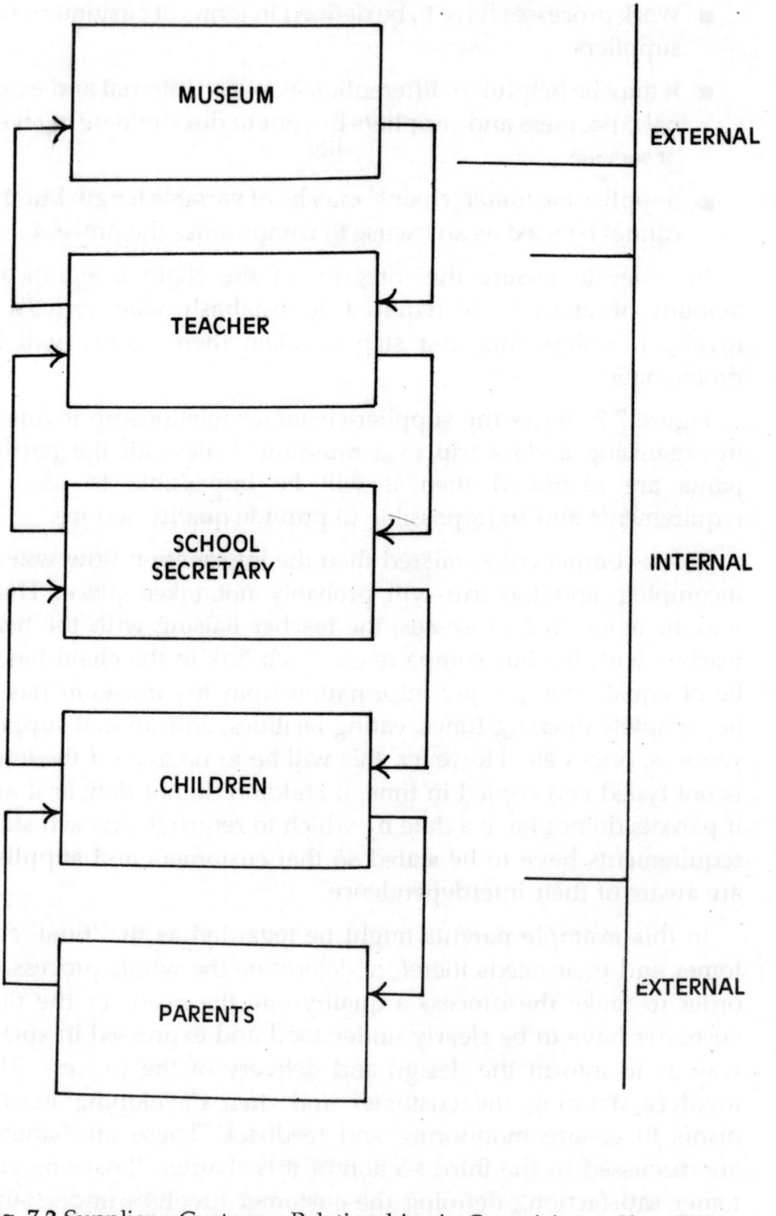

Fig. 7.2 Supplier—Customer Relationships in Organising a Class Trip.

In order to understand your customers you need information about their:

Values	:
Attitudes	:
Educational Level	:
Expectations	:
Preferences	:
Social Situation	:
Commitment	:

Fig. 7.3 Defining the Customer.

Many schools could argue that they have a full understanding their customers. However, care has to be taken in the extent to which this understanding is imposed by teachers, is based on subjective opinion or swayed by political opinion.

The components of defining the customer outlined in Figure 7.3 may be expanded as follows:

- Values: This is the significance attached to the education process in general and the school in particular. It will be reflected in the extent to which education is seen by parents as an investment or an expedient, the importance attached in the school by the community and the credibility it has with other stakeholders. Unless the school understands the value of its customers it is unlikely to be able to deliver quality outcomes.
- Attitudes: In some senses attitudes might be regarded as the manifestation of values—responses to the school displayed behaviour. Attitudes are reflected in the language, involvement and commitment of the school's customers. The school that aspires to provide a quality service to its customers looks to itself first as the cause of behaviour on the part of its clients. Attitudes change and develop in response to the service provided.

- Educational level: Most professionals are so immersed in their expertise that it is possible to forget that the rest of the community does not necessarily share their understanding. Just as teachers are sometimes confused by medical or legal language so their clients can be intimidated by inappropriate language.

No effective teacher would ever dream of teaching a lesson without checking that the vocabulary was appropriate and the concepts understood. The same principle applies to all those with whom the school communicates. This is not to argue for simplification to the point of absurdity but rather effective communication.

- Expectations: Meeting customer expectations is the hall mark of quality—exceeding them is the key characteristic of total quality. However, this means that they have to be known and understood. Expectations are more than requirements—they are the basis of 'delighting the customer'. It is easy for a garage or shop to exceed customer expectations, less so for a school to ensure that every child is happy and fulfilled, achieves at least 5 GCSE passes or gets a job. Yet one of the principal features of successful schools is that they share and express high expectations.

- Preferences: All organisations that provide a service will usually offer a range of options in order to maximise the possibilities of anticipating customer choice. Understanding the broad preferences of customers is a fundamental component of providing a quality service. The details are to be negotiated and developed on the basis of feedback but the broad pattern of preferences has to be established; this might include issues such as uniform, the pattern of the school day, sex education, religious education etc.

- Social situation: The social context of a school will be a major determinant of its response to many of its customers. Prevailing patterns of culture, the ethnic balance, unemployment, the economic situation, social advantage and deprivation will all be significant features in helping to determine a school's response to its community. Schools are often highly expert in understanding the context in which they operate. The difference for a TQM school is the extent to which responses are assumed and derived by teachers or based on real understanding.

- Commitment: Commercial success depends on obtaining and retaining customers. Increasingly schools are in the same situation—failure to recruit and retain pupils will result in the school ceasing to be viable. It is therefore essential to understand the significance attached to education by customers, in order to be able to make the most appropriate responses. Figure 7.4 shows one way of understanding the implications of varying levels of commitment.

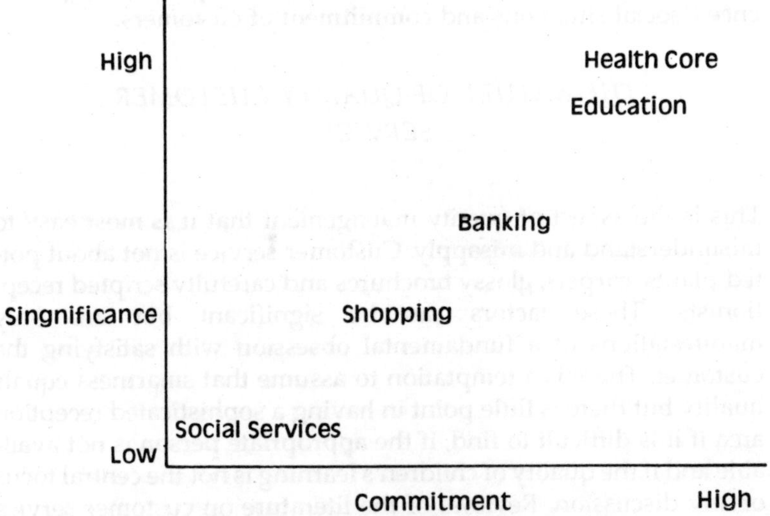

Fig. 7.4 Understanding the Relationship Between Significance and Commitment.

For a relatively prosperous community the relative levels of significance and commitment might appear as shown, however, the situation could be totally reversed in other communities. The commitment of parents will be a direct function of the significance attached to education and this will in turn reflect the six components identified above.

Defining the customer is essential with regard to parents and children and they should be the predominant feature of any such analysis. However, the same process is needed for all customers especially the external ones. There is a potential issue in that perceptions and needs may be in conflict—different groups may have varying expectations. This issue is best resolved by analysis of the particular process and identifying the 'end user' who is then the customer whose needs predominate. This does not mean that managing a quality school is simply a series of conditioned responses. There is an imperative to enhance the service provided, to 'delight the customer' and most importantly to add value. TQM organisations are successful because they build on customer expectations and continually enhance the service provided. However the starting point must be the values, attitudes, educational level, expectations, preferences, social situations and commitment of customers.

THE NATURE OF QUALITY CUSTOMER SERVICE

This is the aspect of quality management that it is most easy to misunderstand and misapply. Customer service is not about potted plants, carpets, glossy brochures and carefully scripted receptionists. These factors can be significant but are only manifestations of a fundamental obsession with satisfying the customer. There is a temptation to assume that smartness equals quality but there is little point in having a sophisticated reception area if it is difficult to find, if the appropriate person is not available and if the quality of children's learning is not the central focus of any discussion. Reviews of the literature on customer service produce lists of strategies, many of which fall into the 'have a nice day' syndrome. However, it is possible to isolate a range of factors which an appropriate to schools.

Conformance to Requirements

This is at the heart of quality management. In essence it means that the service provided is fit for the purpose intended, i.e. it meets the needs of the customer. There are many potential applications of this principle in schools:

- reporting on progress to parents; the information is expressed in such a way as to be comprehensible and comprehensive;

- purchase of text books; they are relevant, up-to-date, written at an appropriate level with a suitable format;
- classroom organisation; facilities and resources are easily available.

This list could be continued indefinitely and it is an important part of the implementation process to find out and deliver their needs. However, the most important potential application is in the organisation of learning. Conformance to requirements does raise significant questions about the delivery of the curriculum. If the needs of the individual learner are considered the starting point to identifying customer needs then a number of issues emerge:

- the need to relate learning strategies to individual ability;
- the flexible use of time to allow appropriate pacing and completion of integrated units of study;
- deployment of the full range of teaching strategies from the most didactic to the most flexible—to be determined by not ideology;
- reviewing the role of the teacher as controller and emphasising the role of facilitator;
- questioning teaching the 'class' when individual outcomes are the determinants of educational success;
- recognition of the importance of intellectual and social skills development being reflected in the organisation of learning;
- ensuring that marking and assessment are formative rather than summative;
- programming options to ensure that individual rather than systems needs are met.

This approach would appear to endorse an open or flexible learning approach and this would appear to be the strategy that is closest to quality principles. However, a quality approach to managing learning is not a matter of prescribing the 'one best way' but rather diagnosing and identifying needs and relating learning strategies to them. What the quality approach does question is the view of managing learning for administrative convenience. As has been mentioned elsewhere in this book the effective primary classroom is probably the closest that education currently comes to TQM.

Continuous Improvement

In terms of customer satisfaction continuous improvement means that suppliers are constantly concerned with adding value. There is an obsession with enhancing and improving every process. This is where professional expertise and development are so important. It is the professional skills and knowledge of teachers and managers in schools that are the principal source of this process. At the most fundamental level it is how the teaching of a particular topic can be improved the next time it is taught, how teaching aids and resources can be deployed to better effect.

This is a natural process for professionals—never accepting the 'status-quo' but constantly explaining techniques to ensure more complete understanding, to improve the language used in materials, to develop activities that help clarify complex issues.

The same principles apply to management processes in schools, education procedures, decision making, INSET days are all capable of sustained improvement over time. The crucial thing is that there is no complacency, no notion of a plateau of acceptability.

Responsiveness

This is one of the most tangible expressions of a customer satisfaction orientation. In practical terms it means a rapid response to complaints and requests. More directly the phone is answered promptly, letters are replied to within a specified time period; more importantly there is a tangible and personal response on the customers' terms. This might mean an 'open door' policy. It certainly means that concerns are given a high degree of seriousness.

In the classroom it means creating the situation where children feel able, and are encouraged to express concerns which are deal with. It also means that ideas and suggestions are incorporated rapidly in order to improve classroom and school processes.

Integration

Customers are fully integrated into the organisation. This means the possible customer response is the baseline criterion in every decision-making process and that customers are physically incorporated in activities. it is better to involve at the outset than to decide, consume and then have to change.

This is much more than encouraging a PTA, holding parents evenings or inviting parents in to help. It is actively, deliberately and systematically informing and involving all customers in processes Low levels of interest are usually explained by low levels of perceived significance. Genuine integration means that customers will be able to see tangible outcomes of their involvement rather than a token acknowledgment.

In practical terms this means maximum contact at appropriate levels; in the secondary school making the form tutor the first point of contact with parents; the notion of the 'open day' needs to be replaced by the concept of permanent openness. The non-teaching staff of the school need to be fully incorporated into all aspects of the quality strategy. Crucially administrative systems and structures should not be used as barriers to incorporation and involvement. Secondary and primary school staff need to visit and exchange as a secondary and college staff. The National Curriculum require partnership through integration if it is to work for the benefit of children. Many schools have found that the best way to deal with bullying, theft, vandalism etc. is not to make more rules but to have the problem, its solution and implementation to children.

This is a classic example of real integration and it is much more likely to succeed because it takes into account the views of the involved and also has their commitment. This is listening to the customer and demonstrating tangible respect.

Focus on Delivery

The quality organisation centres all its resources on those who are in direct contact with the customer. In the case of schools this is obviously the classroom teacher. The focus for concern, support and development has to be those who actually deliver. Their development has to be the central priority and the way in which the school is managed has to reflect the importance of the classroom teacher. They are the management team's most important internal customer.

The best word to describe the relationship between management team and teacher is probably *respect*, i.e. recognition of the central significance of the classroom practitioner.

One of the best ways of ensuring customer satisfaction is to ensure that those with whom customers come into contact have the skills to be able to respond and confide in senior management. This requires support praise, recognition, thanks and trust. In practical terms this means direct and immediate support for teachers in the classroom, budgeting so as to maximise resources at the focal point of the school and the provision of quality INSET to meet classroom needs.

A further manifestation of this is the involvement of senior management by being directly available to classroom teachers and by being involved in the classroom and other aspects of the school on a regular basis. This can take a wide variety of forms, e.g. covering for absence, having a programme of regular cover to create opportunities for feedback—and time for colleagues, taking teachers off timetables for a week to allow time for projects etc.

The crucial thing is that managers do not 'lose touch' and are directly available to improve responsiveness. Much is made in the literature of the quality movement of management by walking about (MBWA). Better than this is MBDTJ—managing by doing the job. This is not to diminish the strategic role of senior management but to stress the importance of keeping close to the customer and seeing the school through its customers' eyes.

Listening to the Customer

Quality customer service can only be achieved through real listening; such is the importance of this topic that it is the subject of the third section of this chapter. Delivering quality customer service is a matter of respecting the uniqueness of each customer, treating them with respect and listening to them.

ENSURING CUSTOMER SATISFACTION

Measuring customer satisfaction is at the heart of TQM—obtaining feedback and *acting on it* is what differentiates TQM from every other management theory. There is a moral obligation on all suppliers to find out customer needs, to seek to meet them and then to find out the extent to which they have been met. There is an equal obligation on customers to articulate requirements and then to participate in monitoring and review. This section is concerned with some of the methods available to gather data, many of these are familiar to most schools—the crucial difference is the extent to which listening takes place and action results.

The following techniques are among the most appropriate for schools:

Suggestion Cards

Invite all the school's customers, internal and external, to suggest improvements. The natural creativity of children can be a powerful force as can parents after two hours spent in school for a total of 20 minutes' consultation with teachers. The only rule is to offer solutions as well as identifying problems. This approach can also be used to solve a particular problem. The important thing is that the cards are seen to lead to action and not used as a spurious form of PR.

Shadowing

Suppliers place themselves in the situation of customers. A form teacher in a secondary school spends the day with her form (and is not allowed in the staff room at break or lunchtime!). A primary teacher joins his former pupils on their first day in secondary school, a secondary school timetabler experiences the fruits of her labours by experiencing the reality of the pro-graph board! Senior staff teach the problem class.

Although the shadow's presence will inevitably distort 'reality' the process does provide the opportunity for experiencing the direct impact of school policies.

Interviews

These can be used with almost any group as the basis for detailed and informed data collection. Talking to small groups of children, inviting representatives of the local community, groups of governors and teachers to indicate how the school might be improved are all potentially powerful strategies to generate ideas, to indicate seriousness and demonstrate commitment.

Surveys

These are probably the most powerful, and potentially most intimidating means of obtaining feedback. They are important because they are capable of quantification and will thus permit comparisons over time. Quantification also facilitates prioritisation. Surveys can be used to:

- collect information about customer needs;
- identify specific problems;
- assess conformity to requirements;
- measure satisfaction.

Thus surveys may be used about a specific lesson, a particular aspect of school life, meetings, evaluation of a course of study, a specific facility (e.g. the library) or views on a current issue (e.g. uniform).

The design of the survey should be determined by the data required but may include:

- open-ended questions; a useful source of data but difficult to analyse;
- closed questions; easy to analyse but limited options);
- rating scales; easy to complete and analyse but requiring careful design.

The data that is collected can be analysed using a variety of techniques such as Pareto Analysis. The results of a survey can provide:

- instant feedback;
- diagnosis of specific problem areas;
- indications of satisfaction and success:

- decisions about priorities for action;
- evidence of commitment to customer satisfaction.

Team Meetings

Almost any team can contribute to feedback by having a regular agenda item concerned with feedback to suppliers. It may be appropriate to constitute terms for the specific purpose of reviewing services provided. A team may also invite some of its customers to attend its meetings on a regular basis. Aspects of some lessons, e.g. personal and social education can be devoted to the provision of feedback. This survey is potentially one of the most powerful as it integrates review and feedback into normal operating processes. As confidence grows within a team so feedback will become more detailed and specific.

Although review and monitoring are essential they are symptomatic of a school which is listening to its customers and trying to see itself through their eyes. If the customer chain is fully established then there will be a gradual shift from reaction to anticipation and the school's customers will be fully integrated into all aspects of its working processes. The full involvement of children in this process can be viewed as an important, and living, contribution to their preparation for adulthood by learning how to participate in a wide range of social processes—not least their own obligations as suppliers of products and services. Seeing children as customers in the classroom and school processes also minimises the view that management approaches turn them into products.

SUMMARY

- Quality organisations exist to meet customer needs.
- A customer is anyone to whom a product or service is provided.
- There are internal and external customers.
- It is the responsibility of customers to specify needs and suppliers to meet them.

- Customers need to be defined in terms of a complex range of factors.
- Customer needs are defined in specific actions.
- Customers must be listened to—complaints and concerns must be welcomed.
- A range of techniques can be used to find out about customer satisfaction.
- Children are not products—they are customers.

ACTION

- Identify your customers and find out their requirements.
- Analyse areas of strength and weakness.
- Build review procedures into every process.
- Create a climate for delighting the customer.

8

Cost Analysis of School Education

By this point most readers are no doubt anxious, having read enough about the nature and behavior of costs and about how others are using cost analysis, to get to their own question: How can I apply cost analysis to my problem?

The next four chapters are addressed to this question. Three deal respectively with recurrent costs, especially teacher costs, capital costs, and checking consistency and feasibility. First, however, presents a number of practical suggestions on how to get started on cost analysis, the minimum facts needed, where to look for them, some important analytical and accounting distinctions to bear in mind, and some common pitfalls to avoid.

Obviously, we cannot consider each type of use in detail, much less each local variant. Thus we have chosen the compromise of offering selected suggestions, caveats, methodologies, and illustrations that will be relevant to a wide range of uses and circumstances, leaving it to the reader's ingenuity to adapt them to his own situation.

Space limitations also preclude us from demonstrating the arithmetic of each methodology discussed. Readers who want help on this score are urged to explore the useful two-volume manual by John D. Chesswas, Methodologies of Educational Planning for Developing Countries (Paris, Unesco : IIEP, 1969).

Effective educational cost analysis involves much more than simply knowing the right analytical methods. It also involves choosing appropriate tactics and maintaining good human relations; knowing where and how to get the necessary basic data and how to judge the reliability of different sources; allocating your time judiciously; avoiding certain conceptual and accounting pitfalls; and skillfully arranging trade-offs between economic, pedagogical, and other considerations.

This chapter offers a potpourri of practical suggestions and cautions about such matters, drawn from a wide range of experience and stated in down-to-earth terms. If you are already an experienced hand in these affairs, then we suggest that you scan these pages and move on quickly to the next chapter.

GETTING OFF TO A GOOD START

Your first serious cost analysis assignment may well be a crash operation. Perhaps the deadline will be close at hand for submitting the new draft educational plan, but it must first be costed and its feasibility tested; or a project proposal, must be quickly readied for a mission from the World Bank scheduled to arrive soon; or a major decision on salary policy is impending but its economic implications must first be determined. If you are lucky, you will previously have had a chance to make a more general exploration of costs in your educational system, but this would make you an exception to the general rule.

In all events, getting started right is half the battle. By honoring the following simple rules you may save much time, avoid many difficulties later, and increase the ultimate impact of your efforts.

Clarify Your Objectives at the Outset

Before getting too committed to a particular approach or too buried in a mass of statistics, we suggest that you take time to define clearly the objectives of your exercise, the key questions you will seek to answer, and what you hope to accomplish, being certain that all of these have a direct bearing on real and important issues requiring decisions.

You may find it useful to ask yourself such questions as these: What are the most critical emergent problems confronting this educational system which cost analysis might help to solve? What experts on the scene could contribute to an analysis aimed at solving these problems? Who in particular might be interested in the results of such cost analysis and could put them to effective use? How and when can the results best get injected into the decision making process in order to have a maximum impact on what is decided? In what form should the final results be presented to be of greatest effect?

Consult your Main Clients at the Outset

The best way to answer these questions and to guarantee that your efforts will count most is to bring the potential users of your analytical results in at the takeoff. They include especially the managers and decision-makers who need the help of cost analysis and who alone can put the results into action. Ask them what *they* see as the main problems and questions needing attention. You may not agree entirely with their initial answers and perhaps you can gently persuade them that there are even more important questions to start with. But in all events it is wise to give heavy weight to their views and to meet them more than half way, not only because they may have valuable experience beyond your own, because without their interest and cooperation you may not get very far.

You may, of course, run up against some clients who are so skeptical of cost analysis, or who feel so threatened by it, that they are not prepared to take your questions seriously. If so, the burden of proof will be on you. The best tactic in such circumstances is not to write such people off as "the enemy," but to do your diplomatic best to persuade them to reserve judgment until you have had a chance to demonstrate how cost analysis might help them. There is no more ardent apostle, after all, than a "doubting Thomas" who finally sees the light. It is up to you to furnish the light.

Find Some Able Collaborators

It is well to identify as early as possible some technical collaborators who have skills and access to sources of information that supplement your own. They may include, for example, an able educational statistician and an experienced budget officer in the education ministry, a general economist at the planning commission interested in human resource development, a manpower expert at the ministry of labor, an imaginative demographer at the university or the census bureau, a fiscal expert at the ministry of finance, and a construction cost estimator in the ministry of works.

Things usually move faster and more smoothly, especially in the early stages, if this sort of collaboration is kept as informal and unstructured as possible. To try right at the outset to set up a formal inter-ministerial committee to deal with technical and informational matters often wastes time, creates irrelevant bureaucratic problems, and, worst of all, jeopardizes the essential climate of informal give-and-take among professional colleagues.

Needless to say, in these matters of tactics you must be the judge of your own particular situation. But the main point holds in all circumstances: to be a successful cost analyst one must be not only technically competent but able to work well with others in an atmosphere of professional objectivity and mutual respect, regardless of traditional bureaucratic obstacles to easy communication.

Use A System Approach from the Outset

To identify all the key questions that should be answered by your inquiry, whatever its objective, we suggest that you view the matter in its full context, using the broad perspective which systems approach affords.

To illustrate, let us suppose that your first assignment is to cost a proposed new teacher training project whose aim is to increase the supply of fully qualified teachers and thus upgrade the qualifications profile of the teaching corps. Since an international capital loan is being considered, you will naturally want to give careful attention to the capital costs involved. But it would be a grave mistake to stop there. The most important issue is not whether your government can qualify for the loan, but whether, if it gets the loan, it can afford the subsequent annual cost consequences. The questions thus posed go beyond capital cost analysis. For example: What would be the effects of this project on the future teacher salary bill and other recurrent costs? Can we afford it without seriously penalizing other educational activities? Is this the best way to upgrade the teacher corps, or are there alternative ways to achieve the same result more quickly, cheaply, and effectively? Finally, taking a longer view, do we run the risk of over-expanding teacher training capacity—once the immediate backlog of demand for trained teachers is met, will the annual demand settle down at a lower level?

The guiding rule suggested by this illustration is that there is no such thing as a narrowly circumscribed, isolated problem for cost analysis. Any much problem is part of the seamless web of interconnecting and interacting elements which can only be seen in proper perspective through the wide-angle lens of systems analysis.

THE MINIMUM NECESSARY FACTS

Once you have identified your objectives and key questions and mapped out your study plans, you will begin in earnest the search for pertinent facts. At first you may be dismayed by how few pertinent facts are readily available. The stockpiles and flows of information are often shockingly deficient even in the most sophisticated educational systems. If you have joined the educational management team from some other field, you may be astonished at how little hard data is available for assessing the system's performance and for planning its future.

But do not be easily discouraged; even in the poorest circumstances, cost analysis can be helpful. As we noted earlier, however, the less adequate and less sophisticated the data you have to work with, the more ingenious and sophisticated you will have to be in using them. Also, the more frequently you will have to substitute judgments and "guesstimates" for hard facts.

There can be no single magic list of the "minimum essential facts" needed for cost analysis in all places and for all purposes. But cost analysts in any situation will find themselves severely handicapped if they do not have at least the following statistics to go on:

- Total enrolments broken down by levels and types of institutions, geographic areas, and, if possible, by individual grade levels.
- Annual number of graduates from each category of institutions.
- Annual number of dropouts and repeaters (shown separately) by type of institution, geographic area, and, if possible, by individual grades.
- Total teachers, distributed by types of institutions and levels, and divided, if possible, by qualification and salary categories.
- Total annual expenditures on each level and type of institution, broken down by recurrent and capital costs and by major sub-categories within each of these (particularly separating teacher costs from other recurrent costs, and new construction and equipment from repairs, maintenance, and replacements).
- A breakdown of annual revenues by source of finance (e.g. central and local government, private grants and fees, etc.) for each main educational sector.

In addition to these more or less standard educational statistics, cost analysis and planning require much information on economic and social trends of a sort that educational administrators have not been so accustomed to using. This includes data on the growth and distribution of national income and public revenues; population growth, migration, and distribution, manpower needs and employment trends; general price, wage, and construction cost trends and changes in the structure of the economy. Such data are usually available in some form in various government bureaus.

Inevitably the facts and estimates contained in your presentations will vary greatly in precision and reliability. We therefore make three suggestions. First, you should not be apologetic or embarrassed about making "crude" and approximate estimates if that is the best the situation allows. But you should always be very candid about it. Policy-makers must be made aware of the possible margin of error in any set of estimates you give them so that they will not treat them as scientifically revealed truth if in fact they are only rough approximations. Second, even where more refined estimates might be possible, rough and ready ones are often sufficient for answering broad questions; to embellish them further would go beyond the point of diminishing returns and be a poor use of your time. Finally, to cover the above situations, we suggest that you adopt a scale of accuracy ratings and attach to each set of figures you circulate an "estimate of accuracy." This will help those who use your findings to make due allowance for whatever margin of possible error they may contain.

STRENGTHENING THE INFORMATION SYSTEM

At the same time that you are struggling to extract the best possible immediate answers from the partial evidence at hand, you should also try to strengthen your information system for the future. But here a word of caution is in order. Beware the statistician who considers that all statistics are of equal importance. In fact, some are absolutely essential, some are useful but not essential, and still others have too little value to justify the cost of collecting them. Thus, a cost-benefit mentality is important when selecting the statistics that should be given priority in improving an educational system's information system. The first question to be asked is: What are the most critical questions to which educational managers need answers, and what specific kinds of facts are essential to providing these answers? Unless the matter is approached in this fashion, great effort may be wasted on the indiscriminate collection of facts that are of secondary importance and may go unused, while certain really essential facts remain uncollected.

Once the different categories of statistics have been sorted out according to their relative importance for decision-making and management, two other questions should be asked: With what frequency and regularity will each particular set of facts be needed? Must they be collected from all educational units or will it suffice to use a sample?

Too often limited data-gathering resources are dissipated on a full census approach to every type of information instead of relying for some purposes on well-chosen samples. Obviously, to get reliable annual totals of enrolments, teachers, classrooms, graduates, and the like, data must be collected regularly from every educational unit. But, on the other hand, if you want to monitor the trend of dropouts and repeaters, for example, or to check the comparative unit costs of different levels and categories of educational institutions, this can be done better and at less cost by using a sample.

The sampling method, however, must be used with sophistication or the results can be very misleading. It is especially important to select a truly representative sample that gives proper weight to each of the categories being studied, and to design any questionnaires or interview forms carefully to ensure that the resulting data are comparable and unambiguous. If, for example, you want to study the comparative costs of different types of secondary schools, you should not take the easy course of loading your sample with prestige schools near the capital city just because they are convenient to visit and keep better records. A true picture requires a cross-section sample appropriately weighted to represent different types of schools—e.g. different sizes, day and boarding schools, rural and urban, academic and comprehensive, private and public, boys, girls, and co-educational schools, and whatever other classifications may be relevant.

The case studies from Morocco, Uganda and Thailand demonstrate the value of sample studies. In all three instances, an examination of a sample of individual school accounts provided important insights into significant cost variations among different categories of institutions that could not have been revealed by full census studies.

CRITICAL RATIOS AND NORMS

Beyond the basic statistics listed above, there are a number of crucial relationships, indicators, and patterns that are invaluable to the cost analyst for a variety of purposes. Some of these can be derived from combinations of aggregate statistics while others require sample studies of institutional accounts. Among the most important are:

- The ratio of educational expenditures to the GNP and to total public expenditures.
- The ratio of teacher costs to other recurrent costs.
- The comparative level and composition of unit costs per student in rural vs. urban schools.
- The comparative cost per student in primary, secondary, and post-secondary education.
- Comparative costs per student (teaching and non-teaching, recurrent and capital) of day schools and boarding schools.
- Comparative costs of full-time and part-time instruction, or of formal technical schools vs. on-the-job training schemes.
- The theoretical cost of a primary school graduate (cost per year X normal number of grades) as against the *actual* cost per graduate (allowing for dropouts and grade-repeating).
- The comparative costs and composition of undergraduate and postgraduate university students, broken down by major fields of study.
- The relative size of classes in different types of institutions and in various subject areas.
- Indicators of space and equipment utilization.

Unit cost figures and ratios such as these do for the educational diagnostician what x-ray photos do for the medical diagnostician; they reveal what is going on internally, how the patient is farming, and what remedial actions may be needed.

It may be useful, when studying the foregoing indicators, to compare them with certain critical norms that have been established on pedagogical or other grounds to see if there are any substantial deviations. We saw, for example, how class sizes in rural primary schools in the Soviet Union were found to be far below the pedagogically acceptable norm, thereby revealing possibilities for achieving economies by raising class size. Similarly, the case study of Makerere University College showed how major economics were achieved by enforcing previously recommended by a group of international experts norms pertaining to staff-student ratio, staff-student contact hours, and the ratio of senior to junior staff. A survey of staff utilization in this instance revealed that, instead of an official staffing establishment of 208, there were 300 professional staff members—many supplied from abroad and not shown in the official budget or staff establishment, yet teaching and doing research.

We saw also how Hungarian and Soviet planners make extensive use of norms for planning and costing, and, in the case of the Soviet Union, for monitoring and controlling costs in individual institutions.

LIMITATIONS OF CENTRAL BUDGETS AND RECORDS

The first data source that a cost analyst naturally turns to is the central education budget. If he is dealing with a centralized educational system, as in France or Tanzania, he merely has to go to the national Ministry of Education to examine the public budgetary records and other central records on teachers, enrolments, facilities, and so forth. But if he is working in a decentralized system, as in India, Brazil, Nigeria, the U.S.A., Germany, or the United Kingdom, he may have to travel further and add pieces together from a combination of national, state, district, and local public accounts.

These central accounts and records (at whatever government level) are a rich and convenient source of data, but they have serious limitations and pitfalls which must constantly be borne in mind. Typically they conceal as much as they reveal because they deal in broad aggregates and averages which hide cost and expenditure differentials of great importance to cost analysts. Thus, for example, they may yield the necessary data for tracing broad trends, but not sufficient data to compute many of the critical ratios and differentials listed above. Moreover, the public education budget does not usually include all of the public costs of education, but at the same time it may include certain non-educational items (such as museums, libraries, etc.).

A further limitation is that public (and for that matter, private) education accounts are usually broken down into expenditure classifications which are not very meaningful for most cost-analysis purposes. Most often they show expenditure by object (e.g. salaries, utilities, supplies, equipment, etc.) but not by function or program objective. Olne can usually piece together the aggregate costs of teachers or supplies, but it is impossible to tell, for example, how much was spent for first graders as against second graders, or for learning to read and write as against learning arithmetic, or for what goes on inside the classrooms as against other school costs.

These shortcomings reflect the fact that education budgets were originally designed to serve the purpose of appropriations bodies and auditors, not the needs of educational planning and management. Members of a legislative committee, for example, can tell from the budget how much more of the taxpayers' money the schools and universities are spending this year than last, but they cannot tell for what specific educational purposes the money is being spent, what results are being attained, or what society is getting for its money. Similarly, a government auditor may be able to catch a thief by examining the budget accounts, but he is not likely to catch inherent inefficiencies in the educational system.

What it all comes down to, as we said earlier, is that cost analysis of the sort discussed in this book has not until recently been of great concern to most educational administrators. Now that it has become essential, budgetary accounts will have to be modified and amplified to serve these new purposes as well as the old ones. It is interesting, therefore, that some educational systems have already begun remodelling their budgets and adding new classifications in order to tell a fuller story and to be more useful for planning and management. The case study on Hungary, for example, shows how the annual budget has been made into a tool for implementing each annual slice of the Five-Year Plan. A few other educational systems are moving toward "program budgeting." We will discuss new types of budgeting further in the final chapter.

Apart from budgetary accounts these are other types of central records of great value to the cost analysis, if they happen to be well kept. They include data on enrolments and completions by year, summary information on teachers, and detailed records on facilities. Educational systems vary greatly, however, in the extent and detail of such central records and in how well they are maintained. This, too, was demonstrated by the various IIEP case studies. Relatively few systems, for example, have the detailed central records on teachers that made it possible to project elementary teacher costs in Tanzania by a more sophisticated and accurate method. We saw in the case of Chile that the absence of up-to-date central records on the disposition of technical teachers concealed a major opportunity for improving efficiency by redeploying teachers. The Moroccan case study revealed a great disparity between what the central files showed about the condition and utilization of individual secondary school facilities and equipment and the actual conditions found in a field survey.

In summary, central educational records on expenditures, enrolments, teachers, and facilities are usually the richest single source of data for the cost analyst, but they do not suffice for all purposes and they contain major pitfalls that must be carefully guarded against. Some of these pitfalls are noted below.

PITFALLS TO AVOID

In measuring today's costs or projecting tomorrow's, you can easily get into trouble unless you are clear at all times *what* costs and *whose* costs you are trying to measure and unless you are careful to include *all* the appropriate costs for the purpose you have in mind. Here are a few tips to help avoid such trouble.

Full Costs vs. Partial Costs

Education budgets, whether public or private, never reveal the full financial costs of education to the economy at large.

The national education budget omits (1) all private costs; (2) the costs of educational activities conducted or supported by other governmental agencies; and (3) the costs of education to lower echelons of government. It may also omit (4) certain costs of formal education within the jurisdiction of the education ministry that are actually carried on the budgets of other governmental agencies, such as contributions to teacher retirement, teacher housing costs, student dormitories, or utility costs.

Thus, if you are trying to measure the full budgetary costs of education supported by *public* funds, you will have to search beyond the national education budget and extract appropriate items from other public budgets as well. If, on the other hand, you are trying to measure the full budgetary costs of education to the nation at large, you will in addition have to collect data (or make estimates) on the budgets of private educational institutions (being careful not to double-count government subsidies to private education).

Even after adding together all the public and private budgetary costs of education, however, you will still not have the full picture of total financial costs of education to the economy. The main item missing will be the financial outlays of students and their families for such items as transportation, meals, school uniforms, books, and so forth, which are not reflected in educational budgets.

For many purposes, of course, you will not need to include all of these financial costs of education, and even when you do, you can use rough estimating methods for some of the smaller elements (such as financial costs to families). What is important, however, is that you know when you are leaving something out and that you make your clients aware of the fact.

Financial Costs vs. Opportunity Costs

In a strictly economic sense, the financial costs of education usually understate the real economic costs to the whole economy. As noted earlier, the real costs to the economy are measured by the *opportunity costs* of education, that is, by the value which the resources used in education would have in the best alternative uses. This, in effect, is what the economy foregoes or sacrifices in terms of other goods and services in order to have education.

To illustrate, if a certain technical school had not been built, the same capital might have gone instead into a new factory. Likewise, the teachers and students might instead have been employed in producing goods or services of some sort which sold in the market. The factory would presumably have earned interest on the capital. The teachers and students would have earned incomes. The Gross National Product would have been that much larger. The production thus lost (measured by the interest and earnings forgone) represents the real economic costs of the technical school to the economy.

If it were possible to get a precise measure of the opportunity costs of education (which ordinarily it is not), there is no reason to suppose that they would coincide exactly with the financial costs discussed above. In most circumstances they would be higher, especially because financial costs make no allowance for "income foregone" by working-age students attending school. Much depends, however, on the conditions of employment in the economy. If there is high unemployment, then possibly the income foregone by students is zero because their real alternative to going to school might be unemployment. It is conceivable that in such conditions the teachers themselves would be earning much less outside of school, in which case their teaching salaries exceed the opportunity costs to the economy.

For most purposes it is sufficient for educational cost analysts to work with financial costs, and more particularly with institutional budgetary costs. But the opportunity cost notion is important to bear in mind, particularly when one is considering the true costs of education to the economy. This would be the case, for example, in doing a broad cost-benefit study which seeks to differentiate the social benefits accruing respectively from primary, secondary, and university education. It would also be the case when economic planners and top authorities are trying to achieve a more or less optimum allocation of scarce resources between education and other sectors.

Costs to Whom

It should be clear from what has just been said that the cost analyst should always ask himself: *Whose* costs are being dealt with in this particular analysis? Is it concerned only with financial costs to the central government, or to all levels of government combined, or with private financial costs as well? Is it concerned only with financial costs, or with the full, real costs to the economy? Is it concerned only with costs to the domestic economy, or to foreign economics too? The latter distinction becomes important where foreign and is a big factor. For example, the examing the over-all educational expenditures of certain

African countries whose educational systems are heavily dependent at the moment on external assistance, it is important to know to what extent the figures include or exclude such assistance; otherwise the true burden on the local economy and taxpayers cannot be properly assessed.

On this point we should also mention the distinction between the cost of foreign aid to a donor nation and its economic value to the recipient country; the two are seldom the same. The cost to the donor country is measured in terms of its own prices, wages, and salaries and usually includes substantial transport and other special costs. The value of the particular item of aid to the receiving country, on the other hand, should be measured in terms of as own prevailing costs and what it would cost to do the same thing on its own.

Take the case of a Peace Corps teacher who is sent to an African country. Let us suppose (hypothetically):

(1) that the total cost of this teacher to the United States, including training, transportation, and salary, etc., averages out to $12,000 per year; (2) that the host government pays $500 per year toward the teacher's local maintenance; and (3) that the total cost of an equivalent local teacher (if available) would be $2000 per year. From the point of view of the host country, the value of the aid received in the form of this teacher is $1500 ($2000 minus $500), despite the fact that the cost to the sending government was much higher.

This same proposition holds with respect to capital assistance. A new technical school, fully equipped, might cost a donor nation $2,500,000 (using its own equipment and high-level manpower), but the recipient government might have built and equipped an equivalent facility for only $1,500,000 (using entirely domestic personnel and materials at local prices and shopping in the world market for the best buys on equipment).

The practical point is that you should always try to segregate foreign costs from domestic costs, and in assessing the real value of foreign aid, you should cost it in terms of local equivalent value rather than the actual costs to the donor.

Hidden Costs

Whether one is dealing with the public or private costs of education, or with domestic or foreign costs, it is important to keep an eye out for hidden costs which do not get reflected in the budget. Certain of the unbudgeted private costs mentioned earlier, such as family outlays for books, school meals, and transportation, are hidden costs. The salaries of the foreign professors at the University of East Africa who were rendering teaching services but were not included in the university budget or the official staff establishment were important hidden costs. A very common hidden cost these days is the "free" broadcast time received by schools from private or public television stations for instructional programs. The service may be free so far as the school budget is concerned, but it is a real cost to someone else, and the day may come when it will be a real cost to the school budget itself.

Thus, one important reason to keep these various hidden costs in view is because later on they may no longer be hidden. When the "inexpensive" foreign teachers are replaced by indigenous teachers, or when the experiment in television instruction succeeds so well that the schools need their own broadcast station, these real costs suddenly show up on the educational budget. A good rule to remember is that nothing an educational system uses is truly free if it would have a real economic value in some alternative use.

Transfer Payments

The opposite of leaving out an important cost is to count the same expenditure twice. This happens if one is not careful in dealing with so-called transfer payments. Broadly speaking, a transfer payment is simply a conveyance of purchasing power from one institutional or individual pocket to another without any real expenditure taking place which would generate additional national production and income. The educational cost analyst needs to be especially alert with respect to two particular possibilities. The first is where the national government makes educational subsidy payments, usually from the Ministry of Education's budget, to local governments or to private schools, which in turn spend the money on school buildings, teacher salaries, and other educational purposes. The payment from the ministry's budget is merely a cash transfer; it does not actually buy anything. It only becomes a real expenditure when spent by the local government or the schools themselves. Care should be taken not to count the same money twice when combining public and private or national and local educational expenditures.

The second possibility is the granting of student scholarships, fellowships, and bursaries which are then spent by the students for tuition fees, dormitory charges, and the like. When payment is made to the students, it is merely a transfer; the real expenditure occurs only when the students buy something with the money. Often, however, university budgets show both the transfer payment (under "student assistance" or some such label) and the costs of the educational services which the students partially pay for with the grants (e.g. room and board, staff salaries, etc.). This is a perfectly legitimate (even if sometimes an illogical) accounting procedure for universities to use, but it can trap the unwary cost analyst into double- counting. He should eliminate such transfer payments in computing the real costs of education.

Unit Cost of What Unit

The term "unit cost" can also be a trap if one is not careful. It is used most often to mean the annual cost per enrolled student. But there are a variety of other types of unit cost measures that come in handy for certain purposes and it is important to keep them straight. The include, for example:

- The total cost per graduate
- The capital cost per student place
- The capital cost per occupied student place
- The average cost per teacher
- Cost per classroom
- Cost per school
- Cost per course
- Cost per square or cubic foot

It all depends what the most appropriate unit is for costing the particular item with which you are concerned. If you are costing the number of pencils and textbooks needed, or the food bill, then the individual student is the most appropriate unit because in these cases cost varies in direct proportion to the number of students. But if you are estimating requirements for teachers, or for desks, maps, globes, and various other items of classroom equipment, then the classroom is usually the best unit, since the staffing and equipment requirements vary with the number of classrooms rather than the number of students. In estimating heating and lighting costs, square or cubic footage may be the best unit.

As we saw in the case of the Soviet Union, several different norms are used for estimating educational costs and for making educational budgets, based on a variety of costing "units," each selected to fit best the particular item being costed.

To avoid confusion it is a good idea when using the term "unit cost" to be explicit about what kind of unit cost is in questions, unless this is already clear from the context.

Joint Costs

As the name implies, joint costs are common costs shared by a number of different educational units or activities. The teacher is a joint cost for all the students in a class; the principal and his secretary are joint costs for all the students in the school; maintenance of the building is a joint cost for the regular daytime classes and evening adult classes using it; and the Ministry of Education is a joint cost for all the schools in the system.

Difficulties often arise when it becomes necessary to allocate joint costs to different users of the same service in order to calculate their respective total or unit costs. There is no standard solution for all cases; the cost analyst simply has to devise the most reasonable basis he can in each instance, taking care not to use a more elaborate and time-consuming method than the circumstances warrant, and being sure to apply consistently whatever formula he adopts.

The simplest method in many situations is simply to divide up the joint cost according to the number of students in each category affected, or by the number of classrooms or teachers or schools, as the case may be. We suggest that in disposing of joint cost problems, you content yourself with a pragmatic solution that seems reasonable and not get bogged down in metaphysical debates with your colleagues over, for example, how to divide school inspector costs between older teachers and younger teachers, or between first-grade and second-grade students.

When do Costs Occur

Another tricky problem you will encounter is how to allocate costs by time periods. This problem arises mainly when dealing with capital costs, but it also applies to research and development costs.

For illustration, take the case of a new university science building, built with a loan, which required three years to construct. While under construction it tied up considerable capital that was yielding no return. Two questions immediately arise: First, to what year or years should this capital outlay and the interest charges be assigned for purposes of making a time series of capital expenditure? Second, in computing annual capital costs in subsequent years, how should this building be treated?

The best way to handle the first problem is to apportion the three-year capital outlay and interest charges among the three years on the basis of actual cash disbursements in each year (if this information is available), since this gives the most accurate picture of what really happened. If you use this preferred method, however, it should also be followed for all other capital outlays in your time series; otherwise the series will not be consistent and comparable from year to year. Alternative methods would be to assign the full amount of a new capital project either to the year of authorization, or to the year when construction was started, or to the year of completion. These solutions give a deceptive picture of actual capital outlays, but an accurate one of capital authorizations, construction starts, or completions. Decide which it is you want to show and be sure to state clearly what method you have used or your readers may be misled.

The more important question is how to charge this new capital outlay against educational costs in the future. If you are computing the total cost per student (capital plus recurrent), it would obviously make no sense to charge the full capital costs to the first crop of students. The right approach for this purpose would be to amortize the cost (including interest) over the building's useful lifetime and apportion it annually to all the students who use it over time. We will return to the subject of amortization when we discuss capital costs.

We should also mention in this connection that it is always preferable when using budgetary accounts to take year-end figures of actual expenditures rather than beginning of-the-year authorizations, again to get a more accurate picture of the reality. A budget, after all, is only a forecast of things to come, and until they have actually come and gone, the figures shown are purely hypothetical.

Research and Developments Costs

These are the special costs involved in undertaking a new departure—such as a major experiment or innovation—which will hopefully succeed and become generally applied. Such costs behave in special ways and present special timing problems, similar to but more complicated than a new building.

It is important to distinguish between the "starting-up" costs of such undertakings, which are "one-time-only" costs, and the longer-term "normal" costs that will be reached at a later stage.

As we saw in the Barbados team-teaching case, for example, the five-year experimental phase involved relatively high costs for outside advisors, special teacher training, and other items associated with the experiment itself. Moreover, the experiment applied to only a small fraction of the pupils in the system, hence cost per pupil ran high. But the projected cost per pupil after the experimental phase dropped sharply, first, because the initial research and development costs would then be eliminated and, second, because team teaching would be extended to all schools and its overhead costs would be spread over a much larger number of students.

It is generally true that the cost per student during the starting phase of a major educational experiment or innovation is abnormally high. If these costs are mistakenly regarded as an indicator of future costs, the experiment might be thrown out on grounds of not being economically feasible. It is essential, therefore, to develop two sets of cost projections, the first applying to the developmental period and the second showing the anticipated "normal" costs beyond this period.

This serves two important purposes: it prevents initial prejudice against the innovation; but it also guards against wishful thinking, for the fact may be that the longer-range normal costs, though lower than the initial costs, may still be too high to be afforded. To take an extreme example, there is little doubt that African children could learn a great deal in computerized classrooms, but there are the gravest doubts whether this new technology could be afforded once the experimental period was over, regardless of how impressive the pedagogical results might be.

The IIEP publication on new educational media which we mentioned earlier demonstrates in detail the principle of high costs per student during the developmental phase of television instructional programs, followed by substantially lower unit costs later.

So much for the various pitfalls and accounting puzzles you are likely to encounter. We will conclude this chapter with some comments on the important matter of "trade-offs" in which you will inevitably find yourself heavily engaged.

THE NATURE OF TRADE-OFFS

If educational systems did not live in a world of limited resources (including time, the most fixed resource of all), there would be little need for cost analysis. But they always have and always will, even in the most affluent nations. Therefore the managers of educational systems are constantly having to make choices between alternative ways of allocating and combining the resources available to get the best results.

What makes these choices so difficult is that several sets of variables, measured on quite different scales, must all be weighed simultaneously. It is not the simple matter, for example, of minimizing costs regardless of the educational consequences. Nor is it the simple matter of getting the best conceivable pedagogical results regardless of the cost. Rather it is the much more complicated matter of striking a good balance between the pedagogical considerations on the one hand and the costs and other feasibility considerations on the other. This means that educational planners and decision-makers are constantly having to make trade-offs, and to do this well they must examine each situation through the lens of a systems analysis.

To bring the subject down to practical terms, let us take a few homely examples:

- A financial limit is imposed on a draft educational plan which had envisaged a large expansion of both primary and secondary education. Cost analysis shows that with the limited additional funds available 1000 university students could be added, or 3000 secondary students, or 15,000 elementary students, or some combination of all three within these limits. In this case there must obviously be a trade-off among students at different levels, requiring a Solomon-like judgment. The cost analysis does not provide the answer, but it defines the parameters within which the answer must fall.

- A classroom teacher devotes an hour each to reading, writing, and arithmetic every day, and the rest of the time to other subjects, recreation, and rest periods. She is pleased with the progress her class has been making on reading and writing but perturbed by their slower progress in arithmetic. Should she reallocate time, reducing the amount spent on reading and writing in order to improve arithmetic? Or should she steal extra time for arithmetic from the other subjects, recreation, or rest periods? The costs here are in terms of time, not money, and the outputs are in terms of student learning results, health and educational diversity. This is the sort of trade-off situation teachers are confronted by all the time.

- A primary school, handicapped by resource scarcities and poor quality results, would like to add another teacher in order to reduce class size, and also have a substantially enlarged supply of books and other self-instructional materials. But it does not have enough money to do both and so is forced into a trade-off between adding the teacher or adding instructional materials. The question, of course, in which will improve learning results the most. Again cost analysis *per se* cannot decide the answer. It can only define the parameters of the choice so the decision can be made on pedagogical grounds.

Our case studies offer a variety of other illustrations of trade-offs between pedagogical, economic, and other factors. The school consolidation option in the rural areas of Norway and the Soviet Union involved trade-offs between lower unit costs and improved pedagogical results in larger school units as against the social and psychological advantages of having children attend school in their own village. The Barbados cost analysis identified a series of options to school authorities on how to spend a given amount of money, leaving them to decide which were the best ones pedagogically (see Figure 8.1). It is interesting that in Poland, where the choice was between alternative approaches to teacher training, and in the Ivory Coast, where the choice was between using two different grades of teachers in conjunction with television instruction, the authorities in both instances knowingly elected the higher-cost option. In short, they traded what they though would be significant pedagogical advantages for economic resources, thus in all probability imposing a future sacrifice on some other parts of the educational system.

Most of the suggestions and caveats presented in this chapter apply whether you are dealing with recurrent costs or capital costs, and to any purpose your cost analysis is meant to serve. With these in mind, we will move on now to an examination of problems and methods relating particularly to recurrent costs, and from there to the treatment of capital costs.

Proposed program item		Possible trade - offs.				
A one - week workshop	Is equivalent In cost to	Reduching of supervision load from five to four new schools per supervisor	or	$400 equipment and supplies for each of ten schools	or	One additional trained teacher (Year's salary) for the project
One week's visit by an overseas consultant	Is equivalent In cost to	An Additional teacher ads for the project as a whole	or	$175 equipment and supplies for each of ten schools	or	$0.45 per pupil for materials
etc.		etc.		etc.		etc
etc.		etc.		etc.		etc.

Fig. 7.1 Possible Trade-offs in the Barbados Team-teaching Project.

9

Capital Costs

When capital costs are spread over a period of years, they typically account for only a modest fraction of total unit cost per student. Nevertheless, they deserve the careful attention of planners and cost analysts for several reasons:

- Capital outlays usually involve large lump-sum expenditures, raising special financing problems. Borrowed capital funds must later be paid back with interest, thus mortgaging future revenues for years to come.
- Apart from debt service, the creation of additional facilities increases future operating revenues; the cost of using and maintaining a new educational facility often equals its initial capital cost every three to five years.
- The layout and location of new facilities can impose severe constraints on educational technologies and logistical patterns in years ahead, thereby inhibiting needed changes and innovations and perpetuating old inefficiencies.
- The planning of new facilities provides a strategic occasion for maximizing the utilization of both existing and future facilities, which is a major key to improving over-all educational efficiency and holding down costs.
- The creation of new facilities for new programs in any one sector of the educational system has major repercussions, including cost impact, on other sectors. Unless these are identified, assessed, and provided for in advance, the new

program may later create severe difficulties elsewhere and encounter setbacks.

For all these reasons, educational planners and managers need sharp eyes and sharper pencils when dealing with capital costs.

IDENTIFYING AND MEASURING CAPITAL COSTS

Practical accounting problems arise in distinguishing between capital costs and recurrent costs. Conceptually, the distinction is clear enough. Capital costs are associated with durable educational inputs—particularly land and site utilities, buildings, furniture, and equipment—which give service for more than a single fiscal year; recurrent costs involve services and supplies that can be consumed within a single accounting year. But the practical line of demarcation must often be drawn arbitrarily and can create confusion in accounting systems.

By the above definition, for example, books are capital items because they usually last for several years before needing replacement. Thus it is common practice to treat the initial bulk purchase of textbooks and library books for a new school or university as a capital outlay; but it is equally common practice to treat the purchase of additional books and replacements thereafter as a current expense. The latter violates a theoretical nicety, but in this case no harm is done so long as the same accounting method is used consistently, every one understands what is going on, and the books actually get bought.

However, the treatment of major repairs and replacements which prolong the life of existing capital items is another matter. If these irregular and frequently sizable expenditures are not adequately provided for on schedule (which is what often happens when they are treated incorrectly as current costs and thrown into direct competition with teacher costs), the result can be serious physical deterioration of capital, disruption of educational programs, increased inefficiency and costs, and lowered productivity. To avert this risk, educational systems should set up a special capital reserve account for major repairs and replacements that can be added to annually and drawn upon as needed, independently of the recurrent budget.

Educational systems in developing nations will be well advised to keep a special foreign currency reserve earmarked for the prompt purchase of replacement parts for imported equipment, as well as a minimal inventory of critical spare parts. Each time a machine breaks down, the educational process may remain disrupted for many weeks, due to the time-consuming process of obtaining an official allocation of foreign exchange, and of ordering and awaiting delivery of the needed parts.

The following basic concepts will help you unravel confusing accounting records and avoid errors in measuring capital costs.

Capital Stocks vs. Capital Flows

The stock of capital is the inventory of buildings, equipment, and other capital items existing *at a given point in time*. It is like a reservoir that can be drawn down (by depreciation) or replenished and enlarged by new inflows. The value of an educational system's capital stock can be measured by depreciating the *original* cost of each item in the inventory at an appropriate rate (adjusted for major repairs, additions, and replacements made in the interim). Alternatively, it can be measured by estimating the *replacement value* (what it would cost today to replace the facilities), *minus* depreciation. Or it can be measured by its estimated *market value*, if appropriate evidence is available for making such an estimate.

These distinct concepts and measurements—of capital stock at a particular time, of capital inflows over past years, and of new inflows needed in future years—are basic tools for a variety of practical purposes. You will need them especially for estimating total unit costs per student in different parts of the educational system, for measuring the full costs of education to the economy, for comparing the relative merits of alternative courses of action, for costing individual projects, for projecting future capital fund requirements, and for applying cost-benefit tests.

Depreciation and Amortization

In addition to the stock and flow concepts just mentioned, there is the important concept of spreading the costs of capital items over their useful lifetime in order to allocate a proper share of these costs to each time period and to each group served. This method is essential to determining the total unit cost per student (recurrent cost *plus* capital cost) and to making cost-benefit assessments.

Capital costs can be spread over time by applying an appropriate *depreciation* charge to each year, the rate of depreciation varying with the expected useful life of each item. But this is not the whole of the story; for most purposes interest costs should be added to depreciation costs, resulting in a figure of *amortization* cost. Even when there is no interest cost shown in the budget, it is important in estimating full capital costs to include an imputed interest charge (reflecting what the capital would earn in some alternative use in the economy). In this manner you can arrive at an *imputed rent* for all capital facilities which can be used for estimating total education costs (or unit cost per student) in any one year or over a period of years.

Budgetary Costs vs. Full Costs

The caveats regarding public and private costs, as well as budgetary costs versus costs to the economy, apply with special force to capital costs. Remember always to ask the operative questions: What kind of costs do I want to measure? And costs to *whom?* If, for example, you are only concerned at the moment with estimating capital requirements to be met through government budgets (which will often be the case), it is legitimate to ignore private capital outlays and the full costs to the economy, so long as you are aware of these omissions. On the other hand, if your aim is to measure the nation's *total* capital outlays on education, you must include an estimate for private outlays. Or, if you are attempting to assess the full costs to the economy, you must estimate the opportunity costs of *all* capital used by education, including both the existing stock and any new inflows.

Domestic vs. Foreign Costs

When you are projecting future capital requirements, it is vital to distinguish between those to be met from domestic resources and those that hopefully will be financed by foreign resources. Often it is also desirable to set a value on foreign-supplied facilities in terms of their equivalent *domestic* costs (by shadow pricing) instead of using the actual cost to the foreign donor or lender. This is important, for example, if you are assessing the value of the present capital stock, or if you are estimating what it would cost to replicate, with domestic resources, a pilot facility supplied from abroad.

The several distinctions made above can help you untangle budget forms and accounting records which, from the cost analyst's point of view, frequently "mix apples and bananas." It often happens, for example, that the official education budget includes both debt service on facilities built in the past and capital funds needed to build new facilities. If you include both these figures in an annual time series of capital expenditures, you will be guilty of double-counting. Choose whichever best serves your purpose, but never add them together. There are many similar accounting pitfalls that the above concepts can help you avoid.

CONSTRUCTING A TIME SERIES OF CAPITAL EXPENDITURES

One of your first exercises should be to construct an annual time series of capital outlays, running back several years. This will put the past in perspective and shed useful light on the future. It can be done fairly easily. Capital outlays from public funds can usually be extracted without great difficulty from public budget accounts. But to get a full national picture you will have to add in private outlays as well. These private figures are generally hard to obtain and you may have to estimate them. You can do this quite simply if you have annual figures on the number of new classrooms or the amount of new space added to various types of private education. Apply to these physical quantities the cost factors derived from public construction experience with similar types of facilities. The resulting estimate will be rough, but it will usually suffice. (Again, remember not to double-count public subsidies for the construction of private education facilities.)

We suggest the following guidelines for constructing a time series of capital outlays: (1) use *actual expenditures* where possible rather than budgetary allotment figures; they are a much more accurate measure of what actually happened; (2) separate expenditures on new facilities and equipment from expenditures on major repairs and replacements that simply maintain old facilities; (3) break down the capital total at least by education levels and, if possible, by categories of institutions (e.g., general secondary schools vs. technical schools, rural vs. urban schools, etc.); (4) in addition, make an annual breakdown by *sources* of capital funds, separating especially funds from domestic and foreign sources, from public vs. private domestic sources, and from different levels of government; (5) once having put the whole picture together in terms of *current* prices, translate the series into *constant* prices, using an educational construction cost index as a price deflator.

These breakdowns will provide a picture not only of the over-all trend of capital outlays but, equally important, of any changes in the pattern of allocation within the educational system (which has important implications for the future pattern of recurrent costs), and changes in the pattern of sources of capital funds (which may provide important clues to future financing possibilities).

Do not be surprised if the resulting time series of capital flows shows a very erratic movement of outlays from year to year. A variety of factors cause sharp annual fluctuations in capital outlays: discontinuities in the flow of foreign aid, spasmodic decisions to launch major new educational programs, ups and downs in the economy and in the flow of public revenues.

The figures from a diversified sample of countries given in Table 9.1 demonstrate the unevenness of capital outlays. The first column shows the percentage of total (public) educational expenditures in 1965 that was represented by capital expenditures. The second column shows the highest percentage for capital expenditures in any year between 1960 and 1965. It is evident that 1965 was the highest capital outlay year for seven of the countries whose figures are identical in the two columns. But for some of the others there is a marked difference between 1965 and the year of highest capital outlay. The extreme case is Mali, whose capital expenditures ranged from 4.2 percent in 1965 to 38.6 percent in the highest year. Niger ranged from 5.1 percent to 17.2 percent.

Table 9.1

Capital Expenditures as a Percentage of Total Public Expenditures on Education (16 Sample Countries)

	Capital Percentage in 1965	*Highest Percentage Over 1960–65*
Ethiopia	16.1	22.8
Kenya	8.1	8.1
Mali	4.2	38.6
Niger	5.1	17.2
Argentina	7.2	7.2
Ecuador	13.7	13.7
Guyana	13.6	13.6
Uruguay	9.2	9.2
China	14.4	14.4
Japan	24.0	25.6
Pakistan	42.0	46.0
Malaysia (Sarawak)	22.0	25.7
Austria	20.9	20.9
Czechoslovakia	9.5	24.8
Denmark	24.3	25.4
Finland	18.7	22.0

Source: Data compiled on the basis of the Unesco Statistical Yearbook, 1967, Table 2.16.

Caution should be exercised in making inter-country comparisons from the evidence in Table 9.1; the figures are not strictly comparable because of differences in national accounting practices. It may be, for example, that some of the developing nations reported capital outlays from both domestic and foreign sources, while others included only domestic; some countries may have included repairs, replacements, and debt service charges along with expansion of facilities, while others did not.

It is a fair deduction from Table 9.1, however, that most of these countries were undergoing rapid educational expansion between 1960 and 1965, for if they were merely maintaining existing capacity, their capital outlays would undoubtedly have been a much smaller percentage of their total educational outlays. It is also a foregone conclusion that these high capital outlays would create higher recurrent costs in subsequent years.

DETERMINING PHYSICAL CAPITAL NEEDS

In order to project the capital funds required for a new planning period (say, five years), you must begin with an estimate of physical needs. These include: (1) necessary repairs and replacements to maintain existing facilities in good condition; (2) modifications and additions to existing facilities and equipment to support qualitative changes in educational processes and programs (such as the introduction of instructional television, team teaching, more ample laboratory facilities, etc.) and (3) net additions to present capacity in order to accommodate more students (either by enlarging existing institutions of the same site, or by building separate new facilities).

The first component (repairs and maintenance) is best estimated on the basis of a full physical survey of all existing facilities, resulting in a schedule of needed repairs and replacements for each institution. Where this is not feasible, the second-best method is to survey a representative sample of institutions, classified by age, size, function, type of construction and equipment, and climatic conditions; then apply the repair and replacement needs derived from this sample to the whole establishment. If this sampling approach is not feasible, then you will be forced to use a much cruder method, based on recent past expenditures for repairs and replacements (adjusted upward if there is reason to believe that there has been considerable deferred maintenance in the past). Even for this crude method, it is important to secure, if possible, a full list of existing facilities (perhaps from central records of the ministry), classified according to the same characteristics as those suggested above for a sample survey. With the help of an experienced building engineer, you can work out a set of repair and replacement norms to apply to each category. Obviously the older institutions, those made of materials that deteriorate more rapidly, and those with more complex equipment (such as a technical school), will have the high repair and replacement requirements. Your total estimate may seem small relative to capital requirements for new construction (if your educational system is expanding rapidly), but the matter nonetheless deserves careful attention because skimping on maintenance can eventually result in eroding existing capital assets and can prove to be an extremely expensive way to "save" a little money in the short run.

The second type of capital requirement (involving qualitative modifications of existing facilities) has to be estimated on an *ad hoc* basis, program by program. If, for example, a new science program for secondary schools calls for new types of laboratory equipment, the requirements will have to be worked out and costed in terms of a list of needed equipment, the number of schools involved, and a time schedule for procurement and installation. Estimating the capital requirements for installing instructional television is somewhat more complicated, but the basic method is essentially the same. It is more complicated because a greater variety and complexity of equipment is involved (at both the broadcasting and receiving end); because it may be necessary to provide electric power sources to some schools and to modify classroom space for efficient reception; and because repair facilities may also have to be created.

The third type of capital requirement (to expand existing facilities and create new ones for handling an increased number of students) in quantitatively the most important when an educational system is expanding rapidly, and therefore deserves your greatest attention.

The greatest mistake usually made in projecting the capital requirements for an expansion program is to assume (tacitly) that existing facilities are already being utilized to the hilt, and therefore that the stock of facilities must be expanded by the same percentage as the expected number of students. This, in fact, is rarely the case. Even in systems where some classrooms are grossly overcrowded, many others may have undersized classes. Moreover, it if often possible, as we have seen, to accommodate more students in existing facilities by modifying the academic time schedule. Hence we would strongly recommend that a space utilization survey be conducted before an attempt is made to calculate the need for new facilities and equipment. In short, before scarce resources are committed to building new facilities, every effort should be made to ensure that the best use is being made of the old ones.

A survey of secondary schools in some African countries by Unesco's Regional Educational Building Institute illustrates what a space utilization survey may reveal. The study in Morocco showed that "in almost all the schools surveyed, the available number of spaces is more than that required by a considerable margin... in the general classroom category by an average of 17.45 percent, in the science laboratory category by an average of 33.33 percent, and in the special classroom category by an average of 15 percent."

A similar survey in Ghana concluded that "in all space categories dealt with, it is apparent that provision has been made for more spaces than what is actually required to meet the needs." The average excess capacity in general classrooms was 28.69 percent, in special purpose classrooms 42.69 percent, and in science laboratories 33.33 percent.

Such figures, however, must be interpreted cautiously, for it is never possible to achieve 100 percent utilization, even in the best-managed educational system. There are a number of reasons: schools in one area may be losing students to another area; new schools are en route to becoming filled up but are not as yet fully; daily absentees leave desks unfilled; the academic time schedule itself imposes substantial idle time on all facilities. Even after allowing for such factors, however, there is usually a sizable cushion for improving the use of expensive, scarce facilities. By bringing the facts of under-utilization to light, cost analysts can encourage decisions in favor of greater efficiency.

There are limits, of course, to what can be achieved without impairing educational effectiveness. Where these limits are must be determined case by case in each locality. But, in making such determinations, it is important that they be based on rational evidence developed by practical experimentation and observation, not simply on traditional practice and educational mythology.

Once plans have been made for the full and efficient use of *existing* facilities and the need for a net increase in facilities has been established, the next problem is to choose the best size and location for the new structures; to decide when to add to existing facilities (which is usually cheaper) and when to create new ones; to strike the right balance between different types of facilities (e.g. day schools vs. boarding schools); and to plan the optimum use of new facilities, for example, by adopting efficient time schedules, by using technical schools in off-hours for adult training, and other schools for general community purposes. By exploring and costing all such alternatives, cost analysts can help blaze a trail toward more and better education for more people.

ESTIMATING THE COSTS OF CAPITAL EXPANSION

Once the *physical* needs for new facilities have been established, the next step is to estimate what it will cost to meet them. Here again the best methods to use will depend on the particular purpose and circumstances. If you are costing a specific project, such as a new teacher training institution, for which specifications have already been drawn, the costing should be much more refined and tailored to the specifications than if you are making an over-all estimate of capital fund requirements for a whole five-year national educational plan.

The Role of Physical Norms and Prototypes

Even over-all capital requirements estimates, however, must be tied to some sort of physical specifications; otherwise, they are meaningless. Such physical specifications in turn must be related to what will go on in and around the new buildings, what educational aims and functions are to be served, what educational process is to be used, and what types of learners are to be served, including how many and for what periods of time. Thus, for example, projecting costs for primary schools obviously involves a very different set of physical norms than costing secondary technical schools or an agricultural college. In short, capital cost estimates must be based either on specific architectural plans or, for more general estimating, on a series of models or prototypes that fit the variety of physical requirements foreseen in the forthcoming plan period.

The more varied these prototypes are to fit varying categories of circumstances, and the further the over-all enrolment projections can be broken down into these categories, the more accurate the capital cost projections will be. In a typical developing country, it would be desirable to have standard cost estimates for at least the number of prototypes shown in Table 9.2.

Table 9.2

Illustration of Standard Cost Prototypes

	Cost Per Pupil Place	*Single-Shift Enrolment Capacity*	*Capital Total Cost*
Primary			
Single-room school (rural)			
2 classrooms (rural)			
3 to 6 classrooms (rural, semi-rural)			
6 to 12 classrooms (urban)			
Over 12 classrooms (urban)			
Secondary (day)			
6 or less classrooms			
7 to 12 classrooms			
Over 12 classrooms			
Technical schools			
Secondary (residential)			
12 or less classrooms			
Over 12 classrooms			

The classifications shown in Table 9.2 obviously must be adapted to the educational structure and practices of each country. A British-type system, for example, might classify secondary schools by the number of "streams." Where appropriate, various prototypes of post-secondary institutions (such as teacher training colleges, advanced rural institutes, etc.) could be added to the list. Universities or other major institutions, however, are likely to require separate, tailor-made estimates, since each one is so individual.

Before discussing how to cost these prototypes, a brief word is in order about new trends in setting physical standards for schools.

Traditionally, physical standards for school construction have either been extremely haphazard or excessively rigid. The rigid ones have typically been defined in such terms as the minimum or maximum floor space required per student; the ratio of window space to square-feet of working area; minimum-maximum ceiling heights; required number of doors per room; the proportions of classroom space, corridor space, and other types of space; number of toilet stalls and playground area per 100 students, etc. In the extreme, a single school design has been imposed by the central ministry on every community, whether it fitted local conditions or not.

Times are changing rapidly in these respects, however, toward a golden mean between the extremes of full laissez-faire and total rigidity. In a number of countries (the United Kingdom is a good example), teams of imaginative architects, educators, engineers, and cost analysts have been fashioning new approaches to the more efficient design, construction, and utilization of educational structures, and to enhancing their aesthetic and psychological features as well. One of the outcomes has been the creation of *performance* or *functional* standards as distinct from the old-fashioned, rigid *physical* specifications that leave little room for local ingenuity and adaptation. For example, instead of specifying a fixed ratio of window space to floor space, the new norms simply indicate the minimum strength of light required in all working areas, leaving it to the ingenuity of architects and lighting engineers to determine how this functional norm can best be met in a given situation. Similarly, local educators and architects are given latitude (within a prescribed cost ceiling) to make trade-offs between classroom space and other space (e.g. administrative offices, corridors, cafeteria, auditorium) that will provide maximum flexibility and educational advantage.

We strongly recommend that educational planners and cost analysts try to keep informed about new ideas on school building, through the publications and advice of such organizations as the Unesco regional school buildings centers, the Educational Facilities Laboratory in New York, and ministries of education in such countries as France, Spain, and the United Kingdom that have been fostering new approaches to school construction.

Costing Project Designs and Prototypes

Once an achitectural plan has been sketched for a particular facility, it is usually the task of professional cost engineers to develop a detailed cost estimate for the project. But prior to that stage, rougher cost estimates must be worked out by general educational cost analysts (with whatever help they can get from construction experts). For the most part this means arriving at the best possible "standard costs" for the various prototypes referred to above, along with certain "adjustment factors" that can be applied to these nationwide standard costs to allow for regional cost variations, interim price changes, or any other important differentials. For some purposes, however, such as costing innovations and qualitative changes in existing facilities, other methods must be used.

By and large, the best unit to use for expressing the costs of different prototypes is the *capital cost per student place*. Once this figure is determined, it can be applied to the number of additional students that must be provided for in each category (e.g. rural primary students, secondary boarding students, etc.) to determine the over-all capital funding required for each category.

The advantage of using the cost per student place (as against the cost per classroom) is that it averages out differences in the sizes of classes and classrooms in different schools, as well as variations in the ratio of classroom space to other space. For the same reason, cost per student place makes the best costing unit for setting cost limits and enforcing them, without typing the hands of architects and local school authorities. The case study on school construction in the United Kingdom is highly informative on this point.

When it comes to costing the installation of a television system, however, the number of classrooms and the cost per classroom (rather than the number of student places) is a better unit to use for costing the television sets, whereas the number of school broadcast hours required to cover desired portions of the curriculum is the best unit for determining the size and cost of the broadcasting facilities needed.

The costing of furniture and equipment, whether for prototypes or specific projects, calls for an appropriate list of items to fit the requirements of a given size and type of facility. Appended to this chapter is a typical list for a secondary school. The bill of equipment and furniture should be costed at the best prices available on items meeting minimum standards.

The best way to establish standard costs for prototypes is on the basis of recent actual costs for a sample of projects as representative as possible of those to be built in the future. (If future structures are to differ drastically from previous ones, a different method of costing may be required.) If possible, the sample for each prototype should include no fewer than a half dozen cases in order to average out wide variations, particularly in land, site preparation, and site utility costs (which usually vary much more from project to project than construction and equipment costs). The sample cases should be analyzed uniformly, with the following minimum cost breakdown:

- Land acquisition (total area and per square foot)
- Site clearance and improvement
- Installation of site utilities and services
- Construction of structures
- Equipment and furnishing
- Architectural and other fees

The cost data from the sample cases for each prototype can then be analyzed, aggregated, and expressed in various useful ways, as illustrated in Table 9.3. Take note that the projects in the sample will probably have been built at different times; hence an educational construction price index will be needed to translate them into comparable prices before they are averaged and entered on a summary table.

Analysis of the various samples should also provide a standard set of geographic differentials in land and construction costs that can be used in calculating deviations from the nationwide standard costs when costing regional components of overall national construction plans. The construction price index can be used to adjust for cost increases occurring since the base date for the standard costs, and for projecting future increases.

Table 9.3

Examples of Standard Characteristics and Costs of a Prototype Urban Primary School

1. Typical number of student places		________
2. Cost per student place	$	________
3. Land area (mean average)		________ sq.ft.
4. Total building area (mean average)		________ sq.ft.
5. Costs (actual)		
(a) Land and site survey	$	________
(b) Site improvement and utilities	$	________
(c) Construction materials	$	________
(d) Construction labor	$	________
(e) Construction cost per square foot	$	________
(f) Equipment, furniture, etc.	$	________
(g) Architects' and other fees	$	________
(h) Total	$	________
6. Costs (percentage breakdown)		
(a) Construction		________ %
(b) Architects' and other fees: ________ % of (a)		________ %
(c) Equipment and furniture		________ %
(d) Land and site survey		________ %
(e) Site improvement and utilities		________ %
(f) Total		100 %

The standard costs and price adjustment factors described above can be used not only for costing an over-all national school expansion plan, region by region and level by level, but also for making initial rough cost estimates for more limited sub-systems, including even individual projects. A worksheet for calculating the costs of a sub-system is shown in Table 9.4.

Table 9.4

Summary Worksheet for Calculating Capital Costs of Expanding an Educational Sub-system

A. Category of facility ______________________

B. Typical enrolment capacity ______________________

C. Breakdown of costs:

1. Standard cost of structure	________
2. Site improvement and utility services ________% of (1)	________
3. Total (1 + 2)	________
4. Adjustment of (3) for interim cost increases ________ %	________
*5. Adjustment of (4) for regional cost differences ________%	________
*6. Architects and site supervision fees ________% of (5)	________
*7. Cost of land and site survey ________% of (5)	________
8. Standard cost of furniture and equipment	________
9. Adjustment of (8) for interim price increases ________%	________
*10. Adjustment of (9) for regional price differences ________ %	________
11. Total cost per institution (5 + 6 + 7 + 10)	________
12. Total cost of projected program ________institutions X (11)	________

*Components of total cost (11).

Methods similar to those outlined above were used in Thailand in 1965 to estimate the costs of building three similar vocational schools (each to accommodate 450 students) in three different locations. The results are shown in Table 9.5. It will be seen that the construction and equipment costs, based on standard costs, are very similar for all three schools, except that the construction costs of School 2 run 10 percent higher than the other two because of regional cost differences. The land, site improvement, and utilities costs, however, vary widely. The latter three items should always be looked at in combination. Often a "bargain" on the land cost can be much more than offset

Table 9.5

Three Estimates of Capital Costs of Similar Vocational Schools in Thailand (1965) (Costs in Thai Bahts).

	School 1	*%*	*School 2 (same as 1 plus 10 per cent increase due to geographic location)*	*%*	*School 3*	*%*
Construction costs						
1. Space for administration, classrooms, and library	1,710,000	17.1	1,881,000	14.8	1,710,000	15.2
2. Workshop	2,760,000	27.6	3,036,000	23.9	2,280,000	20.7
3. Cafeteria	550,000	5.5	605,000	4.8	550,000	4.9
4. Dormitories	1,704,000	17.0	1,874,000	14.8	1,704,000	15.1
5. Staff housing	700,000	7.0	770,000	6.1	700,000	6.2
6. Sanitation services	1,305,000	13.0	1,435,000	11.3	1,305,000	11.6
Total	8,729,000	87.3*	9,601,000	75.5	8,249,000	73.0
Construction cost per place	19,398		21,337		18,331	
Other costs						
1. Site improvements	400,000	4.0	400,000	3.1	1,240,000	11.0
2. Utilities	400,000	4.0	200,000	1.6	600,000	5.3

	School 1	%	School 2 (same as 1 plus 10 per cent increase due to geographic location)	%	School 3	%
3. Equipment	500,000	5.0	500,000	3.9	500,000	4.4
4. Land	—		2,000,000	15.7	700,000	6.2
Total	1,300,000	13.0	3,100,000	24.4	3,040,000	27.0
Grand total	10,029,000	100.0*	12,702,000	100.0	11,289,000	100.0
Total cost per place	22,287		28,226		25,088	

*Totals do not add up correctly, due to rounding.

by high site improvement and utility costs. In the Thai case, School 3 had land costs of only 700,000 bahts compared to 2,000,000 bahts for School 2, yet their *combined* land, site improvement, and utility costs were roughly equal (2,540,000 bahts vs. 2,600,000 bahts).

International Norms and Comparisons

Unfortunately, we can offer no tidy international norms for educational capital costs, or any standard ratios between the major components of such costs, which an individual nation can use to assess its own past performance and future costs. As we have seen there are often substantial variations in cost conditions even within the same nation. The variations are much greater between nations. In a poor nation, for example, construction labor may be relatively cheap compared to the costs of materials and equipment (especially if much of the latter must be imported), whereas in a rich country quite the reverse may be true. Similarly, the costs of land and materials may be much cheaper relative to labor in one developing country than another, because it has a lower population-land ratio and a more abundant supply of trees, clay, and other raw materials to use for construction. Thus, each country must establish its own appropriate costing norms.

This is not to say, however, that countries cannot profit greatly from one another's experience in educational construction and costing. Quite the contrary is true, as our international collection of case studies has shown.

SOME PARABLES ABOUT CAPITAL COSTS

We will conclude this chapter on capital costs with a few parables which have had many counterparts in reality and sum up many of the basic points made earlier.

Parable One: A Tale of False Economy

School authorities in a certain community decided to substitute lower-cost roofing, siding, and flooring materials in their new school in order to cut costs. The savings released funds for a much-needed playing field and everyone was pleased—until it turned out that the savings were false. Within a few years after the new school was opened, the *extra* costs of janitorial services, frequent repainting and repairs, not to mention replacing the storm-torn roof of the new school, added up to five times the "savings."

The moral of this particular parable is that a penny saved in building a school is not always a penny earned; it is sometimes the cause of losing many more pennies later.

Parable Two: The School That was Too Well Built

Having learned their lesson, the same school authorities built their next school of the best materials, rugged enough to outlast their grandchildren. Its floors and walls were thick, solid, and soundproof; all surfaces cleaned easily and never needed repainting or repair; the roof could laugh at any storm. It was more expensive, of course, but the extra costs were expected to be recouped many fold by later savings on custodial and maintenance costs. And indeed they were, to the great relief of each year's operating budget. Once more everyone was pleased—until one day the unexpected happened.

Research studies based on a wide range of experiments in other school systems convinced the school authorities that their pupils would learn much more at little or no extra cost if certain innovations were adopted, including team teaching and instructional television combined with self-instructional "programmed" materials. An exciting new world of learning opened before their eyes, until they suddenly realized that their solid new school stood in the way. Its traditional, cell-like classrooms, built to accommodate thirty students and a teacher using nineteenth-century pedagogical methods, prevented the flexible redeployment of space and people that was required throughout the school day to take full advantage of these promising innovations.

A compromise solution was reluctantly adopted. It meant that the new technologies would have to be adapted to the building, not the building to the new technologies, and this reduced their effectiveness considerably. And since they did cost something extra, it was doubtful that, on balance, the school's cost effectiveness had been improved.

The moral is that old-style buildings can prevent progress; new educational facilities should be planned to accommodate whatever new and better teaching technologies may come along, perhaps even before the new school is finished.

Parable Three: The Right School in the Wrong Place

School authorities in a newly independent nation concluded that their colonial-type academic secondary school was obsolete and irrelevant to local needs; hence they launched an experiment involving a new type of multi-purpose school that combined prevocational training and university preparation. Careful pedagogical planning went into the project and enthusiasm ran high; if the new model succeeded, it would light a new way for the whole system.

Unfortunately, it did not succeed; quite frankly it failed miserably and set educational progress back several years in the process. It was not because the pedagogical planning was unsound or the resources inadequate. Basically it was because this "lighthouse" school, for quite accidental political reasons, was located in a remote site where students could not get to it easily and where its light could not be seen by other school people. For some years its enrolments ran well below capacity, causing its operating costs per student to be inordinately high. To remedy this situation, expensive boarding facilities were added to accommodate distant students. This remedy worked, the school became filled, but now its costs per student ran even higher because of the board and room costs. By now, unfortunately, disenchantment with the whole idea of multi-purpose secondary schools had spread throughout the land—mostly for the wrong reasons—and the classical academic high school continued to be the national model, despite the generally acknowledged fact that it was a misfit.

The obvious moral is that new schools should be located for the convenience of students, not politicians. Educational planners can help in this matter by demonstrating clearly the comparative costs, convenience, and pedagogical advantages of alternative locations—so clearly that political leaders will appreciate the risks they run by insisting that a costly school be put in an irrational location.

Parable Four: The Strange Case of Too Many Schools

A poor nation with a dispersed rural population finally achieved its cherished goal of universal primary education, only to be disappointed. The costs were high and kept mounting, yet the educational results were notoriously poor. Close analysis showed why: paradoxically, the nation had built too many schools.

It had continued the ancient custom of a school for each village, but meanwhile many villagers had been moving to cities and there were too few students to fill the classrooms of the rural schools. The result was a low pupil-teacher ratio and abnormally high costs per student compared to urban schools, but, unhappily, poorer learning results because the best teachers preferred the cities where they could work with better equipment, a richer curriculum, and other teachers without being professionally isolated.

In due course, the government adopted a plan to abolish the small traditional schools over a period of years (as older teachers and school buildings reached retirement age), replacing them with new medium-sized schools serving a combination of neighboring villages. This added some new transportation costs, but they were offset by lower instructional costs per student in normalized classes. More important, the teachers preferred these somewhat larger schools; so did the students, and they learned more. Naturally there was at first considerable local opposition to the school consolidation scheme—no village likes to lose its school. But soon the satisfaction of parents and children with the superior performance of the new schools lessened the opposition, and taxpayers generally were pleased by the lower unit costs. The government took these lessons into account as it planned a new campaign for expanding secondary education.

The moral of this story is that the romance and nostalgia which adults often feel for the one-room village school can impose heavy penalties on their children's education and on the public purse. A prerequisite for being able to afford good schools (and universities) is that they be of at least the minimum size that is economically and pedagogically viable.

Parable Five: An Educational White Elephant

A handsome new technical school in a developing country was dedicated jointly by the prime minister and the foreign ambassador with great hope and enthusiasm. But, sad to say, it soon became an embarrassment to both. The reasons, in retrospect, were plain to see.

The ambassador's nation, in all good faith, had met its promise to deliver a fine new technical school, as modernly equipped as the best at home. To be sure, it had cost more than expected because the policy of "tied aid," which the ambassador's country insisted upon, had required importing many of the materials, virtually all of the equipment, and much of the expert manpower from back home, at much greater cost than if the recipient country had been given the money outright and allowed to build the school in its own way. But all this was now past and paid for. The real problem and the cause of the embarrassment was the high running cost, which the recipient nation had to shoulder and could ill afford.

No one had looked into these very seriously, they had been too preoccupied with the initial capital costs. Also, too little attention had been paid to the practical problems of recruiting, training, and paying local technical teachers, of which there were virtually none. Not surprisingly, much new equipment still stood around in crates, unused, while other equipment soon broke down for lack of proper care and maintenance—all because of a lack of trained personnel. Most troublesome of all, local employers complained that the graduates of this new technical school did not fit their needs; they were over-trained or mistrained for local types of work; and they came on the job with inflated expectations of becoming shop supervisors overnight.

The moral of this sad parable is that educational gifts sometimes turn into white elephants that can eat poor educational systems out of house and home. The best way to avoid a white elephant is to discover his costly feeding habits in ample time to avoid getting stuck with him. With a modicum of tact and diplomacy, it is usually possible to obtain instead a hard-working elephant with a good disposition and more moderate appetite, who fits into the local scene more comfortably.

Parable Six: The Accordion Schools that Saved Money

The educational planners in a developing country, with the help of demographers and manpower economists, plotted the changes likely to occur in the student population over the next decade, by age and geographic distribution, as well as changes in the employment patterns of the economy. Their analysis showed that certain currently pressing educational and manpower demands could be expected to subside after a few years, while other types could be expected to increase.

Once the large backload of demand for primary education in various urban neighborhoods was worked off, for example, demand would stabilize at a lower level. Meanwhile, population transfers from particular rural areas would diminish their educational demand but correspondingly raise the demand in certain urban areas. Similar ups and downs could be foreseen in the demand for various types of technical and professional training—not least of all in teacher training itself.

Thus, it became evident that if educational capacity were planned simply to fit today's pattern of demand, it would be out of joint with tomorrow's pattern. The result would be unused capacity in some places, and not enough in others. To avert such costly maladjustments and mis-investments, the country adopted a new and imaginative strategy of educational expansion. It was based on a distinction between "permanent demand" and "temporary demand," and a corresponding distinction between permanent capacity and temporary capacity. To illustrate: there was a projected need for 100 new secondary teachers per year during the next five years to meet present deficits and expansion requirements; but after that requirements would decline steadily to only 400 new teachers per year to meet replacement needs and to support a slower rate of expansion. Hence, the permanent demand would be for about 400 new teachers a year, but for the time being there was an additional temporary demand of 600 per year.

The strategy had two prongs. One was to provide lasting solutions for permanent needs, but less costly provisional solutions for temporary needs. Thus, for example, the construction of new teacher training facilities would be limited to an output capacity of only 400 teachers per year, while provisional and less satisfactory quarters (e.g. old army barracks, estate houses, etc.) were adapted and borrowed professors were used to train an additional 600 teachers to meet the peak demand.

The second prong of the strategy involved the "accordion principle." In some neighborhoods where demand for primary and secondary education was expected to grow steadily over the years, new "modular" schools were built to which additional modules could later be added. This required buying and developing larger sites than were needed in the short run, but avoiding the premature construction of school space. Over the years this would save on capital costs. Conversely, in areas where the school population was expected to decline, demountable classrooms were installed.

These were sturdy prefabricated structures, also modular in design, that could be moved by trailer from "surplus" to "deficit" areas. The initial efforts to design and develop these demountable units ran into a variety of technical problems, but once they were overcome and factory production got underway, the cost per classroom (including moving) fell below the cost of a "regular" classroom. Needless to say, many people, including many educators, at first opposed the idea of "standardized" demountable schools, considering them somehow dehumanizing and unaesthetic. But they relented as it became evident that these units were not only educationally efficient but that each could have its own distinctive personality. The modular units could be arranged differently to fit the contours and conditions of each site. Moreover, students and teachers in different villages and urban neighborhoods were soon competing in making attractive landscape designs, planting shrubs and flowers, introducing novel color schemes, fashioning outdoor sculptures, and otherwise beautifying their respective schools.

The obvious moral of this final parable applies as well to all the others: in planning educational facilities these days, unconventional thinking and great ingenuity are called for, backed up by good pedagogical judgment, alert planning, and competent cost analysis. Temporary solutions should be devised to meet temporary needs, but even to meet enduring needs, flexible solutions should be sought. For if there is to be a revolution of teaching-learning technologies, as there clearly must be, this will require a kind of architectural flexibility and ingenuity that will not suffocate new educational ideas and practices.

10

Economies of Scale

INTRODUCTION

THE rate of increase of student numbers in higher education has been remarkably steady since the beginning of the century in both England and Wales and the USA, with a doubling every 15 and 17 years respectively. However, there are now indications that the rate of increase is becoming greater. It has been calculated that in 15 West European and North American countries, the doubling period of total student enrolments in higher education in the period immediately prior to 1966 was, with only one exception, between 6–10 years (Edwards, 1971).

Thus there is nothing revolutionary in projections made by the UK Department of Education and Science with show the student population of British universities doubling to an estimated 394,000 in 1981. (DES, 1970, p. 22). Nevertheless, taxpayers may be startled by the absolute size of the financial commitment that this expansion would involve—a rise in real expenditure in 1971–1972 from £300 million (including capital and current items and student maintenance), to an estimated £573 million (DES, 1970, p. 33). These same taxpayers may insist upon the possibility of a university education for their burgeoning families, but do they need to pay on this projected scale? Our work at Bradford seems to reveal that they do not.

To get this answer we have used the techniques of Output Budgeting; part of what the Americans call Planning Programming Budgeting Systems (PPBS). The methodology involves attributing the total cost of university operation to the units of the various outputs produced—first degree graduate by discipline, post-graduates and research. In this paper, however, we are concerned only with first degree graduates.

Any approach to attributing costs to particular courses is unavoidably complicated and open to criticism at every stage. In practice, virtually every resource used by the university contributes to more than one course and nearly all costs are, in one way or another, joint costs. Academic staff teach and pursue research; technical staff service teaching and research laboratories; classrooms, laboratories and item of equipment are used by students on different course; materials are purchased on behalf of Schools of Studies and it is difficult to find the course for which they are ultimately used, and so on.

Nevertheless, we have tried to discover how each of these components contributes to the expense of producing each student in each discipline at the University of Bradford and to enumerate the potential economies which we believe are revealed.

We deal with: (1) the components of these costs per student (2) potential economies in academic staff costs and (3) potential economies in teaching accommodation costs.

COMPONENTS OF COST PER STUDENT

These components we classify as:

1. Capital and maintenance costs;
2. Teaching costs;
3. Administrative; library, student facility, general and miscellaneous costs.

Table 10.1 illustrates the way in which total cost per student for the various courses at Bradford is divided between the three classes of components.

Capital and maintenance costs represent in imputed rent for the use of classrooms, laboratories, libraries, office and student

Table 10.1

Total Cost Per Student at the University of Bradford (1969–70)

Course	*Capital and Maintenance Costs*		*Teaching Costs*		*Administrative, Library, Student Facility, General and Misc. Expenditure*		*Total Cost Per Student*
	£	*% of Total*	£	*% of Total*	£	*% of Total*	£
Laboratory based courses							
Chemical engineering	908	35	1089	43	560	22	2557
Civil engineering	1030	41	956	38	523	21	2509
Electrical engineering	1278	36	1769	49	556	15	3603
Mechanical engineering	1768	44	1679	42	544	14	3991
Applied biology	849	27	1639	53	622	20	3110
Pharmacy	1446	44	1329	40	519	16	3294
Chemistry	1915	49	1332	34	627	17	3874
Colour chemistry	1888	48	1517	39	513	13	3918
Materials science	1134	31	1874	51	672	18	3680
Ophthalmic optics	1011	34	1484	49	504	17	2999
Applied physics	1375	36	1635	46	672	18	3682
Textile science	1245	40	1290	41	621	19	3156

Course	Capital and Maintenance Costs		Teaching Costs		Administrative, Library, Student Facility, General and Misc. Expenditure		Total Cost Per Student
	£	% of Total	£	% of Total	£	% of Total	£
Classroom-based courses							
Business studies	710	34	693	32	711	34	2114
Modern languages	818	34	748	32	820	34	2386
Social sciences	548	34	475	30	609	36	1632
Applied social studies	676	36	419	22	812	42	1907
Mathematics	907	39	744	33	656	28	2307
Statistics	563	31	613	35	599	34	1775

facility space, such as refectories and social facilities. The rent comprises annual interest at 7 percent and amortization payments over 50 years on the insured value of buildings and non-teaching equipment, together with maintenance costs. The annual cost of each building in the University is then allocated to the different kinds of room (classrooms, laboratories, offices, etc.) in proportion to the area that each type constitutes of the total usable area of the building, but with a weighting factor to allow for the greater cost of constructing laboratory space.

The general cost of laboratories and classrooms was distributed over different undergraduates following different courses in proportion to their use by each of these students. This involved a detailed study of the timetables of teaching rooms and took full account of the use of space in one School of Studies by students from other Schools.

The cost of academic staff offices was distributed in direct proportion to the relative amounts of time devoted to various activities by members of staff. The division of staff time between undergraduate teaching and other activities, such as post-graduate teaching and personal research, was based on the results of a survey carried out in 1968 in which staff kept a diary of their activities for a term-time week. The subsequent division between courses was based on a study of teaching timetables.

The cost of administrative offices and student facility space was divided equally over all students except those on "thin-sandwich" courses who were weighted one half. The cost of library space was also divided equally over all students, but with post-graduates weighted two.

Teaching costs comprise academic and technical staff salaries, super-annuation and insurance, the annual value of teaching equipment, and expenditure on materials used in teaching. The cost of academic staff was divided in the way already described. The cost of technical staff was attributed to different courses in proportion to the relative areas of teaching and research laboratories, and of their use by different courses, since it was found that their number correlated closely with laboratory area per discipline.

Table 10.2

Directs Costs Per Student at the University of Bradford (1969–70)

Course	Teaching Space		Academic Staff		Technical Staff		Secretarial Staff Plus Offices		Equipment and Materials		Total Direct Costs	% of Total Cost
	£	%	£	%	£	%	£	%	£	%	£	%
Laboratory based Courses												
Chem. eng.	580	32	617	34	204	11	128	7	268	15	1797	70
Civil eng.	613	37	458	28	240	14	93	6	258	15	1662	66
Elect. eng.	882	32	1073	38	352	14	144	4	344	12	2795	77
Mech..eng.	1388	44	981	31	452	14	120	3	240	8	3187	79
App. biology	416	19	946	43	339	15	145	7	354	16	2200	70
Pharmacy	1026	42	549	22	474	19	114	5	306	12	2469	75
Chemistry	1482	49	600	20	432	14	187	6	300	10	3001	77
Colour chem.	1465	47	785	25	432	14	156	5	300	9	3138	80
Mat. sci.	618	23	982	37	472	18	164	6	420	16	2656	70
Ophth. opt.	624	28	815	37	354	16	123	5	315	14	2231	74
App. physics	859	32	743	28	472	18	164	6	420	16	2658	72
Textile sci.	777	34	696	30	468	20	224	11	126	5	2291	73

Course	Teaching Space		Academic Staff		Technical Staff		Secretarial Staff Plus Offices		Equipment and Materials		Total Direct Costs	% of Total Cost
	£	%	£	%	£	%	£	%	£	%	£	%
Classroom based courses												
Bus. studies	284	24	486	41	42	4	204	17	165	14	1181	56
Mod. lang.	258	22	624	53	64	5	176	15	60	5	1182	50
Soc. sci.	188	24	406	52	18	2	114	15	51	6	777	47
App. soc. stud.	116	17	327	49	24	4	136	20	68	10	671	35
Mathematics	339	27	652	52	0	0	172	14	92	7	1255	55
Statistics	126	14	544	62	0	0	144	16	69	8	883	50

Similar techniques were employed with respect to the cost per student of staff, stock and equipment in the university administration, library, students' union, and so on.

The results of the foregoing calculations for the academic year 1960–70 varied widely between different courses at the University of Bradford. Laboratory-based courses in science and engineering were considerably more expensive than classroom-based courses in social sciences (see Table 10.1). The cost of educating an undergraduate to first degree level in science or engineering ranged from £2509 in the lowest discipline to £3991 in the highest, as against £1632 to £2386 in different social science disciplines.

Annual capital and maintenance costs varied between 27–49 percent of the cost of educating a student to first degree level, depending upon the course involved. Teaching costs were between 22–53 percent of the total, while residual and miscellaneous expenditures ranged from 13–22 percent of costs per student for laboratory-based courses, and 28–42 percent for classroom-based courses.

The comparisons between laboratory-based and classroom-based courses were even more marked when overhead administration and other costs, which apply to all the University's students regardless of discipline, were taken out of the calculations. Then direct costs per student in classroom-based courses ranged from £671 to £1255 in the different social and mathematical sciences as against £1662 to £3187 in science and engineering.

Table 10.2 shows the total direct cost per student for each course, and its principal components. The percentage figures measure the proportion which each components forms of total direct cost.

STAFF COST ECONOMIES

With Increased Enrolment

It seems difficult to make economies in the foregoing cost components with present level of student enrolment. Greater promise appears to lie in the possibility of reduced costs per student with the projected expansion in numbers over the next decade.

We, therefore, made detailed studies of the teaching structure of nine courses. This involved analysing for each course; (a) the annual contact hours, i.e. the number of hours teaching that a student receives each year; (b) the number of optional subjects embodied in the course, from which students may select a limited number; (c) the size of teaching groups regarded as educationally acceptable by the School of Studies; (d) the relative balance of lectures, classes, laboratory sessions and tutorials within the total contact hours.

From this data we calculated the total number of teaching meetings that must be provided at the present enrolment. We then postulated for each of nine courses successive increases in enrolment, by one student at a time, up to more than twice the present number, calculating the number of teaching meetings that must be provided at each level of enrolment on each course, if the appropriate professor's maxima regarding student numbers per type of meeting were observed. Assuming a constant staff teaching load, then the number of academic staff required, and therefore the total academic staff cost of the course, is directly related to the number of meetings. We next divided the number of meetings at each level of enrolment by the number of students to obtain the number of meetings provided per student and therefore the academic staff cost per student.

Figure 10.1 shows the proportionate change in academic staff cost per student as enrolment increases on the Civil Engineering course from its present annual intake of 66. For convenience it is expressed in index form with the value at the present enrolment equal to 100. We term this the Staff Cost Index.

For all the nine courses studies the Staff Cost Index exhibits the same form—falling as enrolment increases, but with periodic upward jumps corresponding to those levels of enrolment at which a series of teaching meetings must be duplicated because a laboratory class, seminar or tutorial reaches the maxima designated by the professors involved. The rate of fall, the points at which the jumps occur and the size of the jumps, vary from course to course, but the pattern is similar. The moral is clear—if

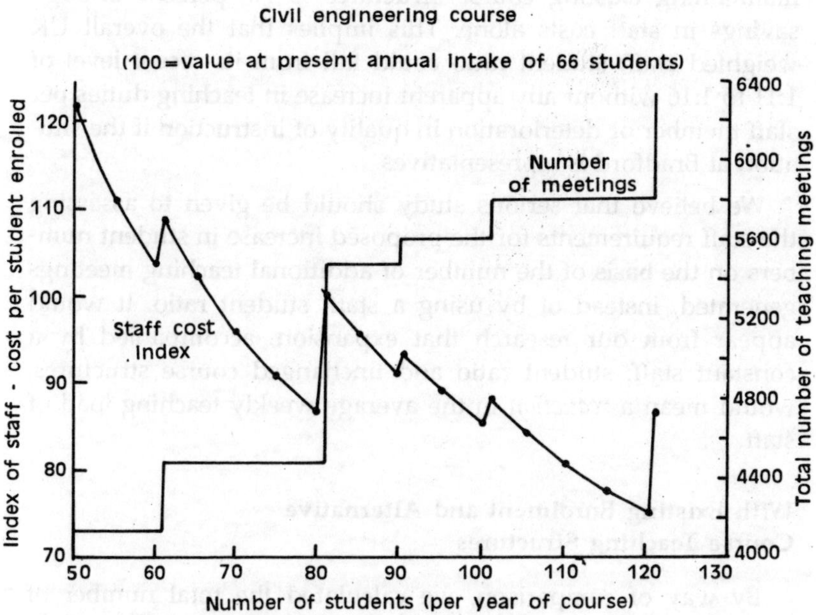

Fig. 10.1 Academic Staff Cost Per Student.

expansion is to occur it should be to a level of enrolment corresponding to a "trough" rather than a "peak" on the Staff Cost Index.

It seems that, for nine courses examined, the per student cost of providing teaching staff falls by a minimum of 18 percent and a maximum of 48 percent when enrolment is increased to the "trough" nearest to twice the present number. This saving in staff cost may be achieved without increasing the number of hours per week which each staff member teaches, or reducing the number of hours of instruction which each students receives. This may be done in spite of the fact that the size of seminars, tutorials and laboratory classes are held at a level which professors or their representatives think reasonable. In other words, these economies arise from expanding numbers in lectures where direct student-teacher exchanges do not normally take place. The average saving in total cost per student achieved by a carefully chosen approximate doubling of numbers, whilst maintaining existing course structures is 7.7 percent through savings in staff costs alone. This implies that the overall UK weighted staff: student ratio could fall from its recent level of 1:11 to 1:16 without any apparent increase in teaching duties per staff member or deterioration in quality of instruction if the situation at Bradford is representatives.

We believe that serious study should be given to assessing the staff requirements for the proposed increase in student numbers on the basis of the number of additional teaching meetings generated, instead of by using a staff: student ratio. It would appear from our research that expansion, accompanied by a constant staff: student ratio and unchanged course structures, would mean a *reduction* in the average weekly teaching load of staff.

With Existing Enrolment and Alternative Course Teaching Structures

By way of comparison, we calculated the total number of teaching meetings that would have to be provided for each of the nine courses at their present enrolments as the values of the parameters listed in Table 10.3 were varied. From the number of teaching meetings we calculated the number, and therefore the cost, of academic staff required and the consequent effect on total cost per student.

Taking the nine courses together and using the costs outlined in the previous section as a base, the following results were obtained. A 20 percent reduction in contact hours per student caused average cost reductions per graduate of 5.1 percent. A reduction by two in the range of optional subjects offered per degree course saved between 1 and 4.8 percent of cost per graduate. Yet increasing the maximum size of teaching groups by 60 percent did not reduce per student costs by more than 1.7 percent on any but one of the courses examined. Similarly, replacement of small tutorials by lectures and classes produced an average saving of only 2.7 percent.

As an illustration, Table 10.3 represents some of the results obtained for the undergraduate course in Social Sciences.

Table 10.3

Changes in Cost Per Student in Social Sciences in Relation to Changed Course Structures

	Change in total contact hours (%)					
	+ 40	+ 20	Present number	− 20	− 40	− 60
Change in cost per student (%) (− = saving)	+ 11.4	+ 5.7	0	− 5.7	− 11.4	− 17.0
	Number of optional subjects					
	2 more	1 more	Present number	1 less	2 less	
Chnge in cost per student (%) (− = saving)	+ 3.7	+ 1.7	0	− 2.0	− 4.8	
	Change in size of teaching group (%)					
	− 40	− 20	0	+ 20	+ 40	+ 60
Change in cost per student (%) (− = saving)	+ 10.5	+ 5.0	0	− 3.7	− 4.5	-- 5.7

It may be seen that the savings from any reasonable alteration in course structures at the present level of enrolment are considerably less than 7.7 percent saving expected from a doubling of the number of students.

ECONOMIES IN TEACHING ACCOMMODATION COSTS

Space cost economies of scale exist as a result of what appears to have been a good deal of overbuilding at the University of Bradford in recent years. This probably also applies to a greater or lesser degree to the British university system as a whole.

The current situation in the courses we examined at Bradford is that teaching is taking place in laboratories for only 41 percent of a 32-hr basic teaching week, and classrooms are in use for only 52 percent of the time. Furthermore, in most Schools of Studies the teaching week consists of only 33 weeks a year.

Laboratories

That cost of laboratories forms between 11–35 percent of the total cost per student on science and engineering courses. Any economy of scale in this factor is to lead to a significant savings in total cost.

In the majority of the Schools studies, an increase in enrolment sufficient to bring laboratory use up to 80 percent of a 32-hour week would reduce total costs per student by between 7–19 percent. If this 80 percent utilization were extended to a 60-hour week, the total cost per student could be reduced by 10–34 percent of the present cost. Table 10.4 shows the reduction in each of five courses investigated.

However, there are a good many practical problems involved here in time tabling, setting up experiments and inducing academic staff to work outside the normal working week, even though the objections of the latter might be met by some supplement to salary provided out of productivity savings.

Furthermore, the increases in student numbers required to achieve 80 percent or even 60 percent frequency of use are considerably in excess of anything at present envisaged for the University of Bradford, or of the likely availability of suitable students.

The University is conscious of the apparent under-utilization of laboratories, and is at present conducting a large scale survey of laboratories in all Schools of Studies. This is attempting to measure the capacity of laboratories (the maximum number of students that could reasonably be accommodated at one time) their frequency of use, the number of students present when the laboratories are in use, and the factors inhibiting improvements in their utilization. Preliminary results suggest that the frequency of use may be rather lower than the 41 percent quoted above and indicate occupancy factors of 60–70 percent when the laboratories are actually in use.

Classrooms and Lecture Theatres

We went on to analyse the use of classrooms and lecture theatres in the main building of the university in terms of the frequency and occupancy factors. This building is the University's

Table 10.4

Reduction in Total Cost-per-Student in Relation to Increased Laboratory Utilization*

% Laboratory Utilization and Length of Teaching Week	*Pharmacy*		*Colour Chemistry*		*Electrical Eng.*		*Applied Biology*		*Applied Physics*	
	Total Cost per Student	*% of Existing Cost*								
	£		£	%	£	%	£	%	£	%
Existing	3294		3918		3703		3110		3682	
60% at 32 hr	2957	90	2802	71	3151	87	2999	96	3275	89
70% at 32 hr	2777	84	2737	70	3054	85	2917	94	3215	87
80% at 32 hr	2671	81	2694	69	2994	83	2885	93	3131	85
80% at 40 hr	2593	79	2649	68	2938	81	2837	91	3083	84
80% at 50 hr	2536	77	2613	67	2898	80	2816	90	3039	82
80% at 60 hr	2497	76	2586	66	2878	80	2801	90	3023	82

* This relates to greater frequency of use only. No account is taken in these figures of the proportion of places that are unoccupied when the laboratories are in use.

largest and the level of its utilization is greater than that for the University's buildings as a whole. Nevertheless, its classrooms and lecture theatres were only used on average for 55.3 percent of 32-hour week. Even when rooms were in use, only 52.0 percent of the available seats were occupied.

It is evident that considerable economies in cost per student year could be obtained if building design and timing were to be more closely related to a academic plans. For example, Figure 10.2 shows the discrepancy between the size of rooms required and the capacity of the rooms available in the main building. Of a total of 619 meetings scheduled each week during the academic year 1971–72, 423 (69 percent) were held in rooms within a greater size range than was actually required. More detailed analysis showed that 334 meetings (54 percent) were held in rooms of more than twice the required size, including

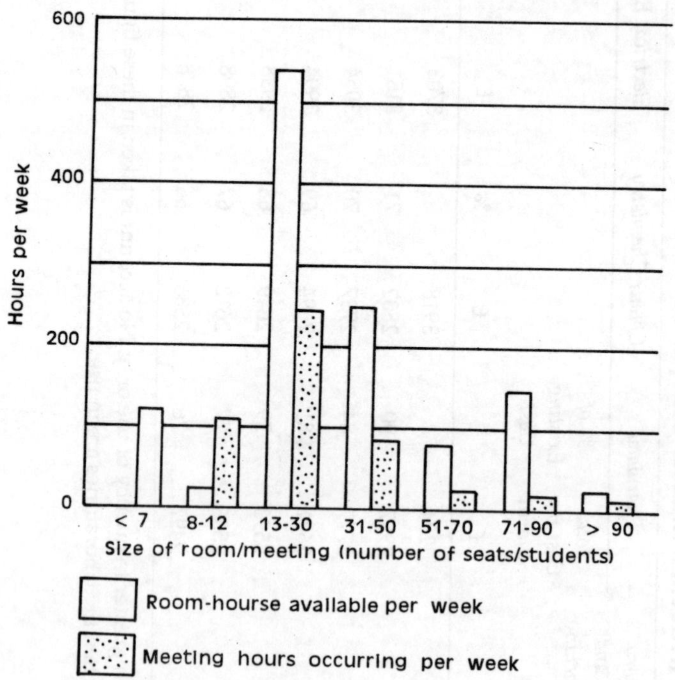

Fig. 10.2 Room-hours Available and Meeting-hours Occurring Per Week, Analysed by Size of Room/Meeting, 1971-2.

142 (23 percent) where the rooms were at least four times too big.

Table 10.5

Room Requirements in the Main Building

Range of Meeting Size (No. of Students)	*No. of Meetings of this Size Scheduled per Week*	*No. of Rooms Required (with 66.7% Frequency of Use)*	*No. of Rooms Available*
7	125	6	—
8–12	110	6	1
13–30	252	12	17
31–50	71	4	8
51–70	28	2	2
71–90	24	2	5
> 90	9	1	1
Total	619	33*	34

The total of 33 rooms required is an overestimate, as it is obtained after all the elements of the total have been rounded up to the nearest integer. If the elements are added to two decimal places, and the total rounded up, a figure of 29 is obtained. (Applying the 66.7 percent directly to the 619 meetings also gives 29 rooms.)

Table 10.5 shows the number of rooms of each size which are actually required assuming the 66.7 percent frequency factor regarded as normal by the UK University Grants Committee (UGC) within 32-hr week. A comparison of the last two columns shows the differences between the rooms actually available in the main building and those which were really required during the academic year 1971–72. As a result of this study, some of these surplus classrooms are being altered during the present vacation. Two of the 31–50 seat rooms and four of the 13–30 seat rooms are being converted into a total of seven 12-seat classrooms, five 7-seat tutorial rooms and seven staff offices. By rescheduling the small meetings in the new small rooms it is hoped to release a further three classrooms in the 13–50 seat ranges during the 1972–3 session for non-teaching uses.

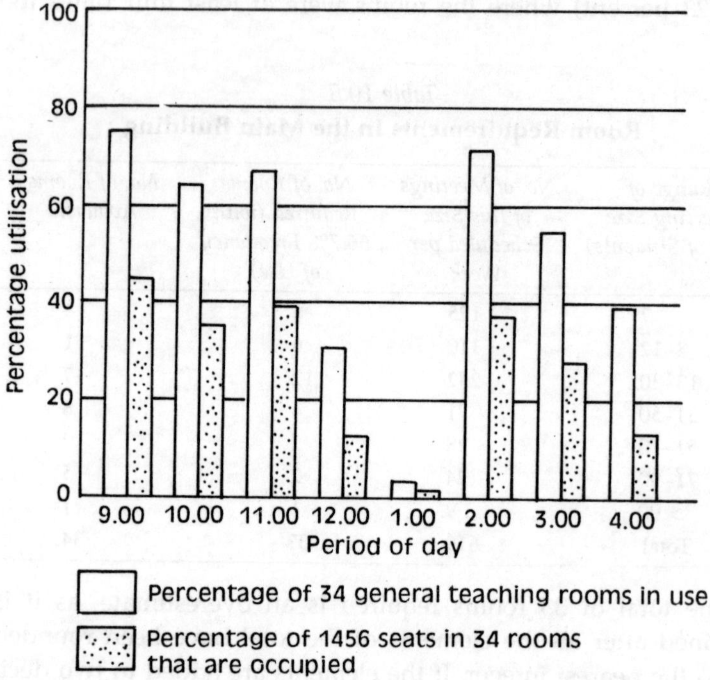

Fig. 10.3 Room and Seat Utilization in the Main Building by Hour of Day—1971–2.

Figure 10.3 further demonstrates how the aggravating factor of low seat occupancy compounds the overall under-utilization arising from the low frequency of classroom usage. The situation varies widely at different hours of the day. Considerable potential economies of scale would therefore exist with increases in enrolment which used classrooms and seats in accordance with the varying percentages of capacity detailed in Table 10.6), and which follows the pattern for potential laboratory use outlined in Table 10.4.

It is again clear from Table 10.6 that costs per student-year at Bradford could be substantially reduced given the various postulated rooms x seat-occupancy factors. This might be achieved either by expanding enrolment on existing courses, or by transferring the surplus teaching accommodation to other uses or to new courses. It might, however, be difficult to get the precise

Table 10.6

Percentage Saving in Total Cost Per Student in Relation to Improved Utilization of Classrooms

Course	*Percentage Saving in Total Cost*					
	60% Freq.	*32 hr week 70% Freq.*	*80% Freq.*	*40 hr week 80% Freq.*	*50 hr week 80% Freq.*	*60 hr week 80% Freq.*
Chem. Eng.	1.9	2.3	2.6	3.4	3.7	3.9
Civil Eng.	3.8	4.1	4.4	5.0	5.2	5.3
Elec. Eng.	1.7	2.0	2.2	2.7	2.9	3.0
Mech. Eng.	1.3	1.6	1.9	2.8	3.0	3.2
Biology	0.9	1.2	1.3	1.8	1.9	2.0
Pharmacy	0.7	0.9	1.1	1.7	1.8	1.9
Chemistry	0.9	1.3	1.6	2.5	2.7	2.9
Colour Chem.	1.8	2.1	2.2	2.6	2.7	2.8
Materials Sci.	3.2	3.4	3.5	3.9	4.0	4.1
Oph. Optics	0.5	0.9	1.1	1.8	2.0	2.2
App. Physics	3.2	3.8	4.2	5.3	5.6	5.8
Mod. Langs.	2.2	2.8	3.3	4.6	4.9	5.2
Social Sci.	4.0	4.6	5.0	6.1	6.5	6.7
App. Soc. Stu.	2.3	2.8	3.2	4.4	4.7	4.9
Maths.	2.6	3.7	4.6	7.1	7.8	8.3
Statistics	1.7	2.5	3.0	4.7	5.2	5.5

An occupancy factor of 75% (i.e. the UGC norm) is assumed in all cases.

required increment in student numbers in this respect or to time-table in accordance with the exigencies of an 80 percent utilization factor. In any event, the reader may choose whatever percentage of capacity he thinks reasonable when identifying potential economies per student year from Table 10.6.

It might be argued that the 33-week working year is not sacrosanct, and it is clear that further economy would lie in using the buildings for 48, rather than 33 weeks per year. This could permit an intake of two groups of students per year. This is already done on several of the "thinsandwich" courses at the University of Bradford, and doubling the throughput of students per year goes a long way towards cutting the cost.

We calculated the savings per student year in this respect with a conversion of what are now 33-week courses to two intakes over a 48-week year. The possible cost reductions range from 4-12 percent with the pessimistic assumption that all costs other than for accommodation increase pro rata with the increase in student numbers. The greatest savings are, of course, in the laboratory- based courses. If, on the other hand, we optimistically assume that there will be no increase in library expenditures and student facility space and only a 50 percent increase in technical staff expenditure, equipment and material costs, cost per student fall by between 18–24 percent of laboratory-based and 15–19 percent for classroom-based courses.

The savings from greater utilization of buildings either more intensively, or for more hours per week, or more weeks per year, are thus substantial. On the other hand, our investigations showed that any "reasonable" reduction in building standards and costs could not be expected to yield more than a small fraction of these sorts of savings. A 10 percent reduction in the capital cost of buildings and non-teaching equipment, for instance, would result in reductions in total cost per student of only 1.7–3.1 percent.

Quinquennial Expansion Plans

Current expansion plans within the University confirm our view that considerable economies of scale exist. This was seen to be so when we costed the plans for six existing courses during the 1972–77 quinquennium. These costings were based on estimates of staff and other resource requirements made by professors or their representatives, and were in no way influenced by any of the potential economies identified by the research reported on above. It was calculated that, taken together, professors' proposals for a 66 percent increase in student numbers on the six courses could be met with an increase in total costs of only 14 percent. The cost of each additional student (the incremental cost) would be only 22 percent of the present average cost, with the result that the average cost per student on these courses would fall by 31 percent over the quinquennium. Figure 10.4 shows for each of the six proposals, the cost per student in 1969-70, and after expansion in 1976–77; and the incremental cost for each of the additional students. It is assumed that surplus accommodation is brought into use during the existing teaching hours and years, and that course structures remain the same. (Figure 10.4)

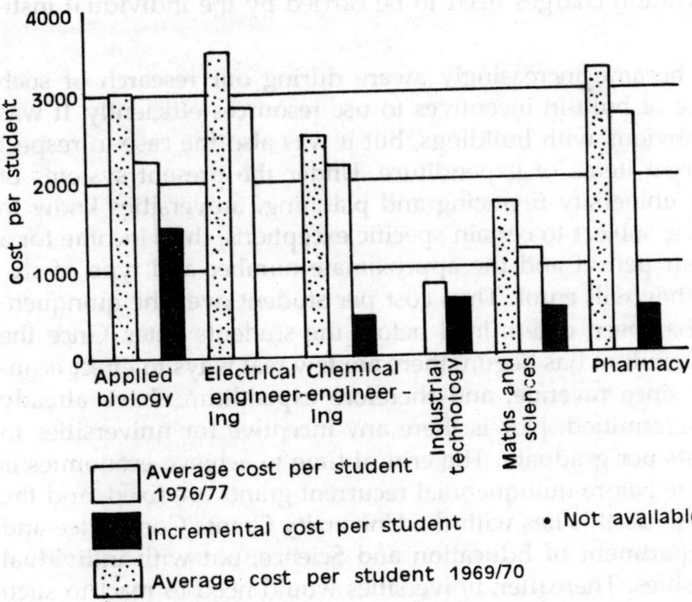

Fig. 10.4. Average and Incremental costs of six expansion proposals for the Quinquennium 1971-72

CONCLUSIONS

It seems that considerable potential economies of scale exist in higher education if the University of Bradford is in any way representative. If enrolment is doubled or thereabouts with present accommodation surpluses and course structures, then average costs per student may fall by between 11–38 percent, depending upon the course involved and the assumptions made. Further substantial cost reductions would arise with a course structure which handled two intakes a year.

It is evident that building plans have been sanctioned in a manner which fits university requirements more like a *sack* than a *glove.* Architects and academic planners should now be joined in providing tailor-made building programmes over time. Unfortunately, the universities themselves cannot be relied upon to do this. They have no incentive to economize on space-use where buildings are construed as free goods and no interest or amortization charges need to be carried by the individual institution.

We became increasingly aware during our research of such absence of built-in incentives to use resources efficiently. It was most obvious with buildings, but it was also the case in respect of current items of expenditure. Under the present systems of British university financing and planning, universities know in advance, subject to certain specific exceptions, their income for a five-year period and the approximate number and type of students they will enrol. Thus cost per student over the quinquennium has been determined before the students enter. Once the quinquennium has begun, there are few real ways to effect economies, since revenue, and therefore expenditure, have already been determined. Nor is there any incentive for universities to cut costs per graduate. The critical time to achieve economies is therefore before quinquennial recurrent grants are fixed, and the power to do this lies with the University Grants Committee and the Department of Education and Science, not with individual universities. Thereafter, universities would need to react to such economies by implementing them as painlessly as possible.

Finally, we would emphasize that the nation would be getting the worst of both worlds if it reduced the projected rates of expansion mentioned at the outset, while roughly maintaining the present grant per student year. Fortunately, there are signs that this will not happen and the considerable economies of scale which we have here identified may, perforce, become of interest throughout the British university system.

11

Making Decisions

INTRODUCTION

THE systems approach and its application to planning in higher education have long been the target of exhaustive discussion in administrative circles, as have such topics as the use of operations research, computer methods and the need for management information systems. After reading the current literature on the administration of higher education, one might conclude that decisions are never made except perhaps on the most capricious grounds. To date, no study has been made of the alleged shortcomings of our present planning processes. Does a new approach really need to be considered?

In this chapter I will attempt to answer that question by making at least an informal analysis of the method by which decisions are now made and of how that method compares with the systematic planning procedures so often proposed. I will then suggest a way in which the systems approach can be applied in higher education and will indicate what processes would be involved in effecting such a change. Finally, I will point out a few of the problems and some of the advantages of systematic planning.

PLANNING: A DUAL DEFINITION

We must look at planning from two points of view, that of the decision-maker or top administrator and that of the analyst or planner. The word has slightly different meanings in these two contexts.

For the decision-maker, planning is making decisions which commit the institution far into the future. Decisions about facilities (particularly special-purpose facilities), the hiring of tenured faculty and the implementation of a major new educational program, for example, are planning decisions.

Some decision-makers hire assistants, called "planning analysts," who gather and analyze data to facilitate the decision-making process. Thus, from the point of view of the planning analyst, planning is the collection, organization and analysis of information in support of planning decisions.

THE CURRENT PLANNING PROCESS

Decisions are indeed made and plans created and implemented in present-day higher education, but these tasks are now accomplished by a process most aptly described as a series of negotiations (see Cyert and March, 1959). In other words, the various people involved in the decision process bargain with each other to arrive at a common position, thereby making the decision.

Although real stories of such negotiation are readily available, an especially vivid picture of this method is delineated in the novel *Poetic Justice*, by Cross (1970). The setting is an American university, which includes an extension college. The main characters are the Dean of Arts, who is also the Chairman of the English department and the Dean of the extension college. The story takes place soon after the campus has been shaken by a series of riots and uprisings, as a result of which the senior members of the faculty and administration decide to "restructure" the curriculum and some of the regulations. No attempt is made, however, to define what this restructuring is or what it is meant to accomplish. *The absence of explicit goals is typical of the negotiating mode of planning.*

The Dean of Arts takes the opportunity to suggest that the extension college must be eliminated, his explicit reason being that the university should limit itself to degrees based on full-time participation on the campus. He attempts to carry out this aim through a series of bargains and negotiations with other members of the faculty. In the words of one character, "Dean Cudlipp (the Dean of Arts) had a lot of favors to trade." *Trading of favors is a prime basis for negotiating*. Typical are such trades as, "you vote for me as department chairman and I'll support your request for an increased budget."

The dean of Extension, of course, insists that the extension service is a vital contribution to the community and a proper one for the university, sharply pointing, by way of justification, to the fact that the students of the extension college did not participate in the riots. As the novel progresses, he proceeds to strengthen his position by involving a female professor from the English department, thereby obtaining support within his opponent's own home ground. It seems that the lady has dared to allow extension students in her regular classes. He invites her to luncheons and makes it a point to enlighten her about the current school politics.

Here the novel contains a superb description of an English department faculty meeting, which is cleverly terminated by parliamentary procedures when the Dean of ?arts feels he is losing his argument over the question of the extension college.

And so the negotiations ensue. At one point, the lady English professor, now won over to the side of the Dean of Extension, asks a colleague why the other colleges, such as engineering and the sciences, bother to support the extension programs. She is told:

> "The secretaries in these various colleges take jobs in order to attend the extension college free: no extension, no secretaries.
>
> It is really extraordinary the way one works one's ass off for important ideas and principles, only to find that decisions are made in the end for reasons and by people who have no more at stake in the quality or general movement of education, that I have in the changing rate of arbitrage.".

As the plot thickens, the Dean of Arts dies under mysterious circumstances that look like murder, and, of course, some members of the college of extension are suspected. (I suppose murder is the ultimate form of negotiation!) However, it turns out that the death occurred for unrelated reasons, and at the conclusion of the novel it is still not clear whether the extension college is to continue its existence, though the implication is that it will survive.

THE SYSTEMS APPROACH

Let us suppose that the university in the above example had handled the question of creating and continuing an extension college, using a more systematic approach to planning, an approach that takes advantage of modern management and technical processes.

First, systematic planning assumes that planning decisions are made on a cyclical basis, every year or two. Thus, decisions are not triggered by crises, such as riots or an arbitrary dictum to "restructure." Rather they are examined on a regular basis so as to build a desired future and prevent crises. As part of the cyclical process, there are a series of specific planning analyses. I will review these analytic steps briefly.

The first step is to predict the environment. This means that a conscious effort is made to try to predict what demands might be made on the university. In our example, predictions could have been made of the number of students likely to attend the various colleges and programs. There would be a basis, thereby, for deciding, independent of faculty desires, whether or not the various colleges were providing a service desired by the community. An important feature of the systems approach is that predictions and forecasts are made by explicit, formal processes. There are often mathematical operations, computerized procedures which are called models. This formality ensures communicability. Anyone familiar with the procedure and having the basic data can repeat the prediction. All assumptions in the forecasts are explicit, if one takes the time to study the procedures.

The second step in a systematic planning approach is to predict the future status of the institution. This step describes how the university will operate and will meet various demands if no new planning decisions are made. Formal methods are used here also to predict such factors as faculty levels, number of students served, total costs of operations and comparisons of costs with revenues. Ideally, an estimate of the quality of the educational output should be made, but in connection with the present example, it would be impractical to make such a formal calculation. Planners could, however, estimate for the next five years the student enrolment in the extension college, the cost of operating the college and the number of graduates. These estimates would provide a "base case," or a guideline from which to judge the possible need for new decisions.

The third step of the planning process is to compare the predicted status with goals of the university. The assumption, of course, is that these goals have been established and have been made explicit, a point to which I will return below. If one of the goals is service to the community, then, obviously, the extension division may be a valuable program. On the other hand, if a particular goal is to promote basic research, then the extension division may be less essential. An examination of the base case prediction reveals the gaps between what is likely to happen and what we wish to occur.

The planning process proceeds with step four, the conscious development of alternatives to move the institution closer to the desired future. We might suppose, for example, that a goal of service to the community has been established, but there may be some alternatives to a classroom-oriented extension college. At this point, we enter a phase that is sometimes called program planning, the design of these alternatives. One alternative might be to eliminate the extension college. Another might be to give certain students a special status in the regular college programs. A third choice might be to develop some sort of independent study and test program, that is, a school without classrooms, for part-time students.

In this step, the alternatives are carefully designed and thought out. The description of each includes specifictions of resource requirements and expected outcomes or results plus a scheme for implementation and operation over the planning period.

Step five in the planning process is to make an unbiased comparison of these alternative plans with the established goals. Predictions are made for the operation of the university, as for the base case, but it is now assumed that one or more of the alternatives has been adopted. These are the same kind of computations and estimates as those indicated in step two, but now we take new decisions into account. This procedure allows the comparison of alternatives in terms of resource requirements and in terms of the accomplishment of goals. Where possible, the predictions are made by formal techniques, which are used also for searching out the best combinations of alternatives. This last step involves the difficult problem of relating program (or alternative) goals to overall institutional goals.

Finally, the specific alternative to be implemented are selected—a decision is made. Then the descriptions of the alternatives are used as a basis for preparation of budgets and authorization of program changes.

SUMMARY OF THE DIFFERENCES BETWEEN NEGOTIATED AND SYSTEMATIC PLANNING

Before we consider the possibility of a transition from present methods of planning to those based on systems analysis, it would be well to regard some basic differences between the two techniques.

In negotiated planning the goals are often not stated. Each negotiator prefers to leave his "fall back" position or ultimate goal a mystery so that he has room to maneuver and bargain. In systematic planning, both the goals and the measures of performance for judging progress toward the goals are to be made explicit and public. Most desirable, the goals are agreed upon by all parties before the planning starts.

The two methods also differ as to the use of data. A negotiator releases only those data which support his cause. The hope is that the combined effect of the data presented by various factions will ultimately bring forth a more or less total picture. In actual practice, however, many positions are not fully represented. Many parties to the negotiations do not have the resources to collect and organize even the data that would support their own case. In systematic planning, there is a common analysis group who collects, organize and presents data for all to use. The data are to be made public and available to all interested parties. While this procedure is expensive, it does eliminate arguments about data, although not about its interpretation.

In negotiating, comparisons between alternatives, to the extent that explicit alternatives are presented at all, are made during oral arguments. In systematic planning, these comparisons are made by predicting the consequences of each alternative with formal analytics. All analyses are presented in writing and are available for study and for recalculation with differing assumptions.

Regarding the processes involved in making the decision, both methods are alike. By either one, value judgments are required to set goals (and in a few cases, to make predictions). The systematic method uses hard data and computational forecasting where possible, leaving the negotiations to the goal setting areas.

In a sense, the use of systematic planning "raises the level of debate" from arguing about specific alternatives to arguing about goals.

WHAT DOES IT TAKE TO USE A SYSTEMATIC APPROACH TO PLANNING IN HIGHER EDUCATION

Suppose, for the moment, that one wishes to use a systems approach (without assuming that this is the best thing to do in all cases), several steps are required in order to define goals and to set up the data base and the predictive procedures required by the systematic method.

First, the decision-makers involved must agree on explicit goals. Expressions of basic goals are usually vague, such as, "our college should provide educational and research services to the community in which we exist." These goals, then, must be made more specific by agreement on the measures of performance, or *indicators*, which can be used to judge whether or not the system is moving toward the goal.

Indicators for the above-mentioned goal might be: the number of community residents who participate in a college program (perhaps measured by credit hours or contact hours) and the number of man-hours of faculty time devoted to projects designed to improve the community. Furthermore, these goals must be made explicit by establishing *desired levels* for the indicators. For example, the college might decide that at least 20 per cent of its student contact hours should be devoted to residents of the community and that at least 30 percent of its faculty research time should be expended on community-related projects. (An extension service would, of course, contribute to at least one and perhaps both of these indicators and therefore to the goal.) Finally, since there will be several goals and many indicators, the decision-makers must set priorities among the indicators, to determine which deserve the most attention in a given planning phase.

Most "system analysis" projects which fail do so because policy makers neglect to identify indicators and associated desired levels. Without these factors, there is no basis for either creating or evaluating alternatives.

The problem of setting goals in higher education is more difficult than it is in almost any other organization. There are obvious goals related to vocational training, such as the ability of the students to get jobs when they graduate. And there are goals related to the community, in two ways. First, the college, by its very existence, brings activity into the area and contributes to its regional economic product and to its economic health. Second, it can contribute to the community, beyond education. It can design and help implement improvements in community services.

Also, however, a college can be considered as an activity in which the students and/or the faculty participate for its own sake. In a sense, the college is an "art form," which one enjoys as a thing unto itself. It is very difficult to measure this last goal and to relate it to the others. Abstract considerations of this sort contribute to the difficulty of expressing priorities among various goals.

Goal-setting for higher education is further confused by the fact that a college can be considered as two almost separate entities: (1) the faculty, which is responsible for faculty-student interaction (the teaching and learning which go on) and for the research process; (2) the "administration," which is responsible for providing the services that the faculty and students need. Alternatively, the institution can be considered as an integrated whole with a single decision-making mechanism. The choice between these two views is significant. It affects everything from basic organization to the most trivial decision processes.

Yet, in any opinion, goal setting, while critical, is not as difficult as many imply. It faculty, students and administrators can be induced to think about what they really want the university or college to do—what they want the institution's future to be like—indicators which measure goals can be developed. A critical question to ask in this process is, what factors or indicators one would look at so that one could say that the institution is doing a better job than it did in "the past"? If the answers are the result of serious thinking, this question should evoke very explicit indicators, on which there will be general agreement. Differences may arise as to the desired levels and priorities, but the differences will be out in the open and subject to debate.

The second major effort which must be undertaken before systematic planning can be implemented is the development of a good data system. Most of the program planning and budgeting activities frequently proposed are efforts to establish good cost accounting and other data bases. Setting up such information systems is not conceptually difficult, but does take a great deal of time and effort. Perhaps it is largely this fact which inhibits the progress of an institution toward the implementation of systematic planning.

The third major effort required to implement systematic planning is the development of the analytic processes, or *models*, which will allow the prediction of resource requirements (manpower, space, costs), of effects and of other consequences of proposed alternatives. The development of some models is well within the state of the art, but again time-consuming and expensive. There are, however, many efforts underway to provide these models, along with generalized software to facilitate their use (see Casasco, 1970). Prediction of the consequences of behavioral processes or of the long-term economic consequences of alternatives is difficult and requires the judgment of experts.

Finally, of course, implementation of systematic planning requires decision-makers who understand what systematic planning is and how to use the models and data tools available.

In summary, setting up for systematic planning takes a high level of technical effort, concentrated negotiations for setting goals and priorities, money and time.

PROBLEMS WITH THE SYSTEMATIC APPROACH

We have discussed the process of planning and the steps required in preparing to plan by systematic means. To complete the picture, let us take a look at some of the problems which may result from the use of the systematic approach and then at some of the benefits.

The basic problem with systematic planning is that it is completely unfamiliar to decision-makers who have been trained and selected for years as good negotiators. The change from negotiating to explicating goals and analyzing on the basis of formal information is a major one. To some extent, the systematic approach takes away the negotiating base.

The psychological trauma associated with the transfer of orientation from negotiating to systematic planning is quite real and even impedes bringing groups together to establish goals.

As we have noted, systematic planning does involve money and manpower, or only to set it up, but also to operate the complex, extensive data systems. Technicians who can develop and use analytic models must be employed. Time on the part of decision-makers to analyze and absorb the data must be expended.

A more serious difficulty is that the systematic approach, by requiring explicit indicators may focus attention on goals or objectives which are too narrow. The phenomenon of inexpressible goals may be real and there may be alternatives which, though desirable, do not measure up well on a chosen set of quantitative indicators. Good systematic planning does *not* preclude the acceptance of such alternatives, but does tend to make them appear less attractive.

A final drawback to the systematic approach is that our understanding of human behavior is limited, and therefore we have no models or analytic methods for predicting the behavioral consequences of alternatives. In some work my organization [Government Studies and Systems, Inc., Philadelphia, USA] has done with the California Coordinating Council for Higher Education, there arose the problem of predicting the number of students who would come to very late or very early classes. No way was found to model the students' behavior. There was no prior data to serve even simple linear models. Another common educational planning problem is to predict the effect of increased faculty workload on faculty performance (both in educational and in research activities). There are, at this time, no formal ways of making such predictions. Still, systematic planning is valuable in that it eliminates the time required to make other predictions and gives the planner more time for concentration on these critical judgments. Also, an attempt to implement systematic planning pinpoints very clearly the need for fresh inputs in the behavioral area, thereby providing a pragmatic base for exploration by educational researchers.

BENEFITS OF SYSTEMATIC PLANNING

Despite the above problems, the systematic approach does offer a number of benefits. First, it provides a basis for communicating the institution's decisions to outside agencies. The negotiating mode may arrive at excellent decisions (in terms of application of resources to attain goals). But it does suffer from the fact that the negotiator has trouble describing to outsiders why the decisions were made, what alternatives were considered and how those alternatives compared with one another. The systematic approach is explicit. Written justification for any decision is usually inherent in the documents produced as a normal part of the planning procedure.

Because the systematic approach depends on formal processes of prediction and comparison (models), it tends to offer more stability as managers and administrators change. There is less opportunity for the development of a personality cult and more for the continuity of efforts to improve performance and attain goals. (If an institution is already headed in the right direction, this independence of personality is an advantage. If, however, the organization is in serious trouble and needs a major "shakeup," the introduction of a charismatic leader to set new directions may be desirable and should not be precluded by a planning process.)

Because it is never possible to represent all aspects of a problem through negotiations and because there is never time to discuss all major alternatives, the negotiating approach often fails to lead to good decisions, especially in complex, dynamic situations. By reason of its formal, highly organized nature, the systematic approach is designed to produce sound decisions, by making wise use of resources in the attainment of clearly stated goals.

ANALYSIS TO INSTRUCTION

Abstract

The Systems approach to the evaluation of instruction is treated. A mathematical methodology is presented and a discussion is provided of the major aspects of the procedure i.e. definition and scope of the problem, listing of the relevant variables and their measure and construction of the model of the formulation of criteria functions.

A discussion is provided of the advantages of the systems approach and the use of sensitivity analysis is treated.

Introduction

Systems analysis is often used interchangeably with the term *operations analysis.* It refers to a specific analytical technique which consists of constructing a mathematical model of an operation. The model is a set of mathematical equations which enables one to calculate changes in the outputs of the operation resulting from specified changes in the inputs. Thus a model of the operation of building a highway might show that increases 10 per cent in the manpower and 5 per cent in the equipment inputs would result in an 8 per cent increase in the primary output—miles of highway completed per month. The model would allow one to calculate the outputs for any arbitrary selection of inputs.

There is also usually implied in the term, *systems analysis*, the notion of optimizing some aspects of the outputs. The thing optimized is called the *criterion*. In the case of highway construction the criterion might be cost per mile and the optimization would consist of minimizing the cost per mile. It would be done by trying all combinations of inputs and selecting that one which resulted in the lowest cost. There are a number of mathematical devices for simplifying a search of this kind.

A similar phrase, *systems approach*, refers to a much less definitive procedure. It is simply the idea of viewing a problem or situation in its entirety with all its ramifications, with all its interior interactions, with all its exterior connections and with full cognizance of its place in its context. The two ideas are related because a systems analysis attempts to deal with a problem comprehensively; in setting up the mathematical model one uses the systems approach. However, one uses it primarily as a guide and as insurance against overlooking an important factor. The systems analysis does not attempt to be complete in its mathematical model. It attempts to be judiciously selective by including significant factors and omitting or aggregating minor factors in order to keep the model to manageable proportions for purposes of the optimization.

To have a convenient illustration during the course of the paper, we shall refer to a specific hypothetical investigation, namely: to what extent, if any, should films be used in high school biology courses?

Possibility of a Systems Analysis

The first problem to be faced is whether or not the question to be studied is suitable for a systems analysis. The only way to start exploring this problem is to make a quick try at setting up a model. Before that can be done one must decide upon the variables that may enter into the model. With regard to the question of using films in biology courses some of the variables suggested might be: (1) quality of available films; (2) quality of teacher; (3) capability of students; (4) proportion of class time devoted to films; (5) budget for biology course; (6) cost of films and related costs; (7) selection of material to be presented by films; (8) composition of instructional program (conventional classroom teaching, laboratory work, demonstrations, TV and radio); (9) time of day class meets; (10) size of class; (11) standing of school in its football league; (12) teacher's measurements (if female).

Without considering the relevance of these variables let us merely inquire into whether they are measurable. Certainly, the last few can be put directly in numerical terms. The first variable is not easy but critics do measure quality of films very roughly as one-star, two-star, three-star, etc. Unfortunately, critics are not altogether consistent in these ratings so that the best we can hope for is only a crude measurement. Similarly with the second variable, about the only quantitative measure we can hope for is some kind of consensus of persons in a position to make good judgments about the teacher's performance. The third variable is less troublesome; the average score of the class on some aptitude test might be used. Better still, one might devote two variables to this factor and use both the average and the standard deviation of the scores to measure capability of class. Moving on to the seventh listed factor, one would need really an infinite number of variables to give a logically complete description of all the ways material could be selected from the course to be presented on film. However, reasonable people could probably agree on a classification of the subject matter which would allow this factor to be represented by half a dozen or so well-defined variables. The eighth listed factor suffers from the same kind of difficulty and also needs four variables merely to measure the time allocation to the different teaching means.

Thus the investigator faces at the outset the problem of whether his question is amenable, as a practical matter, to quantitative analysis or whether such an analysis would be forced. Forced, that is, in the sense that so many quantities rest on human estimates and judgments that perhaps one might just as well admit that the whole question is largely a matter of judgment and treat it by qualitative rather than quantitative analysis.

As a general rule it may be safe to state that the amenability of a question to quantitative analysis usually varies inversely with the generality of the question.

When an investigator decides that his question is not completely suitable for the systems analysis technique, he must then face the problem of whether some portion of his analysis might be a systems analysis. It is a problem which is largely a judgmental decision resting on the extent to which the analyst believes the outcome of such a systems analysis will substantiate important aspects of the qualitative analysis of which it will become a part.

Configuration of the Analysis

The scope of an analysis is ordinarily limited by resources of one kind or another (e.g. time, money), thus presenting the analyst with the problem of what shall be include in and what shall be omitted from the investigation. The avenues available for limiting an investigation are: (1) omitting variables; (2) aggregating variables; (3) restricting the range of variables.

Omission of variables is primarily accomplished on the basis of the judgment of the analyst after careful consideration of his real goal and evaluation of the apparent relevance of each tentative variable to that goal. Rare happy occasions do occur now and then when a brief preliminary analysis will immediately establish the importance of certain variables to the central problem.

Rather than omit variables altogether, analysts often prefer to combine apparently correlated variables into a function or index of some kind which then enters the analysis as a single variable. Thus, in the list of twelve variables given in the preceding section, perhaps the last four could be aggregated into an index of environmental state with some variables making positive and some making negative contributions to the index. Again, considering the eighth factor (composition of instructional program), the matter of selection might be combined so that the eighth factor would be simply the proportion of time not devoted to conventional teaching. The fourth factor (time devoted to films) might then be merely a proportion to be applied to the eighth factor.

An analysis can be very effectively limited without great cost in information content by limiting the range of variables either in extent or by restricting a continuous variable to discrete values. Thus the fourth factor might be limited to the range 0–0.50 and might be further limited to the four values 0.05, 0.10, 0.20 and 0.40 if the analysis seemed to be getting unduly complicated.

The Economic Factor

School boards know how expensive education is, how tight educational budgets are, how difficult it is to squeeze more money out of the taxpayers. There is not much value in informing school boards that their educational systems can be improved by spending more money. They already know that. An investigation which shows that biology students learn more biology when the teacher uses films has missed the point. A meaningful practical question is this: if the teacher's salary is reduced so that she must be replaced by a poorer teacher and if the money thus saved is used to buy film equipment and rent biology films to be used by the poorer teacher, what then is the

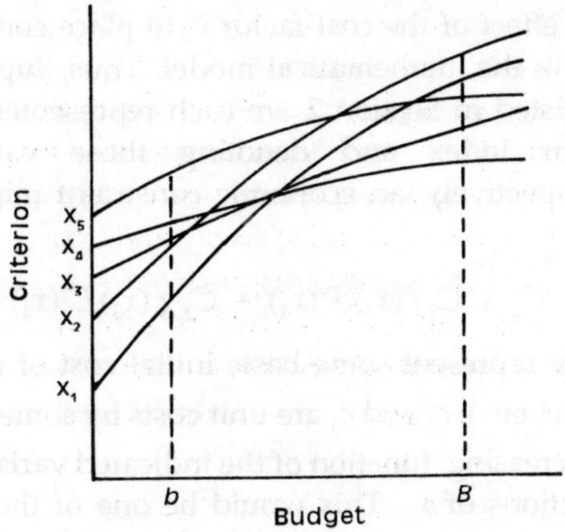

Fig. 11.1

effect on the amount of biology learned by the students? In other words, school boards must allocate resources; additional resources allocated to one sector must be subtracted from another sector. Boards need guidance for making such exchanges profitably from the point of view of overall educational goals.

There is another reason that costs must almost inevitably be a factor of every investigation. It is that conclusions often depend strongly on the operating level of the systems. Recommendations for a wealthy school system will usually differ quite significantly from recommendations suitable for a needy school system. For geometrically-minded persons the accompanying figure demonstrates the idea. The vertical axis measures some reasonable criterion such as amount of biology learned by students and the horizontal axis represents the total budget level of the school system. The curves represent different components of the criterion; one would expect them all to be monotonically increasing with increasing budget. However, they will surely not be increasing at the same rate except in pathologically improbable circumstances. Thus the curve marked x_4 may indicate that a priority portion of money should be devoted to biology films at budget level b but that biology films may be at the bottom of the list at budget level B (which might include an excellent biological laboratory).

The primary effect of the cost factor is to place constraints on other variables in the mathematical model. Thus, supposing the twelve factors listed in Section 2 are each represented by a single variable or index and denoting those variables by $x_1, x_2, \ldots\ldots\ldots, x_{12}$ respectively, an economic constraint might appear as follows:

$$x_3 = C_1 + C_2 f(x_1) F(x_4) + C_3 g(x_2) G(x_4)$$

in which c_1 may represent some basic initial cost of using films (buying projector, etc.); c_2 and c_3 are unit costs by some definition; $f, F,$ and g are increasing function of the indicated variables; G is a decreasing functions of x_4. This would be one of the equations comprising the mathematical model of a systems analysis.

Relations Between Variables

There are several problems involved in relating the variables of an analysis. There is first the problem of deciding what are the legitimate equational relations. An example is given in the preceding paragraph. That example was easy to write down from straightforward logical considerations. Others are not so easy to write down. What relation does "capability of students" fit into? How about "standing in football league," for another? Sometimes one has difficulty finding enough relations; sometimes one can put together too many. In the latter case, a mathematician must be called in to determine a complete set of independent relations.

Having one way or another determined a suitable set of relations, it is necessary to come to specific definitions about the functional forms that enter into the relations. Thus the equation above contains a function $f(x_1)$ which is said to be an increasing function of x_1. This says only that the cost of films increases as the quality of films increases. How does it increase? Linearly? In that case the function would be of the form $ax_1 + b$. This cannot be right. After the most lavish appropriation for a film which meets the director's every demand, will additional funds continue to increase quality at the same rate? Of course not. We need a function which increases steadily at lower values of x_1 but then levels off rapidly as one approaches high quality levels. The final choice might be made by having a mathematician supply a set of functions which have roughly the shape desired and then to have an expert in film production choose one from among that set.

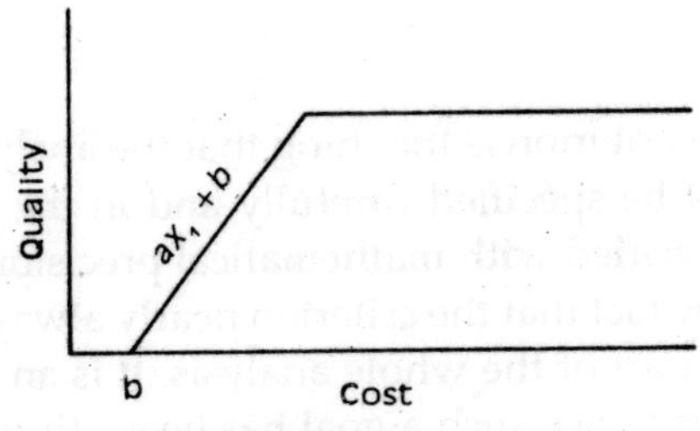

Fig. 11.2

After the equations have been determined and the functional forms selected for all the terms of the equations, one next faces the problems of fixing all the parameter values in the functions. The parameters are the constant (non-variable) elements in the functions and equations. In the illustrative equation above, $c_1, c_2,$ and c_3 are parameters. It is possible that the function $f(x_1)$ might be taken to be linear over a limited range and then horizontal thereafter so that it would have the appearance shown in the accompanying figure with the slant portion given by $a x_1 + b$. Here a and b are parameters; b represents the cost of the very poorest quality film one could make. The parameter, a, measures the rate at which cost increases with quality; there might be some problem in determining what its numerical value is. All the functions will have parameter values to be pinned down.

Some will require some digging through the literature; some, it will appear hopeless to determine except by the device of asking some expert to supply an educated guess. This last, incidentally, is a common and approved method of determining parameter values; it is upgraded, if possible, by obtaining several guesses from several experts in order to get an indication of their consistency and hence the reliability of the value used.

We have not been discussing solely the systems analysis in this section but also the qualitative analysis. A qualitative analysis must concern itself about all these things, the nature of relations, the elimination of dependent relations, the shapes of functions, the ranges of possible parameter values, the probable effects of all these on the criterion. An investigation which does not do these things is not an analysis but merely a pontification.

The Criterion

We recall that the criterion is the thing that the analyst is trying to optimize. It must be specified carefully and in the case of a systems analysis, specified with mathematical precision. Making the task difficult is the fact that the criterion nearly always seems to be the most elusive part of the whole analysis. It is an expression of an overall goal and once such a goal has been stipulated it rarely looks just right.

One aspect of the difficulty may be called the problem of philosophical pursuit. As an illustration we may suggest with respect to biology films that the goal is to optimize the proportion of classroom time to be devoted to films. To what purpose? Well, we want to maximize the amount of biology the students learn. Oh. So the real goal is to maximize the amount of biology learned. Yes, that's it. One thing you might do is drop history and maths so that three hours per day could be devoted to biology. No, no, no. The real goal is to maximize the amount of biology that can be taught in one hour per day. Oh? Even to the point of draining resources from the coaching of cheer leaders? God forbid! No! The real goal is to teach an amount of biology appropriate to a balanced education. What is a balanced...?

And so on and on the issue can be pushed until one is debating the fundamental aim of education. It is to impart knowledge and information? Or, is it to generate understanding? Develop analytical skills? Develop capacities for imaginative creativity and ingenuity? Develop the capability of making sound judgments and decisions? Or is it all of these? If so, in what proportions or priorities? There is, of course, no point in getting off into this thicket. The investigation is certainly not going to settle these large matters. It is merely intended to shed a little light on the advisability of using films in teaching biology. The final statement of the goal should reflect that fact as accurately as possible and as consistently as possible with the general beliefs of the day about the larger matters. It is a good rule of thumb to phrase the goal about one level above that of the investigation in order to be sure that it does fit its immediate context. In a similar vein, the commander of an infantry company makes his decisions in the light of the goals of his battalion commander but does not wander off into the theater commander's plans or the national war aims.

The criterion must be a function of the variables in the analysis. That is why some of the variables are there in the first place—the criterion depends upon them. The other variables are there because those required by the criterion are entangled with them. One view is, then, that the criterion determines the model; certainly that is true to the extent that there is rarely anything to be gained by carrying along variables which do not affect the criterion either directly or indirectly.

Let us assume, for illustrative purposes only, that a suitable criterion for the film problem is maximization of the amount of biology learned as a function of the budget allocated to the one-year high school biology course. Restricting ourselves for simplicity to the first six variables only, we would seek (in symbols):

$$Y(x_3, x_5) = \max_{1,2,4,6} Y(x_1, x_2, x_3, x_4, x_5, x_6)$$

Where Y is the amount learned and is to be maximized over the first, second, fourth, and sixth variables. The actual maximization could not of course be carried out until the precise functional form of Y is specified. How does the amount learned by students vary with the quality of the films (x_1)? With the quality of the teacher (x_2? And so on. To perform a qualitative analysis we must have at least some reasonably reliable impressions about how learning varies with these factors.

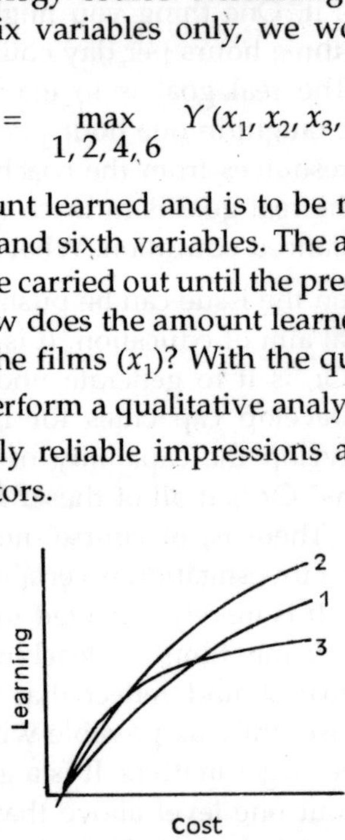

Fig. 11.3

A very common problem in developing a criterion is that there is no suitable single criterion but two or more factors that one would like to optimize simultaneously. For example, one might desire not only to maximize the students' learning of biology but also to minimize the total cost c of giving the biology course. These two quantities work in opposite directions so that it is impossible to achieve both ends. Considering learning, y, (e.g. measured by an achievement test), and cost, c, for a fixed teaching system, the amount of learning might vary with cost along a curve such as one of those plotted in the figure. The curve labeled 2 is everywhere better than that labeled 1 because for any amount of learning it has lower cost and for any cost it gives more learning. But curves like 3 ruin any chance of selecting a system on the basis of the simple kind of comparison possible between 1 and 2. One must face the issue of how the criterion shall exchange dollars for achievement points and use a criterion perhaps of the form:

$$kY - C$$

if a constant exchange ratio k is to be used over the whole range of the variables. Thus, and this is generally true, multiple criteria must be combined into a single index or function before the optimization stage of a systems analysis can be carried out.

CONCLUSIONS OF AN ANALYSIS

The advantage of a systems analysis over a qualitative analysis are never so apparent as in the evaluation of the results of the analysis. The systems analysis with its precise mathematical statements is not an easy place to hide unconscious assumptions. Furthermore, a systems analysis can be subjected to a *sensitivity analysis* which is a replay of the whole analysis with modifications in some of the judgments and estimates that went into the construction of the model. Frequently very many replays of the analysis are done with whole sequences of variations in functional forms and variations in parameter values so that the analyst can see how seriously the results of the analysis depend on some of the less certain components of the analysis.

With all this, the role of judgment is nevertheless quite large in a systems analysis and it may be worthwhile to recapitulate some of the places where judgment has intruded: (1) definition of scope of problem; (2) specification of amount of resources to be devoted to investigation; (3) listing of relevant variables; (4) selection of factors to be included; (5) selection of factors to be excluded; (6) selection of factors to be aggregated; (7) selection of aggregating functions; (8) decisions restricting ranges of variables; (9) construction of model; (10) selection of functional forms; (11) estimation of parameters; (12) selection of criterion;

(13) specification of criterion function; (14) selection of statistical design if data are to be gathered; (15) allocation of study resources to data gathering; (16) design of sensitivity analysis; (17) evaluation of sensitivity analysis. The eighth item may involve a number of decisions regarding selection of a standard model versus construction of a special model, regarding the handling of random variables by stochastic methods or simply by expectations, regarding a single analysis or a sequential analysis or the advisability of preliminary analyses, regarding the feasibility of more elaborate models considering the resources available.

If a systems analysis rests so heavily on judgment, what of a qualitative analysis? It rests practically 100 per cent on judgment. It may marshal hundreds of indisputable scientific facts and deploy them most ingeniously at strategic points of a coldly logical argument, but those facts were selected by judgment and the paths of that logical structure were selected by judgment from an infinite network of conceivable paths. Another analyst would never duplicate it.

The beauty of a systems analysis is that another analyst will frequently come fairly close to duplicating it. And the structure of the analytical procedure allows the two analysts to determine just where and why their analyses diverge. Often they will be able to come to some agreement or reasonable compromise that satisfies them both. In any case, there will eventually result, after publication and a period of review and criticism, some generally accepted position among professionals in the field as to what, approximately, the situation is. In this way there can be built up a body of verifiable quantitative knowledge about some of the complex processes and operations with which education must deal.

12
Models for Thinking

In recent years, the word "model" has been used, or misused, to describe almost any attempt at specifying a system under study in a scientific way. There are differences of opinion about what should truly be regarded as a "model" in the scientific sense. This bickering over fundamentals shows how difficult it is to lay down rigid classifications but cannot disguise the fact that modelling is becoming a widely-used tool in business and industry.

The sort of model we are concerned with is not necessarily, or even usually, a physical representation like the scale models that an aircraft designer makes to test in a wind tunnel. The concentration in industrial and economic studies today is on models in the form of written specifications of the system under study, expressed in logical or mathematical terms. The idea of these models is that they express the inter-relationships between the parts of a system sufficiently clearly to enable its behaviour to be studied scientifically. In particular their object is often to show how the system should be controlled, and to predict its future movements.

USE AND PURPOSE

The applications of such "mathematical" models are many and varied. To take a more-or-less random selection of fields in which recent studies have relied on model- building and analysis, such methods have been applied to forest fire control, labour allocation, the rise of employees through a hierarchy, the behaviour of the stock-market, cloud formation, marketing strategy, the formation of social groups, the operations of an oil company, and traffic control (both air and road). The list could be extended almost indefinitely. There is hardly a branch of science or industry which is not coming under the model-builder's eye (despite the nature of these models, we still speak of "building" them).

It is not obvious at the moment whether or not all these different applications rest on a common body of theory, or a common collection of skills. On the face of it there does exist a set of basic problems and the necessity for a basic expertise shared by all model-building exercises. Whether or not it is possible to write a text book on *the theory of model building*, however, is another matter. The diversity of applications of model-building may have left those outside the fields a little mystified as to what it is all about. Not only do some of the methods used need explaining; some of the myths need exploding.

One important question to be clarified is the purpose of economic and industrial models. The fundamental idea of building models is to mimic the behaviour of a "real-life" system. In doing so, we can get increased understanding of the "real" situation and hence some guidance as to how to control it. What is not attempted is the construction of a microcosm of the system under study which mimics its behaviour in all respects. The systems which are studied are far too complicated to allow anything of this kind.

Models have to be built for specific purposes, not for all possible purposes. This means that there have to be quite different models of the same system, for different purposes. A model of a company for the purpose of planning capital investment, for instance, may be very different from a model of the same company for planning its information flow, and both would differ from a model of its manpower requirements.

Model-builders find it necessary continually to curb their natural ambition to build models of too great a generality. In practice it would seem that the best results are obtained by starting with simple—and by some standards, modest—objectives, and working towards more complicated systems, rather than by starting with attempts at comprehensive structures.

What sort of thing, then, can we fairly call a model? In a sense the organization chart of a company, notwithstanding the fact that it is always out of date, could be regarded as a "model" of the company structure. But, being only a static picture, it is of little use for control or prediction. Such "iconic" models (which include maps and flow diagrams) are, therefore, not of importance to the model-builder except perhaps as a preliminary to his work. He is interested in some sense or other in the movement of the system and in dynamic (as opposed to static) situations.

DISTINCTIONS OF APPROACH

It would be useful to be able to classify the different types of model. At this stage of the subject's development, however, it would be premature to do so. What is possible, and perhaps more relevant, is to compare the different approaches.

For instance, it may be in the nature of the system being modelled that all the relationships can be worked out absolutely precisely. More usually (particularly in economics), some random element is involved, which demands a statistical approach.

Again, some systems lend themselves to being described mathematically by means of general formulae, whereas others are so complicated as to defeat the mathematicians's ideal. In the latter case we can very often simulate the behaviour of the system under a set of different assumptions and, as it were, form a picture of its behaviour by sampling from all the ways it might behave. If solvability is wanting, simulation provides the second line of attack.

There is also a choice between examining the reasons for phenomena and merely describing them. The difference here is more one of degree than of basic approach; it is frequently possible to start with a simple description of a situation, and to analyse it in more detail to find progressively deeper causal connections later on.

A number of such distinctions can be drawn between different classes of model: short-term and long-term; computable and non-computable; macro and micro. But the net result of all these different approaches is always the same—to give some indication of the nature of the system being modelled, as an aid to making decisions about its future.

A NON-IDEAL SCIENCE

Model-building is clearly a way of applying scientific method. It may not be obvious at first sight why it should be regarded as a separate subject. There are a number of reasons:

In the first place, unlike the scientist the model-builder has frequently to deal with concepts to which no concrete units of length, time, mass and so on can be given. In economics, sociology and psychology it is necessary to deal with variables such as value, utility and demand. In some cases these concepts are quantifiable, for example in monetary units, but the units themselves are frequently subject to changes in value so that correction factors have to be introduced. Even in models of manpower, where the primary units are countable human beings, some regard has to be made to quality in order to be realistic.

Secondly, many of the factors appearing in the equations of a model deal with inequalities rather than equalities. In fact, some models of an industrial plant, such as an oil refinery, consist almost entirely of inequality constraints expressing, for example, the maximum capacity of intake, or minimum requirements in output. These situations cannot be dealt with using the "classical" mathematic approach, and a special technique known as mathematical programming has been developed to cater for them.

Thirdly, classical economic theory has been found lacking as a basis for the construction of economic models because it is essentially qualitative. Even when economists did get as far as expressing relationships in mathematical terms, they did so in the manner of equations expressing static conditions. To deduce the dynamic behaviour of a system from such equations is like trying to deduce the laws of planetary motion from the principle of the triangle of forces (which accounts for the fact that mathematical formulation added little or nothing to economic theory). Nowadays, economists realize that the behaviour of economic systems depends critically on the time-lags between stimulus and response. In fact, it has now been shown that the very stability of an economic system may depend on the time-lag between some measure being introduced and its full effect being felt, rather than simple on any causal law relating to the effect of the stimulus.

The length of a time-lag and the pattern of transient phases that follow a change are among the most difficult of economic effects to measure. It is surprising how little is known of them even in the best documented economics. How long, for example, does an alteration in bank rate take to exert its full effect? How far does production lag behind unemployment, or unemployment behind production?

Added to these problems or perhaps causing them, are the difficulties of gathering economic data. In some circumstances it is possible to make up for deficiencies in given data by conducting *ad hoc* enquiries in greater detail. With a few exceptions, economic models built up to the present have had to rely on statistics that are produced by government departments, or central authorities of some kind, for quite different purposes. If governments are going to become seriously interested in model-building there will arise the necessity for collecting data for that purpose alone. This may have a far-reaching effect on the nature of the state's statistical service.

The model-builder is all too aware of the difficulties he faces. However, it would be wrong to paint too black a picture of his situation. It is not necessarily true, for instance, that the behaviour of a complicated system is itself very complicated. Statistics is full of example of this fact. For instance, the circumstances and motivation which go to determine an individual's income are legion. Any model which tried to set out the situation in detail would soon get bogged down in sheer complexity. Nevertheless, the so-called Pareto law of income distributions, which is fairly closely followed in all Western societies, depends on only one parameter, yet it has proved remarkably stable over decades of fundamental change in economic control.

A second source of encouragement to the model-builder is provided by the electronic computer. In fact, it would be an overstatement to say that econometrics and models have become practical possibilities only since the computer was developed. Early writers had many of the ideas, but the practical engineering of the subject had to wait for the technological breakthrough represented by the electronic machine.

THE MODELLER'S VIEWPOINT

As with many of the so-called management science methods, the mere discipline of expressing a situation in terms of a model can frequently advance our thinking about a system. For instance, most businesses have a chain of command expressible by the branching-pedigree type of diagram. The operations represented by this diagram work in both directions; instructions flow downwards, information flows upwards. Decisions at defined levels are made at various points of the network. The attempt to express these operations in a precise way throws up some quite fundamental queries. Is it inevitable, for instance, that the (down-flowing) executive chain should be the same as the (up-flowing) information chain, or the decisional system the same as the executive system? Nature, in designing the human being, has provided at least four different systems for controlling the body (arterial, venous, vascular and nervous) and has linked them in a very intricate and roundabout way. In considering a social or commercial organism, ought we to take a leaf out of her book? I do not know the answers to these questions, not indeed whether there are any answers. The point is that until we think about a situation from a model-building viewpoint such fundamental queries might not arise.

It would be pleasant to be able to offer a simple answer to the often-posed question: "How does one set about building a model?" This is one of those general questions like "How does one design a building?" or "How does one cure a disease?" The answer must be equally general—it all depends on what sort of model, and for what purpose. Granting that, it is still not possible to anatomize the model-building process. Perhaps, when a great many more models of all sorts have been built, it will be possible to lay down rules. At the moment it is only possible to examine the trends.

Certain facts have already emerged. For one thing: although, in limited field, with limited objectives, it may be possible for one gifted individual to have at his command all the skills required to construct and test a model, the larger models must be a matter of team effort. A model of complete economy, for instance, requires the analytical training of the economist, the knowledge of available data of the descriptive statistician, the expertise of the theoretical statistician and perhaps of a specialized mathematician, the skill of the computer programmer, and the common sense of them all. The moral of this seems to be that we are in some danger of spreading our efforts too thinly on the ground. If, as I suspect, there is to be growing interest in the subject of model-building over the next 10 or 20 years, and if the amount of effort which can be put into the subject is limited in time, money and intellectual capacity, it would pay us as a nation (or perhaps some larger community) to strengthen our strong points and concentrate on setting up units for study bigger than the critical mass at which useful results are produced.

Of the many distinctions of type and use that can be made, there is one which may become a source of actual conflict: the difference between models produced primarily as a forecasting tool and those built for control purposes. A model of an economy may be useful to an individual firm to predict its environment, and useful to the government in the actual control of the economy. There is no conflict of aim in devising these cybernetic systems: but there may be a conflict among users in the sense that industry may want to rely on forecasts from a model, whereas government may want to falsify them. It will be interesting to see how this difference in emphasis will influence the development of model-building over the next decade.

13

Educational Law and School Management

Increasingly, those associated with college and university administration need to concern themselves with the legal implications of their activities. One of the more striking evidences of this fact is the growth in the number of full-time attorneys employed on the staff of colleges and universities. Those institutions that do not have counsel on their own staff generally employ outside counsel on a retainer basis. In the past ten years, there has been a very dramatic increase in litigation involving institutions of higher education with legal claims asserted individually or jointly against institutions and against their directors, trustees, officers, faculty, and staff.

What are the liabilities of institutions and what are the liabilities of the trustees in particular? There has traditionally been a legal distinction between corporate directors and university trustees, but one which seems to diminish with the expanding role of university trustees. Both may be said to have a trust or a fiduciary relationship. In the case of the corporate director, this relationship is with the stockholders.

The entire management of corporate affairs is committed to the corporate directors and they are required to act in the utmost of good faith and best judgment and for the common benefit of all stockholders. Stock-holders of corporations can bring suit for a breach of these fiduciary duties. Educational corporations do not have stockholders, nor do they have specific identifiable beneficiaries. Their beneficiaries are a number of groups such as students, alumni, faculty, donors, and the public. They have, consequently, been classified along with nonprofit charitable organizations as charitable trusts. However, public educational corporations are agents of state government and trustees are consequently responsible to state government for the performance of their duties. The trusfee is required to subordinate his personal interest to the diverse group of beneficiaries indicated above. The care taken must be that which a "normally prudent man" would take under similar circumstances, while giving his best judgment.

Following the Cambodian crisis in 1970 and the tragic events at Kent State University, a suit was brought against the Chancellor of Washington University for $7.7 million. The student plaintiffs claimed that the relaxation of normal academic rules and the failure to call police quickly enough during an anti-ROTC demonstration caused them to lose valuable classroom and extra-curricular experience. The trustees and administration of Indiana State University at Terre Haute were sued for $50,000 for failing to take prompt police action against student demonstrators who damaged campus property in the early spring of 1970. Such cases reflect that, although colleges and universities historically have enjoyed a far-reaching legal immunity from many claims, this immunity has virtually disappeared.

Trustees are finding that the heightened emphasis on accountability extends to them as well and they will become increasingly active in their governance role (assuming that the spectre of legal liability does not discourage them from Board participation) because of the extent to which they are pressured to be knowledgeable of and, hence, accountable for the full range of college and university activities. They are faced with the prospect of suits based on alleged neglect of their proper functions of reviewing management, evaluating policies, and providing reasonable answers to deficits and other financial crises.

In recent years, the much publicized circumstances involving speculative investment and pyramiding of endowment funds at one major institution and the virtual collapse of financial administration at another, leading to the resignation of the President, raised questions as to trustee liability. The serious regard for potential trustee liability is evidenced by one university board that provided liability insurance protection for trustees in the amount of $1,000,000.

As another aspect of the increasing number of legal issues confronting colleges and universities, there are at least thirteen major pieces of federal legislation that now govern various aspects of college and university behavior and hence raise compliance issues with legal ramifications. These are:

- The Equal Pay Act of 1963
- The Age Discrimination in Employment Act of 1967
- The Minimum Wage Laws
- The Unemployment Insurance Requirements in the Employment Security Amendments of 1970
- The Social Security Act
- The Health Maintenance Organization Act of 1973
- The employment Retirement Income Security Act of 1974
- Wage and Salary Controls under the Economic Stabilization Act of 1970
- The Occupational Safety & Health Act of 1970
- Regulations Implemented under Civil Laws by the Environmental Protection Agency
- Title VII of the Civil Rights Act of 1964 dealing with Equal Employment Opportunity
- Executive Order 11246, as amended requiring Affirmative Action to Correct Past Discriminations in Employment
- Sex Discrimination Regulations under Title IX of the Education Amendment of 1972.

The distinction between public and private institutions respecting their status before the courts continues to have significance, although the distincuon has become less clear, particularly in relation to the federal courts. In the 1960s a group of students at Alfred University were suspended following an anti-ROTC demonstration. Alfred is a private liberal arts college but is also the host campus for one of the State University of New York contract colleges dealing in ceramics. The court of appeals ruled in this case that the ceramics students (presumed to be students of a public institution) would be entitled to due process and all the substantive guarantees of the Bill of Rights. Liberal arts students would not.

Whether or not private institutions are susceptible to suit before the federal courts and to the guarantees of the Constitution is deemed to depend, at least in part, on the degree of government involvement. Government involvement can be broadly interpreted to include not only fiscal interdependence but also regulation and control. However, even fiscal interdependence is subject to broad interpretation. In one instance, a state court ruled that a private institution was subject to the federal Constitution because of the extensive use of *state* funds to build residence halls, because of the number of students receiving state and federal financial aid, and because of various state and local tax exemptions. The latter two circumstances are clearly widespread. Moreover, private institutions receive nearly twice as many federal dollars as the public campuses. Hence, in legal terms, as well as in other respects (see discussion on public and private institutions in Financing Higher Education) it is not unrealistic to predict that the distinction between public and private institutions is rapidly disappearing.

An inventory of institutional activities can provide an indication to those concerned with college and university administration as to the range of vulnerability or exposure. The categories within such an inventory would vary with the compiler. However, a reasonably representative list would include:

1. Recruitment, promotion, discipline, and termination of personnel;
2. Curricular and research activities (such as, research investigations involving human subjects);
3. Consulting and public services programs;
4. Support services activities and auxiliary enterprises;
5. Student services (housing, food, health, etc.);
6. Student activities;
7. General and financial administration; and

8. Public relations.

The Insurance and Risk Management Committee of the National Association of College and University Business Officers established the following more comprehensive classification of higher education liability perils (Committee Minutes 1974)

1. Criminal Acts;

   Embezzlement—employee dishonesty;

   Environmental—pollution;

   Malfeasance—employee and/or directors; and

   Manslaughter—campus security.

2. Tort (Civil) and Equity Acts;

   Advertisers, authors, and publishers liability;

   Athletic events (players, spectators, coaches), recreational facilities, programs, instructional, intercollegiate contests (events);

   Automobile (including mobile equipment) fleet, drivers, and non-ownership operation;

   Aviation liability;

   Bailee liability (care, custody, and control);

   Boiler and machinery liability;

   Campus security—normal operations, false arrest, and all related internal tasks;

   Construction liability (contractor, students, public, donor, board);

   Dental malpractice—products and services;

   Directors and officers (errors and omissions);

   Discrimination;

   Easement and other property liability—access appurtenances, etc.;

   Ownership liability, rights of others, e.g. eminent domain, etc.;

   Elevators, escalators, including collision liability;

   Employers, including safety and health hazards;

Workmen's Compensation, Federal Employment Liability Act, Long-Shoremen and Harbor Workers, Jones Act, Unemployment Compensation;

Discrimination (civil damages);

Fire—legal liability;

Fringe benefits and employee benefits;

Hold harmless or waiver agreements; consent travel forms, etc.;

Institutional agency—employees, invitees, licensees, trespassers, volunteers, etc.;

Libel—slander, defamation of character, invasion of privacy, etc.;

Liquor law liability;

Malpractice—errors and omissions, negligence;

Medical doctors, dentists, nurses, specialists, pharmacists, paramedics, hospital personnel;

Veterinary medical personnel (institutional personnel);

Clinical practicum, psychological conditioning, counselling;

Audio—speech centers, personnel, etc.;

Nuclear liability—products and general;

Oceanography—maritime liabilities;

Pharmaceutical liability;

Pollution—environmental hazards;

Premises and operations;

Professional liability, errors, omissions, negligence (ordinary and gross) (administration and professional discipline personnel);

Product liability—food services, medical products (blood, prosthetic, etc.);

Program liability—travel, research (foreign and domestic);

Protective liability (contractual in large measure);

Residence liability;

Riot, civil commotion;

Watercraft;

Worldwide premises and program liability.

3. Contractual Acts;

   Artifacts, art objects (bailee, exhibitor, etc.);

   Authority operations;

   Equipment;

   Franchise operations;

   Implied contracts, e.g. catalogs;

   Joint—e.g. affiliation agreements;

   Products and services;

   Real estate—leasehold operations;

   Staff—fringe benefits, tenure, etc.

All of the above constitute areas of activity in which legal advice may be required and which constitute areas of concern for trustees regarding the potential liability of their institutions and their own liabilities.

Without being prescriptive, it is nonetheless possible to set forth several very fundamental principles and caveats in respect to the legal aspects of higher education administration. These are included in the following list:

1. It is important that all those associated with the management of the institution are made fully aware of their potential liabilities. In this connection an SEC investigation report set forth four principal standards of directorial performance that are equally pertinent to college and university trustees:

- Outside directors violate their duty if their presence has no impact whatever on the company's operations or affairs;
- Outside directors cannot blindly rely on the fact that the company employs accountants, lawyers, investment bankers, and other professionals;
- Directors should familiarize themselves with the company's business and question management in more than a perfunctory manner;
- Management must make available to outside directors sufficient information concerning corporate affairs to

enable them to adequately discharge their responsibilities. (See section on Reporting.)

2. Institutional affairs should be conducted in a manner that is fully sensitive to areas of exposure and to potential legal liabilities resulting from institutional activities.

3. Thoughtful consideration should be given to the most effective means of providing adequate legal support to the institution within its resource limitations. Where full time legal counsel is employed by the institution such counsel should be involved in all significant administrative activities and deliberations and not merely consulted on such obvious matters as contractual relationships. While smaller institutions frequently cannot afford to engage full time specialists in many disciplines that are commonly found on the staff of large universities, full time counsel may well be the one area of specialization that an institution can ill afford to forego. The institution that relies on occasional or ad hoc legal assistance is apt to be dealing with potential liabilities in a reactive, rather than preventive manner.

4. Institutions should explicitly establish and effectively implement a thoughtfully conceived and carefully developed program of risk management.

RISK MANAGEMENT

The average lay person practices risk management in his or her every day affairs, frequently on an instinctive basis, without being explicitly aware that risk management is being practiced. The head of household determines the amount of life insurance that is appropriate for family protection, based on a variety of trade-off decisions. The amount of premium cost constitutes an ultimate limitation on the amount and type of life insurance procured.

But there is a wide range of premium cost that will be deemed tolerable, predicated on considerations such as number and ages of children, age and predicted earning power of surviving spouse, and general financial condition of the family, including but not limited to, amount of debt, value of other assets, status of mortgage, and existence or non-existence of mortgage insurance.

A decision on the deductibles when procuring auto insurance will be predicated on considerations such as the age and condition of the car, the potential magnitude of cost in the event of accident and the premium cost. Efforts will be made to minimize risk or to limit premium cost. For example, a woman may elect to keep her expensive jewelry in a vault and to take out day insurance when the jewelry is to be worn for a special occasion. The owner of an automobile involved in an accident may, if there is no personal injury involved, elect not to report the accident to his insurance company and to bear the cost of repair.

Clearly, these same principles have even greater applicability to an institution when considering an insurance program. Some years ago, the curator of a fine arts museum at a prestigious institution was involved in a dispute with the chief financial officer—the kind of argument that business managers all too frequently lose. The overall financial condition of the institution had deteriorated to the point where the financial officer was compelled to examine every potential avenue for reducing costs. It was within this context that premium costs for fine arts insurance came under scrutiny and a proposal was advanced to increase the deductible.

The curator appealed to the President in outraged indignation, contending that the fine arts objects ought to be fully insured because they were priceless and irreplaceable. "Precisely the point," responded the chief financial officer. "if the objects cannot be replaced, all that the insurance premiums can do is to provide funds that will enable us to procure some roughly equivalent substitute. Under those circumstances, since the risk of loss is minimal and the premium cost high, we ought to limit the premium by increasing the deductible." This was one instance in which the chief financial officer prevailed.

Broadly speaking, an institutional risk management program involves:

- a comprehensive identification of exposures and potential liabilities;

- a thorough and continuing evaluation and selection of indemnification coverage which balances premium costs against the level of risk assumed with self-insurance; and
- an institutional style which integrates risk management concepts into the day-to-day administration of the institution so that exposures are reasonably and realistically contained.

Stated differently, the two major components of risk management, when undertaken either by individuals or by an entity such as a college or university, are loss financing and loss prevention. The matter of loss financing is a highly important one for institutions because the sums involved can be quite substantial and the cash flow implications, significant.

There are a wide variety of plans that can be utilized as an alternative to the payment of premiums and passing on the risk or some significant portion of the risk to the carrier. The adoption of these plans is motivated either by financial considerations, such as the substantial premium cost of malpractice insurance or by the fact that carriers may be reluctant to insure certain types of risk.

The essential features of these plans are that they provide an increased cash flow to the institution and involve a greater assumption of risk by the institution. This latter characteristic causes the trustees to be reluctant to depart from the more traditional approach. But institutions have available to them both experience history and analytic tools with which to evaluate that experience, determining the frequency and severity of losses in probability terms, along with the pertinent considerations to determine retention requirements and make other necessary decisions in connection with a self-insurance program. These are essentially the same analytic tools that would be used by an insurance may be required.

An approach to self-insurance that has been used predominantly in the profit sector because of its tax avoidance features, but is beginning to be adopted by some institutions, is the use of a captive insurance company either domestic or off-shore (e.g., domiciled in such locations as Bermuda, the Cayman Islands and the Channel Islands). This is a separate corporate entity formed to provide insurance coverage for its "parent," and third parties. Professionals in the field deem it inadvisable to use a captive unless there is also the intent to insure third parties. In the university sector, this raises issues of unrelated business income. Basically, the captive is a loss-retention vehicle. Identified advantages of the use of a captive are reduction of cost through elimination of unnecessary services or performance of services at less expense, funding of uninsurable or unreasonably priced coverages, and greater control and flexibility in respect to the insurance program. Disadvantages are principally the initial capitalization requirement and the incurrence of limiting company expenses (i.e., expenses associated with normal state requirements that filings must be through admitted carriers).

A prime advantage of a captive insurance company, vis-a-vis a strict self-insurance program, is improved access to reinsurance markets. Off-shore captives have also been used to lessen or avoid the impact of cumbersome or restrictive state regulatory activity.

A Self-insurance program, whether or not associated with the use of a captive insurance company, is likely to stimulate a greater awareness of the necessity for concentrated and systematic attention to the second major element in a risk management program which is loss prevention. As indicated in the discussion on Educational Law, it is possible to comprehensively identify areas of potential exposure associated with the range of college and university activities and to systematically analyze the potential frequency, severity, and likelihood of occurrence.

This analysis is very much a part of the analysis required to determine the most appropriate form of loss financing. The additional ingredient introduced here is the cost of preventive measures that may either reduce the potential of a loss occurrence or minimize its consequences. An important element in any loss prevention program is to induce academic and non-academic administrators to incorporate loss prevention concepts into the administration of their day-to-day activities. For example, does the Dean of Students or other appropriate university official, who is involved in preparations for a rock concert to be held in the campus stadium, give full consideration to all of the potential risk and liability implications and to what preventive measures might be necessary?

In the chapters on computers and on budgeting, the concept of a "chargeback" system is discussed in the context of a budgetary device for properly apportioning the costs of some types of support services. In appropriate instances, it is also an effective device for stimulating effective management. Risk management may be one such area. The apportionment of the costs of an insurance program as part of the operating costs of institutional department and activity centers may serve to make administrators more risk conscious. But whereas in the example of data processing support services it is important that the funds budgeted to a department for this purpose not be susceptible to transfer, it is precisely the potential for transfer to another budget line, or the reverse, that provides the incentive in the case of risk management.

14

Teaching and Bureaucratic—Professional Dichotomy

Reforming Paper Pushers and Avoiding Free Agents: The Teacher as a Constrained Decision Maker

Sharon C. Conley

In the early 1980s, when the current education reform movement began, the assumption emerged that schools could achieve quality education by using bureaucratic strategies to reduce uncertainty in the school and in the classroom (Bacharach & Conley). More recent reports, however, take into account the uncertain nature of teachers' work and the ineffectiveness of these bureaucratic measures (Carnegie Forum, 1986; Darling-Hammond, 1986; Frymier, 1987; Glickman, 1987; Holmes Group, 1986; Timar & Kirp, 1987). Specifically, second- wave reform proponents recommend allocating greater autonomy to teachers, increasing their influence in school and district decision making, and enhancing their professional knowledge and skills (Carnegie Forum, 1986). This chapter examines the problem of maintaining an effective balance between the bureaucratic and professional models of school management in the context of teachers as constrained decision makers.

TEACHERS AS DECISION MAKERS

The need for teachers to make numerous on-the-spot decisions and deal with uncertainty arises from three primary sources. First, the needs of students are variable and constantly changing (Doyle, 1986; Griffin, 1985; Jackson, 1968; Lieberman & Miller, 1978; Lortie, 1975; Williams, 1987;). Second, unlike professionals in such occupational settings as medicine and law, teachers do not have the luxury of serving clients' needs individually. Teachers must operate in the context of a highly interactive group (Berliner, 1983; Doyle, 1986; Shedd, Malanowski, & Conley, 1986). Finally, the goals and purposes assigned to teachers are multiple, ambiguous, and often conflicting (Lampert, 1985; Lieberman & Miller, 1984; Griffin, 1985; Schlechty & Joslin, 1984).

Elsewhere, I have, with my co-authors, described a framework that attempts to capture some of the complexities of teaching by classifying teachers' decisions according to three teaching roles (instruction, counselling, and management) and three functions (planning, implementation, and evaluation) (Bacharach, Conley, & Shedd, 1987). Together, these roles and functions identify critical decision areas in teaching. More specifically, teachers make decisions about increasing the academic achievement of students, meeting the personal "counselling" needs of individual students, and managing groups of students. Similarly, teachers decision making involves not only planning activities but also taking action and evaluating the consequences of action. Indeed, the process of combining different roles and functions constitutes the most demanding and difficult aspect of teaching (Kerchner & Mitchell, 1986; Shedd & Malanowski, 1985).

These observations help us appreciate why professional conceptions of teaching have enjoyed considerable popularity in the second wave of reform. If teachers constantly have to deal with uncertainty and make numerous decisions, it is extremely difficult for anyone except the teacher to plan and coordinate all of these separate decisions. Yet this is precisely what those who hold a bureaucratic conception of teaching hope to accomplish. In the bureaucratic model, "teachers' work is supervised by superiors whose job it is to make sure that teachers implement the curriculum and procedures of the school district" (Darling-Hammond, 1986, p. 532).

The bureaucratic model focuses on simplifying and routinizing the work of teachers, thereby reducing the decisions teachers have to make. In such a conception, the teacher becomes a mere technician, implementing routine solutions to clear and predictable problems. This bureaucratic model requires teachers to use techniques based on research on "effective" teaching to solve classroom problems, but it ignores aspects of the classroom and students that are uncertain or indeterminate (Bacharach et al., 1987). In this context, teachers must rely heavily on external sources for what they teach and "view themselves as ciphers for other people's expert knowledge" (Elmore, 1987, pp. 72-73).

The professional model, in contrast, treats uncertainty as a given in professional practice (Schon, 1983; Fenstermacher, 1987) and emphasizes strategies that help the professional deal with daily uncertainty. The professional model assumes that the teacher is a decision maker who creatively adapts knowledge to unique and varied problem situations, expands skills beyond "textbook knowledge," and continuously refines professional judgment, initiative, and decision making.

Those who adopt the professional model assume that, although experts may identify basic decisions in teaching, they cannot totally delineate teacher's creative integration and adaptation of decisions in response to problems. Indeed, because the problems teachers face do not have prescribed solution, teachers are in the position of risking failure or success in decision making.

MANAGERIAL STRATEGIES FOR EDUCATION REFORM: THE SEARCH FOR A MIDDLE GROUND

The underlying assumptions of the bureaucratic and professional models go far toward explaining many of the reform debates of the past five years. The early reform strategies attempted to reduce uncertainty and thus implicitly bureaucratize teacher's work. Merit pay and career ladders illustrate this point.

Merit pay proposals encouraged administrators to generate, in Tayloristic fashion, "objective" indicators of teachers' performance. In doing so, administrators and policymakers implicitly assumed that teaching activities could be prescribed and delineated by management. In subjecting teaching to detailed specification, merit pay proponents attempted to achieve greater bureaucratic control over teacher's work.

When enthusiasm for merit pay began to dwindle in the mid-1980s, career ladders were heralded as a viable alternative. Career ladder proponents claimed that such plans would rectify the "flat" structure of teaching, provide teachers greater opportunities to develop skills, and help schools and districts make better use of teacher's skills. However, like merit pay, many career ladders ignored the reality of the uncertainty teachers encounter in their work in delineating tasks for teachers and linking detailed job descriptions to each hierarchical level. In one plan, for example, teachers could lose their career ladder status for "refusing to do the duties" prescribed at the next level (Tennessee Education Association, 1984). Consequently, many career ladders did not fulfil their original intent and became a variation of the bureaucratic answer to school reform.

Teachers and school officials recognized immediately the inherent discrepancy between bureaucratic reform prescriptions and the realities of teaching (Frymier, 1987; Rosenholtz, 1986). In many instances, they responded to reform initiatives by circumventing restrictive regulations but, all too often, in ways that could undermine effective school structures and work processes (Timar & Kirp, 1987). For example, many career ladder programs established uniform bureaucratic criteria; therefore, on the day of the evaluation, teachers presented a facade that their work was just as uniform and bureaucratic as expected.

Weick (1976) has maintained that schools are loosely coupled systems. While this metaphor has been useful, the first wave of reform proved clearly that schools could use such mechanisms as career ladders and merit pay to become very tight bureaucracies. The problem is not that school structures are loosely coupled but, rather, that teachers' activities (i.e., roles and functions) are loosely coupled, that is, dominated by uncertainty and unpredictability

In this context, the first wave of reform tried to impose tightly coupled structures on what we know to be loosely coupled work activities. For reform efforts to be successful, they must overcome what is often viewed as an inherent contradiction. That is, while teachers face uncertainty and unpredictability in their daily work, they also carry out this work in a school organization to which they are accountable. If we fail to go beyond this contradiction, we will be constantly beset by the conflict apparent in the first wave of reform—the conflict between the structure of the school organization and the nature of teacher's work.

These observations emphasize the basic incompatibility between the bureaucratic solutions of the early reform movement the complexity (more specifically, the uncertainty) that teachers encounter in their daily work activities. If we begin with the premise that teachers are critical to school improvement, then we must attend to two critical areas. First, we must examine teachers' professional preparation, that is, how teachers are prepared prior to their recruitment. The report of the Holmes Group (1986) dealt with this area in some detail. The second area, teachers' professional development following their recruitment, has received much less attention. Both the Carnegie Forum (1986) and the Holmes Group (1986) discussed it but not in great detail. To date, no clear focus or goal for teacher development exists.

When addressing the development of professionals who work in an organization, we must keep two goals in mind. First, professionals need to be confident about making daily decisions in a context of uncertainty. Furthermore, in making these decisions, teachers must weigh risks and alternatives (Lampert, 1985). Individual teachers who do not weigh alternative decisions but instead repeat routines in a reflexive, not reflective, manner cannot be considered developed professional regardless of the credentials they hold. Second, a developed professional considers alternative decisions within the normative framework of the organization, specifically, within the broad parameters of the organizations' goals and procedures. In this view, the teacher neither follows blindly (i.e., pushes paper) nor totally ignores organizational precedent and context (i.e., acts as an individual free agent).

Figure 14.1 illustrates a continuum of metaphors with the two roles of teacher as paper pusher and individual free agent at the extremes and the role of constrained decision maker occupying the middle. Neither the metaphor of teachers as paper pushers or as individual free agents in consistent with the reality of the professional teacher working in the school. The view of the teacher as paper pusher makes the teacher no more than a bureaucratic extension of the organization as seen, for example, in the teacher-proof curriculum heralded as the direction of the future. Another example is those who see the future of schools as collections of PCs with teachers replaced by floppy disks.

Teachers as Paper Pushers	Teachers as Constrained Decision Makers	Teachers as Individual Free Agents

Fig. 14.1 Continuum of Teaching Metaphors.

At the other extreme, teachers are metaphorically considered to be individual free agents who are granted the autonomy to act independently in the classroom. An example may be found in some of the "open" schools that emerged in the 1960s and early 1970s (Hoyle, 1986), where teachers' expression of their own values and idiosyncratic interests were seen as appropriate classroom activities.

Between these two extremes is the view of the teacher as a constrained decision maker. The constrained decision maker deals with uncertainty by weighing alternatives and taking creative risks, while at the same time being aware that he or she is operating within a specific organizational context characterized by goals, norms, precedent, and colleagues. A central goal for the next wave of reform is to develop teachers professionally as constrained decision makers, avoiding the rhetorical extremes implied in the metaphors of teachers as paper pushers or individual free agents. The notion of teachers as constrained decision makers has direct implications for three critical areas of school improvement: job design, teacher evaluation, and systems of participation.

Job Design

How can teachers' job be designed to be consistent with the image of teachers as constrained decision makers? Those who view teachers as paper pushers would insist that we design jobs according to scientific management principles, specifying detailed steps and procedures to be followed in carrying out the work. On the other hand, those who view teachers as individual free agents suggest that we leave teaching to be conducted "behind classroom doors."

Genuine job design implies creating a work environment that facilitates constrained decision making. For example, Hackman and Oldham (1980) developed a job design model for occupations in general, which is also very useful for dealing with professional occupations (Conley, 1983). The model specifies that five critical job characteristics lead to greater skill utilization and internal motivation of employees: autonomy, skill variety, task identity, task significance, and feedback. Implicit in the Hackman and Oldham model are both dimensions of constrained decision making. Autonomy, skill variety, and task identity allow the professional to cope with uncertainty and process knowledge to facilitate decision making, while task significance and feedback imply constraint mechanisms assuring that the professional operates within the broad normative framework of the organization.

The authors define *autonomy* as the discretion employees have to carry out their work activities. In education, discretion ensures that teachers can deal with classroom uncertainty and take risks. Thus this dimension of job design would ensure that teachers have the flexibility they need to weigh alternatives and make decisions. *Skill variety* is the degree to which employees use a variety of skills and abilities in carrying our their work. As discussed earlier, the work of teaching demands a variety of decision-making skills on the part of teachers, for example, the need to instruct, manage group behavior, and deal with the needs of individual students simultaneously. Job design should enhance, not constrain, skill variety. This characteristic thus directly addresses the issue of task specification and deskilling, which is all too often inherent in detailed job descriptions (Apple, 1987).

Task identity is the degree to which the job involves completion of a "whole task." In education, teachers must be able to "see tasks through" from beginning to end, weighing alternatives that are often needed for taking creative risks necessitated by uncertainty. Jobs should be designed to avoid the fragmentation that we often find advocated by those who metaphorically think of teachers as paper pushers who must be controlled through detailed job descriptions.

While these three aspects of the model deal with teachers' ability to make decisions and take risks, the final two dimensions provide a context of constraint. *Task significance* is the extent to which work activities are viewed as significant to the organization or society as a whole. While task significance can be viewed as a "psychic reward" (Lortie, 1975), it can also be viewed as an implicit organizational constraint that can deter teachers from acting as individual free agents. The more significant the task, the more visibility it has in the organization and the more cautious teachers may be in their decision making and their willingness to take risks. Job design, then, can help make the work of teaching important to the organization as a whole, assuring that teachers operate within organizational constraints. *feedback* is the degree to which the job itself and, to a lesser extent, supervisors and co-workers, provide professionals with direct and clear information about their job performance. In education, through peer review, supervisory communication, and student achievement, feedback also becomes a source of constraint. Taken together ta3k significance and feedback assure that teachers develop professionally as constrained decision makers, not simply as individual free agents operating behind the closed doors of their classrooms.

My description of Hackman and Oldham's (1980) model illustrates how job design may be used to avoid the metaphorical extremes of teachers as paper pushers or as free agents. This logically leads to the second critical question of how to evaluate teachers.

Teacher Evaluation

What kind of evaluation system works best for the constrained decision maker? Those who view teachers as paper pushers simply want to evaluate teachers' output—"counting" the number of papers that teachers produce "New style" merit pay, which links teacher pay to measures of student achievement, is an example of this approach (Bacharach, Lipsky, & Shedd, 1984; Murnane & Cohen, 1986).

At the other extreme, those who view teachers as free agents argue that teaching cannot be evaluated. In this view, effective teaching is an "art" that is dependent on the idiosyncrasies of the free agent and, as an art form, cannot be analyzed or described.

Evaluation systems for the constrained decision maker must place a primary emphasis on evaluating decision-making skills. To the degree that teacher evaluation systems are structured around decision-making skills, teachers, as constrained decision makers, will have a basis for establishing consistent critique and dialogue concerning their professional development. For the constrained decision maker, an evaluation system must accomplish three tasks. First, it must help create a work environment in which the professional teacher can evaluate alternatives, makes decisions, and take creative risks. Many evaluation systems inhibit risk taking and decision making because they specify tasks instead of skills. To evaluate on the basis of tasks is to deprofessionalize teaching and to fail to assure those being evaluated that they will be afforded feedback and opportunities for professional growth.

Second, evaluation systems for constrained decision makers should be developmental rather than remedial. Remedial evaluation systems focus on setting and enforcing minimum standards of performance for teachers, while developmental evaluation systems concentrate on setting "targets" for teacher performance. Goal-oriented, they specify skills that all teachers are expected to develop. Such systems assume that the primary purpose of personnel evaluation in schools is to assure the continued growth of all professional teachers.

Finally, an evaluation system for constrained decision makers must assure that teachers become self-monitoring through peer review. Peer review encourages teachers, as constrained decision makers, to assume responsibility for enhancing the professional growth of their colleagues. Indeed, peer assistance is component of many career ladder programs around the country. However, these plans must also incorporate the first two components of evaluation systems. If mentor teachers simply assure that beginning teachers perform prescribed tasks and activities, or focus only on remediating teacher "deficiencies," it will not matter how many mentor teachers there are. Evaluations will be little more than perfunctory "paper pushing" rather than sources of meaningful feedback.

I have attempted to show how teacher evaluation might be structured to achieve a middle ground between the metaphorical views of the teacher as paper pusher and the teacher as an independent free agent. On one hand, in school organizations, evaluation systems are a source of constraint. Specifically, through peer reviews, evaluation systems can help assure that teachers become self-monitoring. On the other hand, to the degree that evaluation systems are designed to enhance the teacher's decision-making skills, they can also assure that teachers maximize independent judgment and initiative.

Participation

What kind of participation system can be used for the constrained decision maker? Those who metaphorically view teachers as paper pushers maintain that teachers should not be involved in decision making or that participation can be used as a manipulation tactic to gain teacher acceptance of decisions that have already been made (Conley, Schmidle, & Shedd, in press). At the other extreme, those who view teachers as independent free agents maintain that teacher empowerment alone will solve education's problems. The critical question is how to design a system of participation that allows teachers to broaden their decision making beyond the confines of their immediate classrooms without threatening the legitimate authority structure of schools and school districts.

It is critical to make a distinction between decision-making influence and decision-making authority. *Authority* connotes whether an organization member has the final voice in the decision-making process. *Influence* is broader in scope than authority because it connotes informal power (Bacharach & Lawler, 1980). While authority is zero-sum in nature (e.g., one has authority to make a decision or one does not), conceivably all organization members may exercise influence on decisions. Thus, in the context of teacher participation, it should be possible to increase teachers' influence on school decisions without necessarily altering the authority structure of the school or school district.

Teacher decision-making teams can be used to illustrate this point. Malanowski, Kennedy, and Kachris (1986) describe a "professional analysis team" program that was implemented in a school district in New York. The program trained small school-based groups of teachers in problem-solving techniques. The groups met twice per month over a one-year period to work on problems identified through various data gathering and analysis techniques. Moreover, the teams were implemented "without changing the locus of final authority." Thus, while teachers analyzed problems and developed change proposals, administrators retained the final authority for program approval. "This is an essential element [of the teams] because it lessens fear of loss of managerial control and prevents the loss of role and activity coordination, which are legitimate managerial concern" (Malanowski, Kennedy, & Kachris, 1986).

Thus one way of increasing teacher participation is to involve teachers in school and district problem analysis and development of solutions. Only the decision to implement solutions requires final authority. Accordingly, teachers can increase their influence on many phases of decision making, with administrators still retaining final authority for implementation decisions. This illustration serves to sensitize us to the middle ground between whose who maintain that teachers should have little input into decisions beyond their own classroom and those who would "empower" teachers through completely restructuring the authority structure of the school.

BEYOND THE RHETORIC OF LABOR AND MANAGEMENT

I began this chapter by stating that the initial phase of the current reform movement was based on a bureaucratic conception of teachers' work. The assumption was that to "reform" public education, someone, whether a policymakers, state legislator, or administrator, had to determine new and more effective ways of controlling teachers, thereby reducing their uncertainty. The second phase of reform has begun to take into account the uncertain nature of teachers' work and to deal with teachers as professional decision makers. These two phases of reform have introduced two polarities in school management, one based on a metaphorical view of teachers as paper pusher and the other on teachers as "free agents." This dichotomy underlies many of the administrative changes that have been debated throughout the last five years of the reform movement.

It would be all too easy to maintain that, while management views teachers as paper pusher, labor's view of teachers (specifically, the view of teachers, unions) is that of free agents. These accusations have been implicitly tossed back and forth during the past five years of reform. In reality, however, these diametrically opposed positions reflect more of an exercise in polemics than real positions. Most school managers recognize that teachers are professionals who must cope with uncertainty and cannot simply be reduced to paper pushers. Likewise, few teachers' union leaders maintain that teachers should be left to operate as free agents. The problem faced by the past reform movement was that our logic was limited by our metaphors.

In proposing the metaphor of teachers as constrained decision makers, and in illustrating the implications of this metaphor for job design, evaluation, and participation, I have tried to define a realistic middle ground for which the next wave of reform should strive. Unless we begin to strike a middle ground based on management's recognition of teachers as professional decision makers and teachers' recognition that they are accountable to the organizations in which they work, many of our reforms will come to naught.

15

Educational Administration

CHANGING HISTORICAL PERIODS AND CORE VALUES

HISTORICAL periods in school administration carry labels that, with reasonable accuracy, capture the social role and underlying value prescriptions for those occupying leadership positions. In succession, school administrators have been called on to be moral exemplars in the tradition of Protestant evangelicals, social engineers molding the youth of today for the society of tomorrow, and street-level politicians balancing and brokering the demands of potent interest groups. In each of these periods, the problems schools were assigned to solve were presumed to be different, and so, too, were understandings about how school organizations worked and how they were linked to universities. In the last decade, we have seen a renewed emphasis on choice as a central social value. Choice influences school policy decisions as disparate as individualized instruction, magnet schools, and tuition tax credits. If choice became the dominant metaphor of education, it would fundamentally alter the nature of school administration, ushering in a new generation of administrators who are substantially different from their occupational parents.

Historical Periods and Values

Capturing the essence of school leadership with a metaphor is the center-piece of David Tyack and Elizabeth Hansot's (1982) insightful *Managers of Virtue*. For most of the nineteenth century, the role of schools was to further the republican version of the second great religious awakening, joining Christian principles and government. The educator became, in John Dewey's words, "the prophet of the true God and the sharer in the true kingdom of God" (in Tyack & Hansot, 1982, p. 3). Beginning with the Progressive Era, circa 1910, the educators followed the wave of rationality generated by Frederick Taylor's (1911) scientific management movement, and leadership became explicitly tied to authentic expertise in curriculum and school organization. As political reforms divorced school boards from partisan politics, the phrase "neutral professional competence" began to describe the ethos of school administrators as well as that of city managers and other civil servants (Iannaccone & Lutz, 1970).

Beginning in the mid-1950s, the rise of explicit interest groups in education shattered the progressive political consensus. A central vision of education disappeared to be replaced by an era in which politics itself defined the role of educators. If teachers became street-level bureaucrats, to use Michael Lipsky's (1980) phrase, then surely administrators had become street-level politicians, their jobs functionally defined by the necessary brokering of services and balancing of potent interests. Politics became recognized as an explicit part of school administration and political metaphor as part of administrative language (Morgan, 1986).

The Metaphors of Leadership

Each core value shapes administrative practice, thus creating a new metaphor of leadership, a unique problem to be solved, and a distinct attachment to the organizational thought of the time. As Table 15.1 illustrates, if school administrators in the nineteenth century were Protestant evangelicals, those during the Progressive Era were social engineers, and those during the period of discontent were street-level politicians, then school administrators in a choice era will become bureaucratic entrepreneurs.

Table 15.1

Implications of Four Periods of Educational Leadership

	Evangelical Period	*Progressive Period*	*Period of Discontent*	*Period of Choice*
Metaphorical role for administrators	Evangelical ministers	Social engineers	Street-level politicians	Bureaucratic entrepreneurs
Primary problem to solve	Getting organized	Efficient operation	Coalition and organizational maintenance	Engagement of clients and employees
Core values	Morality, industriousness	Achievement	Equity	Liberty or choice
Organizational concepts				
Social system	Closed	Closed	Open	Loose
Authority	Autocracy	Bureaucracy	Polity	Ownership
Rationality	Revealed truth	Categorical	Calculative	Adaptive
Techniques	Charisma	Accounting, field studies	Systems analysis, management science	Network management, empowerment, acculturation
University/field relationship	Developing	Sponsorhip of administrative careers	Elite universities study education, most universities train and certify	Partnership? (not yet developed)

Although they were the forebears of school administration, educational leaders in the nineteenth century were depicted more as advocates of a social movement than as chief executive officers. They formed an "aristocracy of character" that both set the tone and gathered converts for public education (Tyack & Hansot, 1982, p. 7). Their success was extraordinary. In 1850, public schools at all levels accounted for only about half of the funds expended on education; but, by the turn of the century, they had become nearly a monopoly. Leaders did not so much manage as preach a civil religion: "The common school, like the Fourth of July oration, inaugural address, or revival sermon, provided symbols and rituals that strengthened patriotism and pan-Protestant piety."

The social engineers were the proper bureaucrats leading rational, hierarchical institutions. Such an array of public services was possible because schools were depicted as closed systems, worlds unto themselves. Schools used the dominant rationality of the time: correct categorization. Administration existed to create a rational set of categories that could then be put in place throughout a school system, bringing uniformity and standardization that would assure quality. Accreditation standards, teacher certification, and integrated curriculum grew during this era.

Street-level politicians are savvy survivors. They often appear colorless because they have learned the fine art of knowing when to duck, but they have highly developed skills in understanding fundamental interests and satisfying unstable coalitions. Such skills are required to exist in a pluralist and sometimes anti-institutional political environment that simultaneously demands increased public services (such as special education) and a much less institutional environment (such as individualized instruction). The perception of schools as organizations also changed when viewed with open systems theory, which recognizes external demands and supports and a tidal wash of influence between organization and environment. The rationality of administration is one of calculation: thinking problems through before decisions are made. Decision trees, systems analysis, and coalition analysis have become part of the stock in trade of school administration.

Each of these historical periods fashions a different relationship with the university. During the evangelical period, the university relationship was still being developed. However, during the social engineering era, in an explicit effort to professionalize, school administration sought and obtained legitimacy within the university; professors and deans formed the apex of a highly integrated educational elite. University professors became the sponsors and brokers, guiding administrators and also establishing the standards for good schools.

During the street-level political period, the relationship between the universities and the schools bifurcated according the university status. Faculties in elite, research-oriented universities began to *study* education rather than *do* education; and in a curious way, the social distance between the university and the schools became a hallmark of high status among education graduate programs. In the words of one assessment, the message in the graduate schools of education is "Do not prepare teachers or schools personnel or educational administrators. No credit will come to us for dealing with schools that are messy or difficult" (Judge, 1982, p. 41).

Meanwhile, the less selective schools expanded their administrative training programs, many of them offering doctorates and other advanced credentials for the first time. They did not, however, inherit the level of sponsorship formerly enjoyed by the elite schools. School district internal promotion practices, along with requirements for open job posting and antidiscrimination practices, blunted the ability of deans or professors to place students in particular jobs. Also, there were relatively few jobs to be filled as the children of the baby boom passed out of adolescence and into yuppiedom.

"BUREAUCRATIC ENTREPRENEUR": THE CHOICE METAPHOR OF LEADERSHIP

Reduced to the basics, choice involves bilateral selection: Students choose schools, and schools choose students. Choice can be structured in many different ways ranging from vouchers to magnet schools, and the debate still rages over which structures best honor the different values of equity, excellence, and efficiency (see

Kerchner & Boyd, 1988, for a review). However, rather than join the debate over how choice would be provided, this section speculates on the implications of choice as a defining value for school administrators.

If choice were the dominant value, school administrators would become bureaucratic, or public, entrepreneurs, each offering a mix of services and styles of learning designed to attract the students for whom the schools could be most successful. Such an organizational role stands in sharp contrast to that found in the street-level politics era, where administrators were required to accommodate any potent, politically relevant interest. Schools operated under a choice system would require an administrator to attract and hold a clientele but not to serve all comers.

In this environment, schools would be, in some ways, a less protected institution, and like other services that fail to attract a following (family counselling or dentistry, for example), they could face bankruptcy and reorganization. Clients would have an interesting bargaining relationship with schools, one simultaneously more and less powerful than under street-level bureaucracy. Clients could threaten to withdraw children from school more easily than is now the case. But schools could also feel free to release or even expel students and parents whose ideas about education were in great conflict with their own. Schools would, simultaneously, gain more institutional integrity and self-definition and feel pressures toward bland noncontroversiality. Schools that had successfully defined their market would become relatively unresponsive to clients who demanded other options, just as many traditional colleges change only glacially over the years. Other schools that had not been successful in defining a market would find themselves chasing whim, fad, and trend, just as tuition-dependent colleges now do.

Attracting clients and accommodating interest groups are fundamentally different social processes. Whereas interest group accommodation requires that each potent, potentially disruptive group be listened to and answered, client satisfaction requires an individual rather than a group response. Knowing and understanding the client, and creating the cognitive "fit" between client expectation and perception of the school, becomes a central problem.

Organizational Concepts During the Choice Era

In each social period, managerial concepts have been played out within prevailing organizational thought. Thus it is interesting that, in many respects, the current wave of organizational thought about social systems, authority, and rationality has been developed through research into schools and colleges and subsequently applied to corporations and other organizations.

Loose Systems

The idea of loose coupling, or organizations whose parts are not tightly coordinated, grew from observations of how schools and colleges operate. Loose coupling intentionally conveys the image that "coupled events are responsive, but that each event also preserves its own identity and some evidence of its physical or logical separateness" (Weick, 1976, p. 3). This description captures the identity of organizations, such as schools, whose activities are characterized by a relative lack of coordination, planned unresponsiveness, situations when any one of several means will produce the same results, poor observational abilities, and occasions when, no matter what you do, things always come out the same (p. 5). Schools appear tightly coupled in terms of certification (the classification of teachers, students, and topics to be taught) and very loosely coupled in terms of inspection (evaluation, authority, and the technology of curriculum) (Meyer & Rowan, 1978).

Under the rules of bureaucracy, loose coupling equals bad management. But current interpretation finds a virtue in the would-be vice of looseness. Consider the problem of deviant behavior, for instance. Part of the folklore of the firms heralded as excellent in the new management literature is their tolerance of heresy within the organization and even a belief that heresy is necessary to innovation and market response. The phrase *skunk works* was created in these organizations to describe a tolerated but extralegal sub-unit whose inhabitants were busy doing useful things by breaking the organization's own standard operating rules.

Looseness also suggests that too much coordination may be a bad thing. Organizational looseness makes it possible for parts of an organization to function successfully, even when other parts are having trouble. The east coast power grid, whose 1979 failure plunged New York City and environs into darkness, has become the symbol of systems too tight to successfully adapt to an emergency.

Finally, loosely coupled organizations require that we revise our opinions about economies of scale. Large, integrated companies and large schools are no longer seen as models of efficient operation. On the contrary, they are seen as having hurdled into a sea of high transaction and coordination costs while smaller, leaner organizations retained the ability to know and understand their markets. Peters and Waterman (1982), in the best-selling management book of the decade, injected the loose coupling idea into the mainstream of management thought.

Authority through Ownership

Choice as a value legitimates the authority of ownership. As social engineers and street-level politicians, educators acted on behalf of the commonweal and the interest group, both of whom were thought to be surrogates for education's clients (Blau & Scott, 1962). In a choice environment, clients would be expected to pursue their own best interests, and school administrators could flexibly use their resources like proprietors in the private sector as long as they satisfied their clients. Unlike the typical public school principal, an owner can proclaim an attachment to a product or service based on nothing more than personal desire or taste. In a delightful demonstration of this prerogative, a recent article on small brewers quoted Fritz Maytag, president of Anchor Brewing in San Francisco, singing the praises of his barley wine: "It'll never have wide popularity, but I own the place, and I can do what I like. A brewery should have a hallmark—a drink of absolute distinction" (Moon, 1987, p. 84).

Ownership, however, does not necessarily imply a personal economic stake. A human capital investment of self in an idea or vision of a school is altogether as precious a stake as is an investment of physical capital. The central problem for administrators in a choice environment is to gain commitment, matching one's investment of self with the investments of clients and teachers. In this context, ownership becomes broadly spread: corporate rather than a proprietorship.

Successfully creating ownership requires that ownership itself become a motivating factor. Students have to want to work hard and to get into schools that require them to work hard. Teachers have to value their investment in the curriculum. The work itself—teaching, studying, managing—has to carry an incentive value. Extrinsic rewards are a necessary condition in this kind of work but not a sufficient one.

Adaptive Rationality

Ideas about rationality have changed with those about authority. Having the right answers, or being able to figure them out, was the taproot grounding administrative authority in the social engineering and street-level politician periods. However, both educational practice and organizational theory have come to question the existence of unique right answers, and a new genre of administrative texts have started to appear emphasizing leadership in a "non-rational" world (Patterson, Purkey, & Parker, 1986; McPherson, Crowson, & Pitner, 1986). Non-rational in this sense does not mean irrational, and the more apt description is that education appears to be adaptively rational rather than calculatively rational. Educational organizations gain knowledge of themselves heuristically, through trial and error. "What works" in one location or circumstance is not necessarily successful in another. This tendency, already recognized in the literature would certainly be emphasized in a choice environment where matching client and organizational preferences would be paramount to maintaining an orthodox pedagogy.

Managerial Techniques

In a setting characterized by loosely coupled systems, symbolic ownership, and adaptive rationality, school administration would rely on a different set of techniques than those typically emphasized during earlier eras.

Loosely coupled systems require network analysis and management. Because client-responsive organizations are seldom as compartmentalized as existing public bureaucracies, managers will need to analyze the set of interdependencies required for client response. Then, they will have to devote time to create groups of teachers and others with the capability of responding without the high structural overhead and long lag times associated with public bureaucracies. Part of this process involves the management of coupling: choosing those few elements in the organization that will be watched in great detail. These become the touchstones of an organization, almost its trademark, as is IBM's penchant for service (Peters & Waterman, 1982, p. 159). Part of the process is understanding the system maintenance costs of interpersonal and intraorganizational communications implied by networks.

Ownership implies empowerment, that which Kanter (1983, p. 142) calls, "the freedom to act, which arouses the desire to act." The ability to act is created by distributing the "basic commodities" of the organization: its information (data, technical knowledge, political intelligence, expertise); its resources (funds, materials, space, time); and its support (endorsement, backing, approval, legitimacy) (p. 159). Without creating an ability to respond to clients, it is impossible to create the lean, hands-on, close-to-the-client characteristics so prized by writers on entrepreneurial organizations.

Adaptive rationality implies the establishment and management of organizational cultures, whose strong beliefs substitute for bureaucratic rules as an organizational control mechanism (Smircich, 1983). However, cultural norms, unlike bureaucratic rules, have the property of situational adaptivity; they allow teachers, principals, and students to "know" what to do even in the absence of a directive. Cultures are transmitted in story, slogan, and legend, an organizational mythology that often obscures the process of culture creation. Managers create cultures through clear visions, well stated, and by recognizing that mundane events such as visiting class-rooms or conducting weekly school meetings are part of an ongoing process of reality construction.

Schools and Universities

The shape of a new relationship between schools and universities is not yet clear. If choice is constructed along strongly professional lines, as is the case in medicine, the role of the university in legitimating educators' professionalism and in advancing the field of practice is likely to strengthen. No occupation has gained professional status without connection to a university. The growing connection between schools and universities some 70 years ago strongly influenced the development of "neutral professional competence" among school administrators. However, the relationship is not likely to be as one-sided as it once was. Traditionally, we believed that the university's role was largely educative and that education preceded practice. Much professional education is still based on this notion. But in fluid, entrepreneurial organizations, learning continues over a lifetime of practice, and knowledge often flows from the field of practice to the university. The potential for authentic partnership arrangements is a strong one. Although the model of such partnership does not yet fully exist, some interesting trials are John Goodland's national network and Theodore Sizer's coalition of schools.

Is Choice a Likely Metaphor

The emergence of choice as the defining metaphor for school administration is by no means preordained, but it is likely. Choice or liberty is a powerful social value that attracts populists and libertarians as well as traditional conservatives. It is also a public policy option that represents a compromise between other, competing educational values: excellence, equity, and efficiency.

Americans have diverse social values, not easily captured in the two-dimensional liberal-conservative political scale. During the last decade, political theorists have begun to speak of a society in which identifiable groups join with traditional liberals and conservatives but identify with only part of their values. Libertarians share with conservatives an aversion to government intervention. Populists share with traditional liberals a desire for responsible government. Electoral victories require attracting voters from at least three groups and shaping policies that have strong cross appeal.

In education, choice is a particularly potent appeal. The ability to get the kind of education one wants for one's self or one's children serves both as a reward for those with a pedagogical interest and as a means of defusing fights between interests over who should have the ability to impose universal requirements on the system. It is no wonder that a vast array of choices have emerged within public school systems (Lewis, 1987). Schools now offer so many options that they endanger their own ability to form a strong internal identity (Chubb & Moe, 1988). Because offering choice is now part of the established policy arsenal, both clients and policy analysts come upon problems with an expectation of finding options rather than single solutions (Elmore, 1988).

In this respect, the excellence revolution creates a situation of serious and growing political tension. The era of external review and reform initiated in the early 1980s has been, if anything, a frantic effort to re-establish a central political consensus about the purposes of education. The current round of educational reform is ample evidence that those who would alter education have grown intolerant of the belief that some sort of educational truth will emerge from the clash of existing interests.

However, a single definition of excellence is probably impossible. A national core curriculum is highly unlikely, particularly one associated with common set of values, as Doyle (1988) advocates. We are more likely to see the diversity of preference and active educational interests continue simultaneously. These interests grew for very clear historical reasons, namely, the inability or unwillingness of the existing educational establishment to attend to the various needs of handicapped children, inner-city youth, teacher welfare, and other core needs around which advocacy groups have developed.

The idea that a new conception of education administration built on "excellence" would simply override existing interests fails to understand the relationship of each metaphorical era to the previous ones. The administrator of today is the heir of the past, "receiving a handsome legacy from a distant relative" (Tyack & Hansot, 1982, p. 4), and those of the future will labor under history's unseen hand. The metaphor of choice is not so much a repudiation of the past symbol as it is a value that somehow envelops it.

The contradiction between specific interests and general support of excellence will become more apparent when the excellence movement fails to deliver on its promises, as it surely will. The cost of the existing educational reform movement is probably well in excess of the capacity of the states to finance it. In economic terms, we will have created an excess of demand over supply.

The contradiction between social wants and social conditions is, of course, nothing new. What is new, however, is the tendency to resolve these problems through quasi market structures and deregulation. The impulse to provide services and meet client needs that, at one time, would automatically have triggered an appeal to charity or the establishment of a government program is now just as likely to trigger a search for a mechanism that allows people to choose the kind of service they want.

Indeed, the period of educational interests and system responsiveness has increased the expectation that options would be provided. Even the pedagogy built around individual instruction for all children (particularly individual instructional plans for special education students) increases the impetus toward choice.

Choice is an attractive political symbol because it can be made to function as a compromise between the other values. In addition it is attractive to those who value choice for its own sake (Drucker, 1985). Whereas high standards are entirely consistent with the administrative dominance of the progressive era, choice is not. The interest groups—from teacher unions to special education parents—have succeeded in penetrating education to such an extent that individual treatments for children are now considered the norm. Schools are expected to accommodate individual differences in student treatments, and to respect student/parent choice of treatments within the public school setting. As the inconsistency between demands for choice within schools and demands for curricular integrity become apparent, a system of choice between schools is likely to become more widespread. If it does, we will have established new demands upon school leadership and, ultimately, a new metaphor of administration.

16

Students As Active Learners

All too often docile, compliant, and without initiative (p. 54). This is how Theodore Sizer (1984) characterized American high school students at the end of his massive two-year study of high schools. John Goodlad (1983) described "a general picture of considerable passivity among students." The high school teachers surveyed by Goodlad ranked "lack of interest by students" and "lack of interest by parents" as the two most important problems in education.

Studies of time use and time on task in high school show that students actively engage in a learning activity for only about half the time they are scheduled to be in school. Absence rates of 15 percent or more are common. Even when students are in class, the teacher and/or students are on task only part of the time. A study of high schools in Chicago found that public schools with high-achieving students averaged about 75 percent of class time for actual instruction; for schools with low-achieving students, the average was 51 percent of class time (Frederick, 1977). Other studies have found that for reading and math instruction the average engagement rate is about 75 percent (Fischer *et al.*, 1978; Goodlad, 1983; Klein, Tyle & Wright, 1979); for vocational classes it is about 56 percent (Halasz & Behm, 1983), Overall, Frederick, Walberg, and Rasher (1979) estimated 46.5 percent of the potential learning time was lost due to absence, lateness, and inattention.

In 1980, high school students spent an average of 3.5 hours per week on homework. When homework is added to engaged time at school, the total time devoted to study, instruction, and practice is only 18 to 22 hours per week—between 15 and 20 percent of the student's waking hours during the school year. By way of comparison, the typical senior spent 10 hours per week in a part-time job and about 24 hours per week watching television (A.C. Nielsen unpublished data, 1987). Thus, television occupies as much time as learning. Students in other nations spend much less time watching TV: 60 percent less in Switzerland and 44 percent less in Canada (Organization of Economic Cooperation and Development, 1986).

The lack of student interest makes it difficult for teachers to be demanding. As Theodore Sizer has observed: "A lot of the honors students aren't questers. They dodge the hard problems, the hard courses, to keep their averages up" (p. 53). Teachers find it difficult to escape being infected by the lassitude. The students can be cruel if they are not entertained or if they perceive the work load to be too heavy. Ms. Shiffe's class, as described by Sizer, was strikingly similar to one of the classes I visited in my research:

> Even while the names of living things poured out of Shiffe's lecture, no one was taking notes... They did not want to know them and were not going to learn them. Apparently no outside threat—flunking, for example—affected the students. Shiffe could not flunk them all, and if their performance was uniformly shoddy, she would have to pass them all. Her desperation was as obvious as the students' cruelty toward her. (p. 157-158)

How does a teacher avoid this treatment? Sizer's description of Mr. Brody's class provides one example.

> He signaled to the students what the minima, the few questions for a test, were; all tenth- and eleventh-graders could master these with absurdly little difficulty. The youngsters picked up the signal and kept their part of the bargain by being friendly and orderly. They did not push Brody, and he did not push them... Brody's room was quiet, and his students liked him. No wonder he had the esteem of the principal who valued orderliness and

> good rapport between students and staff. Brody and his class had agreement, all right, agreement that reduced the efforts of both students and teacher to an irreducible and pathetic minimum. (p. 156)

Some teachers are able to overcome the obstacles and induce students to undertake tough learning tasks. But for most the students' lassitude is demoralizing. Everyone in the system recognizes that there is a problem, but each group fixes blame on someone else. As one student put it:

> As it stands now, there is an unending, ever increasing cyclic problem. Teacher and administrator disinterest, apathy, and their lack of dedication results in students becoming even more unmotivated and docile, which in turn allows teachers to be less interested and dedicated. If students don't care, why should teachers? If teachers don't care, why should the students? (Krista, 1987)

Yest, it is a classic chicken-versus-egg problem. We assign teachers the responsibility for setting high standards, but we do not give them any of the tools that might be effective for inducing student observance of the academic goals of the classroom. They finally must rely on the force of their own personalities. All too often teachers compromise academic demands because the majority of the class sees no need to accept them as reasonable and legitimate. One must wonder whether, even if salaries were much higher, it would be possible to attract and retain large numbers of teachers who can succeed in teaching difficult material in the face of the obstacles just described.

Student apathy and student motivation are not the entire problem. Parental apathy and parental motivation should also concern us. A comparative study of education in Taiwan, Japan, and the United States shows that *even though American children were learning the least in school, American parents were the most satisfied with the performance of their local schools* (Stevenson, Lee, & Stigler, 1986). Why do Japanese and Taiwanese parents hold their children and schools to a higher standard than U.S. parents?

The U.S. lag in mathematics was revealed by the First International Mathematics Study in 1967. Test scores turned down in 1968. Why did it take until 1981 for a major educational reform movement to get underway? Thus the problem of apathy and motivation is as much a societal problem as it is a parental, a teacher, or a student problem.

REASONS FOR APATHY

The fundamental cause of the apathy and motivation problem is the way we recognize and reinforce student effort and achievement. During the 1960s and 1970s we adopted practices and developed institutions that hid from ourselves our failure to teach, protected adolescents from the consequences of failing to learn, and prevented many of those who did learn from reaping the fruits of their labor. The problem is that although there are benefits to *staying in* school, *most students realize few benefits from working hard in school.* The lack of incentives for effort is a consequence of three phenomena:

- The labor market fails to reward effort and achievement in high school.
- The peer group actively discourages academic effort.
- Admission to selective colleges is not based on an absolute or external standard of achievement in high school subjects. It is based instead on aptitude tests that do not assess the high school curriculum and on such measures of student performance as class rank and grade point averages, which are defined relative to classmates' performances, not relative to an external standard.

Absence of Economic Reward for Effort in High School

The educational decisions of students are significantly influenced by the costs (in money, time and psychological effort) and benefits (praise, prestige, employment, wage rates, and job satisfaction) that result. Any number of empirical studies confirm this (Freeman, 1971, 1976a, 1976b; Bishop, 1977). When asked why they work hard in school and/or why they care about grades, college-bound students typically respond "to get into college" or "to get into a good college." For students who plan to look for a job immediately after high school, however, the situation is different. They typically spend less time on their studies than do those who plan to attend college, in large part because most of them see very little connection between performance in high school and their future success in the labor market. Their teachers, of course, tell them that they are wrong, that they will be able to get a better job if they study hard. But when the students observe the success of prior graduates, they can see that success does not depend on how much they learned in high school. Fewer than a quarter of tenth-graders believe that geometry, trigonometry, biology, chemistry, and physics are needed to qualify for their first-choice occupation (Longitudinal Study of American Youth, 1988). Statistical studies of the youth labor market confirm their skepticism about the economic benefits of taking tough courses and studying hard:

- For high school students, high school grades and performance on academic achievement/aptitude tests have essentially no impact on labor market success. They have
  - no effect on the chances of finding work when one is seeking it during high school
  - no effect on the wage rate of the jobs obtained while in high school (Hotchkiss, Bishop, & Gardner, 1982)
- For those who do not go to college full time, high school grades and test scores had
  - no effect on the wage rate of the jobs obtained immediately after high school in Kang and Bishop's (1984) analysis of High School and Beyond seniors and only a 1 to 4.7 percent increase in wages per standard deviation (SD) improvement in test scores and grade point average in Meyer's (1982) analysis of class of 1972 data
  - a moderate effect on wage rates and earnings after four or five years [Gardner (1982) found an effect of 4.8 percent per SD of achievement and Meyer (1982) found an effect of 4.3 to 6.0 percent per SD of achievement]

- a small effect on the probability of being employed immediately after high school

- In almost all entry-level jobs, wage rates reflect the level of the job, not the worker's productivity. Thus, the employer, not the worker, benefits from a worker's greater productivity. Academic achievement and higher productivity make promotion more likely, but it takes time for the imperfect sorting process to assign a particularly able worker a job that fully uses that greater ability—and pays accordingly.

The long delay before labor market rewards are received is important because most teen-agers are present- oriented, so benefits promised for ten years in the future may have little influence on their decisions.

Benefits to Society of Academic Achievement

Although the economic benefits of higher achievement to the employee are quite modest and do not appear until long after graduation, the benefits to the employer (and therefore to national production) are immediately apparent in higher productivity. Over the last 80 years, industrial psychologists have conducted hundreds of studies, involving many hundreds of thousands of workers, on the relationship between productivity in particular jobs and various predictors of that productivity. They have found that scores on tests measuring competence in reading, mathematics, science, and problem solving are strongly related to productivity on the job (Ghiselli, 1973).

Figure 16.1 compares the percentage effect of mathematical and verbal achievement (specifically, a difference of three grade-level equivalents in test scores or 0.7 grade point average (GPA) points on a 4-point scale) on the productivity of a clerical worker, on wages of male clerical workers (from Taubman & Wales, 1975), and on the wages of young women who have not gone to college (from Kang & Bishop, 1984, and Meyer, 1982). Productivity clearly increases much more than wage rates. *Apparently it is a youth's employer, not the youth, who benefits the most when a non-college-bound student works hard in school and improves his or her academic achievements.* The youth is more likely to find a job, but not one with an appreciably higher wage.

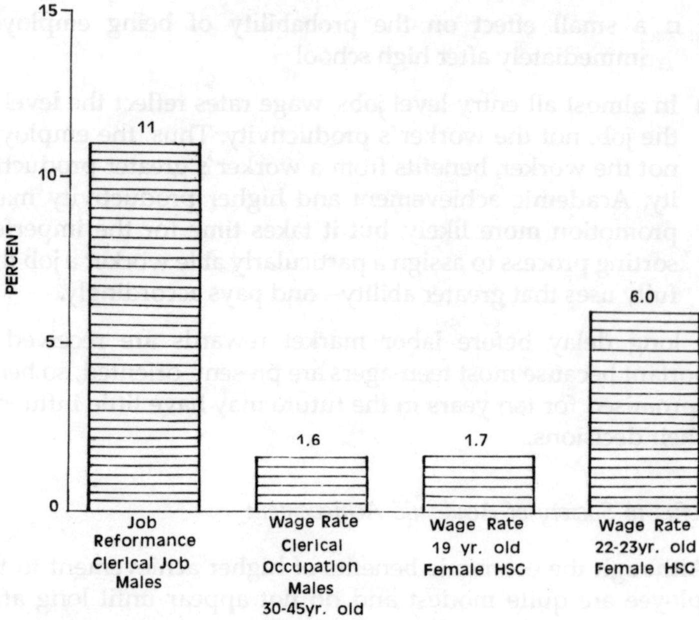

Fig. 16.1 Effect of Academic Achievement on Productivity.

Note: The source of the estimate of the effect of academic achievement on productivity is as follows. Studies that measure output for different workers in the same job at the same firm, using physical output as a criterion, have found that the standard deviation of output varies with job complexity and averages about .164 in routine clerical jobs and .278 in clerical jobs with decision-making responsibilities (Hunter, Schmidt, & Judiesch, 1988). Because there are fixed costs to employing an individual (facilities, equipment, light, heat, and overhead functions such as hiring and payrolling), the coefficient of variation of marginal products of individuals will be considerably greater (Klein, Spady, & Weiss, 1983). On the assumption that the coefficient of variation of marginal productivity for clerical jobs is 30 percent [1.5*(.35*.278+.67*.164)], a .5 validity for general mental ability implies that an academic achievement differential between two individuals of one standard deviation (in a distribution of high school graduates) is associated with a productivity differential in the job of about 11 percent (.5*.74*30%). The ratio of the high school graduate test score standard deviation to the population standard deviation is assumed to be .74.

Why Wage Rates Do Not Vary According to Productivity on the Job

Employers are competing for better workers. Since research demonstrates that academic achievement is a good predictor of productivity, why doesn't this competition result in much higher wages for graduates with high GPAs and achievement test scores? The cause appears to be the lack of objective information available to employers on the applicant's academic accomplishments and skills.

Tests are available for measuring competency in reading, writing, mathematics, science, and problem solving; but court decisions (e.g., *Griggs* vs. *Duke Power Company*, 1971), and pressure from the Equal Employment Opportunity Commission (EEOC) resulted in a drastic reduction in their use after 1971. A 1987 survey of a stratified random sample of small and medium-sized employers who were members of the National Federation of Independent Business (NFIB) found that aptitude test scores had been obtained in only 2.9 percent of the hiring decisions studied (Bishop & Griffin, forthcoming).

Other potential sources of information on effort and achievement in high school are transcripts and referrals from teachers who know the applicant. Both these means are underused. In the NFIB survey, transcripts had been obtained prior to the selection decision for only 14.2 percent of the hiring events in which a high school graduate was hired. If a student or graduate has given written permission for a transcript to be sent to an employer, the Buckley amendment obligates the school to respond. Many high schools are not, however, responding to such requests. Nationwide Insurance, one of Columbus, Ohio's, most respected employers, sent over 1,200 such signed requests to high schools in 1982 and received only 93 responses. Employers reported that colleges were much more responsive to transcript requests than were high schools. High schools have apparently designed their systems for responding to requests for transcripts around the needs of college-bound students, not around the needs of those students who seek a job immediately after graduating.

There is an additional barrier to the use of high school transcripts in selecting new employees—when high schools do respond, it takes a very long time. For Nationwide Insurance, the response almost invariably took more than two weeks. Given this time lag, if employers required transcripts prior to making hiring selections, a job offer could not be made until a month or so after an application had been received. Most jobs are filled much more rapidly than that. The 1982 NCRVE employer survey of employers found that 83.5 percent of all jobs were filled in less than a month, and 65 percent were filled in less than two weeks.

The only information about school experiences requested by most employers is years of schooling, diplomas and certificates obtained, and area of specialization. Probably because of unreliable reporting and the threat of EEOC litigation, only 15 percent of the NFIB employers asked the applicants with 12 years of schooling to report their grade point average. Despite their limited use in selecting employees, employers apparently believe that GPAs are good predictors of future productivity. A policy capturing experiment with a nationwide sample of 750 employers found that employer ratings of completed job applications were more affected by high school grade point average than by any other single worker characteristic (Hollenbeck & Smith, 1984).

Hiring on the basis of recommendations by high school teachers is also uncommon. In the NFIB survey, when someone with 12 years of schooling was hired, the new hire had been referred or recommended by vocational teachers only 5.2 percent of the time and referred by someone else in the high school only 2.7 percent of the time.

Consequently, hiring selections and starting wage rates often do not reflect the competencies and abilities students have developed in school. Instead, hiring decisions are based on observable characteristics (such as years of schooling and field of study) that serve as signals for the competencies the employer cannot observer directly. *As a result, the worker's starting wage primarily reflects the average productivity of all workers with the same set of educational credentials rather than that individual's productivity or academic achievement.* A study of how individual wage rates varied with job performance found that when people hired for the same or very similar jobs are compared, workers who are 20 percent more productive than the average received wage offers that were only 1.6 percent higher than average (Bishop, 1987).

After a year at the firm, the more productive workers were more likely to be promoted, but the impact of reported productivity on a worker's relative wage was still quite low. A 20 percent productivity differential generated a 4 percent wage differential at nonunion firms with about 20 employees and no wage differential at unionized establishments with more than 100 employees and at nonunion establishments with more than 400 employees.

Employers have a number of good reasons for not varying the wage rates of their employees in proportion to their perceived job performance. All feasible measures of individual productivity are unreliable and unstable. Workers are reluctant to accept jobs in which the judgment of one supervisor can result in a large wage decline in the second year on the job (Hashimoto & Yu, 1980; Stiglitz, 1974).

Most productivity differentials are specific to the firm, and this reduces the risk that not paying a particularly productive worker a comparably higher salary will result in his going elsewhere (Bishop, 1987). Pay that is highly contingent on performance can also weaken cooperation and generate incentives to sabotage others (Lazear, 1986). Finally, in unionized settings, the union's opposition to merit pay will often be decisive.

This evidence implies that the benefits of developing one's verbal, mathematical, and scientific capabilities are considerably greater to society than to the individual. Despite their higher productivity, *young workers who have achieved in high school and who have done well on academic achievement tests do not receive higher wage rates immediately after high school.*

The student who works hard must wait many years to start really benefiting, and even then the magnitude of the wage and earnings effect—a 1 to 2 percent increase in earnings per grade level equivalent on achievement tests—is considerably smaller than the actual change in productivity that results.

The Zero-sum Nature of Academic Competition in High School

The second root cause of the lack of real motivation to learn is peer pressure against studying hard. Students report that "in most of the regular classes...[i]f you raise your hand more than twice in a class, you are called a 'teacher's pet'." It's O.K. to be smart, you cannot help that. It is definitely not O.K. to study hard to get a good grade. This is illustrated by the following story, related by one of my students:

> Erroneously I was lumped into the brains genus by others at school just because of the classes I was in. This really irked me; not only was I not an athlete but I was also thought of as one of those "brain geeks." Being a brain really did have a stigma attached to it. Sometimes during a free period I would sit and listen to all the brains talk about how much they hated school work and how they never studied and I had to bite my lip to keep from laughing out loud. I *knew* they were lying, and they knew they were lying too. I think that a lot of brains hung around together only because their fear of social isolation was greater than their petty rivalries. I think that my two friends who were brains liked me because I was almost on their level but I was not competitive. (Tim, 1986)

The primary reason for peer pressure against studying is that pursuing academic success forces students into a zero-sum competition with their classmates. Their achievement is not being measured against an absolute, external standard. In contrast to scout merit badges, for example, where recognition is given for achieving a fixed standard for competence, the schools' measures of achievement assess performance relative to follow students through grades and class rank. When students try hard to excel, they set themselves apart, cause rivalries and may make things *worse* for friends. *When we set up a zero-sum competition among close friends, we should not be surprised when they decide not to compete.* All work groups have ways of sanctioning "rate busters." High school students call them "brain geeks," "grade grubbers" and "brown nosers."

Young people are not lazy. In their jobs after school and at football practice they work very hard. In these environments they are part of a team, where individual efforts are visible and appreciated by teammates. Competition and rivalry are not absent, but they are offset by shared goals, shared successes, and external measures of achievement (i.e., satisfied customers or winning the game). On the sports field, there is not greater sin than giving up, even when the score is hopelessly one-sided. On the job, tasks not done by one worker will generally have to be completed by another. In too many high schools, when it comes to academics, there is no greater sin than trying hard.

The second reason for peer norms against studying is that most students perceive the chance of receiving recognition for an academic achievement to be so slim they have given up trying. At most high school awards ceremonies, the recognition and awards go to only a few—those at the very top of the class. By ninth grade most students are already so far behind the leaders that they know they have no realistic chance of being perceived as academically successful. Their reaction is often to denigrate the students who take learning seriously and to honor other forms of achievement—athletics, dating, holding your liquor, and being "cool"—that offer them better chances of success.

The lack of external standards for judging academic achievement and the resulting zero-sum nature of academic competition in the school also influences parents, the school board, and local school administrators. Parents can see that setting higher academic standards or hiring better teachers will not improve their child's grade point average or class rank. Raising standards at the high school will have only minor effects on how one's child does on an SAT that is purposely designed to be curriculum-free, so why worry about standards? In any case, doing well on the SAT matters only for the small minority who aspire to attend a selective college. Most students are planning to attend a public college, many of which admit all high school graduates from the state who have completed the requisite courses. Scholarships are awarded on the basis of financial need, not academic merit.

The parents of children who are not planning to go to college have an even weaker incentive to demand high standards at the local high school. They believe that what counts in the labor market is getting the diploma, not learning algebra. They can see that learning more will be of only modest benefit to their child's future, and that higher standards might jeopardize what is really important—the diploma.

Only when educational outcomes are aggregated at the state or national level do the real costs of mediocre schools become apparent. The whole community loses because the work force is less efficient, and it becomes difficult to attract new industry to an area. As competitiveness deteriorates, the whole nation's standard of living declines. This is precisely the reason that employers, governors, and state legislatures have been the energizing force behind school reform. State governments, however, are far removed from the classroom, and the instruments available to them for imposing reform are limited. If students, parents, and school board officials perceive the rewards for learning to be minimal, then state efforts to improve the quality of education will not succeed.

INCENTIVES TO LEARN IN OTHER NATIONS

The tendency to underreward effort and learning in school appears to be a peculiarly American phenomenon. In Japan and many European countries, the educational system administers achievement test batteries (e.g., the O Levels in the United Kingdom, or the Baccalaureate in France) that are closely tied to the curriculum. Performance on these exams is the primary determinant of the university and the field of study to which a student is admitted. The credentials that are awarded to secondary school completers signal not only that the individual has passed a particular set of exams, but also the level of the pass. Top companies in Japan and Europe often hire lifetime employees directly out of secondary schools; and performance on these exams, together with teacher recommendations and schools grades, has a significant impact on who is chosen to work at the more prestigious firms (Leestma *et al.*, 1987; Reubens, 1969). Germany has no common national or provincial exams, so grades in school are a crucial determinant of the employer with whom a German youth apprentices and the university and specialty college—bound students are able to enter.

In Japan the best jobs are available only to those who are recommended by their high school. The most prestigious firms have long-term arrangements with particular high schools, to which they delegate the responsibility of selecting new employees for the firm. It is universally understood that when more than one student is interested in a particular job, the student with the highest grades and best exam results is to be referred. The number of graduates that a high school is able to place in this way depends on its reputation and the company's past experience with graduates from the school. Schools with poorly prepared students find it difficult to place them in good jobs. A school that does not live up to this implicit understanding loses the opportunity to make referrals in the future, the following incident demonstrates what happens when meritocratic principles are set aside by the school.

> A couple of years ago, after the school decided to recommend a student for a job, another student told us that he wished to apply for the same firm, and he [and his parents] said he had strong personal connections with an executive in the firm. Although we were not comfortable about doing this, we allowed the second student to apply [and we] withdrew the other [better qualified] student. Later, the firm complained that the student lacked the requisite ability and they have stopped offering a job to us since then. We visited and explained what happened, but, after all, we lost the relation with the firm. (Furikawa, 1986, article written by a teacher in charge of job placement in a high school, quoted in Rosenbaum & Kariya, 1987, p. 10)

Japanese parents know that their son or daughter's future economic and social rank in society critically depends on which high school is attended and on how much is learned in school. Entry into the better high schools depends primarily on the child's performance in junior high school, not on where the parents can afford to live, as in the United States. Because the reputation of the high school is so important, the competitive pressure reaches down into junior high school. Forty-five percent of junior high school students attend *juku*, private schools that provide tutoring in the subjects that will be tested on the exam given to determine the high school to which one is admitted. Because of the importance of the national exams in the allocation of students to high school, colleges, and jobs, learning achievement tends to be measured in relation to everyone else in the state or nation, not just relative to one's classmates in the school. These are the reasons that Japanese parents demand so much of their children and of their schools. It is why Japanese fifth-graders spend 32.6 hours a week involved in academic activities, while American youngsters devote only 19.6 hours to their studies (Stevension, Lee, & Stigler, 1986).

Japanese adolescents work extremely hard in high school, but once they have entered college they stop working. For most students, a country club atmosphere prevails. The reason for the change in behavior is that employers apparently care only about which university the youth attends, not about the individual's academic achievement at the university. *Studying very hard is not a national character trait; it is a response to the way Japanese society rewards academic achievement.*

American students, in contrast, take it easy in high school but generally work quite hard in college. This change is caused in large part by the fact that when higher level jobs requiring a bachelor's or associate's degree are being filled, employers pay much more attention to grades and teacher recommendations than they do when they hire high school graduates. The NFIB survey found that when college graduates were hired, 26.5 percent of the employers had reviewed the college transcript before making the selection, 10.9 percent had obtained a recommendation from a major professor, and 6.5 percent had obtained a recommendation from a professor outside of the graduate's major or from the college's placement office.

If learning were defined by an absolute standard and not by one's ranking in the school, and if the rewards for learning were as attractive as they are in Japan, everyone—students, teachers, parents, and school boards—would behave very differently. Parents would demand that their school be the best and would be willing to tax themselves heavily to achieve that result. The status and salary of secondary school teachers would rise, the requirements for entry into the profession would increase, and standards of teacher performance would improve. If parents were not satisfied with their child's academic progress, they would send him or her to a tutor, just as Japanese parents do. Adolescents would no longer be such reluctant learners.

HOW TO IMPROVE THE QUALITY OF EDUCATION

The rapid gains in academic achievement overseas and declining achievement here spell trouble for the U.S. economy (Koretz, 1986, Bishop, 1989). The problem is so serious and so long-standing that nothing short of radical reform will help. Most of the reforms now underway are desirable, but by themselves they are insufficient.

Proposed reforms of secondary education include stricter graduation requirements; more homework; increases in the amount and difficulty of course material; greater emphasis on the basics (English, math, science, social science, computer science); and improvements in the quality of teaching through higher salaries, career ladders, and competence tests for teachers. Though important, these reforms are limited in that they emphasize changes in the content and quality of what is offered by the school and require the student to work harder, without giving sufficient attention to how to *motivate* students to work harder. Learning is not a passive act; it requires the time and active involvement of the learner. In a classroom with 1 teacher and 18 students, there are 18 learning hours spent to every 1 hour of teaching time. Student time is, therefore, very important, and how intensely that time is used affects learning significantly. Clearly, then, attention needs to be given to how much time and energy students devote to learning.

The key to motivation is recognizing and rewarding learning. Individual learning goals should be established that challenge the student to the maximum extent possible. Achievement of these goals would be assessed by the school and recognized at an awards ceremony. The student would receive a competency profile describing these achievements that would aid in securing employment. If employers know who has learned what, they will provide the rewards.

The second way schools can generate stronger incentives for learning is to restructure schoolwide and classroom recognition of student achievement so that everyone has a chance to be recognized for his or her contribution: Greater effort by everybody makes everybody better off, and there are significant rewards for learning and real consequences for failing to learn. As Theodore Sizer has advocated, "The better the performance, the greater [should be] the latitude given the student" (1984, p. 67). Bloom's theory of mastery learning says that there are no differences in *what* people can learn, only differences in the *rate* at which people learn. Given enough time, almost everyone can achieve mastery. Students who fail to learn on the first try should commit extra time to learning task, with extra classes scheduled after school and during the summer. *Learning* would be defined as gaining in competence and knowledge, not as meeting an absolute standard of performance. The gifted and the handicapped would be stretched, as would everyone else. The reward for effort and for learning would be free time. Schools would be open all day and all year, and enrichment programs designed to attract all students would be offered during the additional time. Everyone would be encouraged to participate, but only the unsuccessful learners would be obligated to participate.

Some might respond to these proposals by stating a preference for intrinsic over extrinsic motivation of learning. This, however, is a false dichotomy. Nowhere else in our society do we expect people to devote thousands of hours to a difficult task while receiving *only* intrinsic rewards. Public recognition of achievement and the symbolic and material rewards received by achievers are important generators of instrinsic motivation. They are, in fact, one of the central way a culture symbolically transmits and promotes its values.

It goes without saying that these reforms involve a radical restructuring of our schools. No-fault adolescence and the zero-sum nature of academic competition would pass from the scene. The incentives faced by everyone in the system would change and this would probably lead to a major increase in public investment in education. The proposed reforms are not simple to implement and they need not be implemented all at once. The following discussion of these recommendations is organized into five sections, dealing with these topics:

1. Improving measures of academic achievement.
2. Getting the peer group to encourage learning.
3. Creating new learning opportunities in school.
4. Generating additional recognition and reward for learning.
5. Helping students obtain good jobs.

Improving Measures of Academic Achievement

Institute Statewide Examinations

States should adopt statewide tests of competency and knowledge that are specific to the curriculum being taught, like New York State's Regents Examinations. If a state does not have such exams, a school district (or the members of each department of a school) could establish its own exams. Such examinations would offer several benefits. They would:

- better inform students and parents about how well the student is doing, and thus help parents work with teachers to improve their children's performance.
- Make the relationship between teachers and students more cooperative, with the teacher and students working jointly to prepare the students for the exam.
- Strengthen students' incentives to learn because they would now be able to signal to their parents and employers their competence in specific curriculum areas.
- Create a data base that school boards and parents could use to evaluate the quality of education being provided by their local school.
- Enable employers to use scores on these examinations to help improve their selection of new employees. If the uncertainties involved in hiring are reduced, expanding employment will become more profitable, total employment will increase, and recent high school graduates will be better able to compete with more experienced workers.

Reform the SAT and ACT Tests

Although national tests are necessary, the Scholastic Aptitude Test (SAT) is not the kind of test that is helpful. The SAT suffers from two very serious limitations: the limited range of the achievements that are evaluated and its multiple-choice format. The test was designed to be curriculum-free. To the extent that it evaluates students' understanding of material taught in schools, the material it covers is vocabulary and elementary and junior high school mathematics. Most subjects studied in high school-science, history, civics, technology, computers, trigonometry, and statistics—are completely absent from the test. As a result, it fails to generate incentives to take the more demanding courses or to study hard. The multiple-choice format is also a severe limitation. National and provincial exams in Europe are predominantly essay examinations. The absence of essays on the SAT and the American College Testing Program's ACT test contributes to the poor writing skills of U.S. students. The test advertises itself as an ability test but is, in fact, an achievement test measuring a very limited range of achievements.

Jencks and Crouse (1982) have made many of the same criticisms of the SAT and have recommended that it evaluate a much broader range of achievements. I support their position. A portion of the test should involve writing an essay. Knowledge and understanding of literature, history, technology and science, and higher order thinking skills should all be assessed.

Colleges should require that students take at least two subject-specific exams. The advanced placement exams are examples of the kind of examinations we need. These exams should not be limited to the multiple-choice format. Foreign language exams, for example, should test conversational skills as well as reading and writing. Students taking science courses should be expected to conduct experiments and demonstrate the use of laboratory equipment.

Certifying Competencies

Schools should provide graduates with certificates or diplomas that certify students' knowledge and competencies, not just their attendance. Competency should be defined by an absolute standard, just as Scout merit badges are. Different types and levels of competency need to be certified. Minimum competency tests for receiving a high school diploma do not satisfy the need for better signals of achievement in high school. Because some students arrive in high school so far behind, and the consequences of not getting a diploma are so severe, we have not been willing to set the minimum competency standard very high. But once they satisfy the minimum, many students stop putting effort into their academic courses. What is needed is a more informative credential that signals the full range of student achievements (e.g., statewide achievement exam scores, competency check lists).

Competency Profiles

Another way to motivate students is to give them feedback on their accomplishments through the mechanism of a criterion-referenced competency profile. Competency profiles are a checklist of competencies needed in a specific occupation that the student either has or can develop through study and practice. The ratings of competence that appear on a competency profile are relative to an absolute standard, not relative to their classmates. By evaluating students against an absolute standard, the competency profile avoids a negative feedback of one student's effort into another student's grade. Unlike the present zero-sum game, it does not discourage students from sharing their knowledge and teaching each other.

A second advantage of the competency profile approach to evaluation is that students can see their progress as new skills are learned and checked off. The skills not yet checked off are the learning goals for the future. Seeing such a checklist get filled up is inherently reinforcing.

With a competency profile system, goals can be tailored to the student's interests and capabilities, and progress toward these goals can be monitored and rewarded. Students who have difficulty in their required academic subjects could nevertheless take pride in the developing occupational competence now recognized just as prominently as course grades in academic subjects. Upon graduation, the competency profile would be encased in plastic and given to the student to serve as a credential certifying occupational competencies.

Gettng the Peer Group to Encourage Learning

Cooperative Learning

One effective way of inducing peers to value learning and support effort in school is to reward the group for the individual learning of its members. This is the approach taken in cooperative learning. Research results (Slavin, 1985) suggest that the two key ingredients for successful cooperative learning are as follows:

- A cooperative incentive structure—awards based on group performance—seems to be essential for students working in groups to learn better.
- A system of individual accountability is needed in which everyone's maximum effort must be essential to the group's success and the effort and performance of each group member must be clearly visible to his or her group mates.

For example, students might be grouped into evenly matched teams of four or five members that are heterogeneous in ability. After the teacher presents new material, the team works together on worksheets to prepare each other for periodic quizzes. The team's score is an average of the scores of team members, and high team scores are recognized in a class newsletter or through group certificates of achievement.

What seems to happen in cooperative learning is that the team develops an identity of its own, and group norms arise that are different from the norms that hold sway in the student's other classes. The group's identity arises from the extensive personal interaction among group members in the context of working toward a shared goal. Because the group is small and the interaction intense, the effort and success of each team member is known to other teammates. Such knowledge allows the group to reward each team member for his or her contribution to the team goal, and this is what seems to happen.

Creating New Opportunities for Learning in School

Turn Schools into All-Day Learning Centers

Schools should remain open after the end of the regular school day. A full range of remedial and enrichment programs, extracurricular activities, and interscholastic sport should be offered. The library should remain open during this period, and the auditorium could be used for showing educational films and videotapes. Extra help would be available for students having difficulty with the core curriculum. Volunteers to provide tutoring and to offer special-interest courses could be recruited from the community. Private teachers of music, art, and other subjects could also use school facilities during these hours. The benefit of this reform is that (1) the regular school day would be freed up for more intensive study of the core curriculum, (2) slower students would be given the extra instruction they need, and (3) the phenomenon of the latchkey child would be significantly reduced or eliminated.

Keep the Schools Open During the Summer

Longitudinal studies of learning have found that the pace of learning slows considerably during the summer and that disadvantaged students, especially, lose ground during the summer months (Heyns, 1987). Experimental evaluations of STEP, a program for disadvantaged youth that combines a part-time summer job with about 90 hours of remediation, has found that adding the remediation to the summer job results in gains in academic achievement of 0.5 grade-level equivalents (Corporation for Public-Private Ventures, 1988). It would appear that summer programs targeted on educationally and economically disadvantaged children are likely to have high payoffs.

A variety of remedial, enrichment, and special-interest short courses should be offered during the summer. Although many of the teachers would be regular school staff, an education degree and state certification would not be required. Private teachers of music, art, athletics, and academic subjects could also offer their own courses at the school. Where appropriate, academic credit would be given for the summer school courses. The school district would provide transportation.

Generating Additional Recognition and Rewards for Learning

A Massive Dose of Mastery Learning

Students who are not learning at the desired rate should be expected to commit additional time to the task after school and during the summer. At the beginning of the school year, school personnel would meet with each student and his or her parents to set goals. Students who are not performing at grade level in core subjects and who do not make normal progress during the school year should be kept after school for tutoring and remedial instruction and required to attend summer school. Assessments of progress should be made at appropriate points during the school year to inform students of their progress and to enable those who are participating in remedial programs after school to demonstrate that they are now progressing satisfactorily. Course grades and teacher evaluations would be a central part of the assessment process, but there should be an external yardstick as well. This might be a competency checklist, a mastery test keyed to the textbook, or an examination specified by the state, by the school, or collectively by the teachers, in that grade level or department. The assessment tools would be established at the beginning of the school year. The external yardstick helps ensure that students perceive the standard to be absolute rather than relative to others in the class, and helps create a communality of interest between teacher and student. Teachers need to be perceived as helping the student achieve the student's goals, not as judges meting out punishment. Final decisions regarding who would be required to attend summer school could be made by committees of teachers, possibly with some administrative representation. Because students will want to avoid being required to get remedial instruction after school and during the summer, this will be a powerful incentive for them to devote themselves to their studies.

Honoring Academic Achievement

Schools should strengthen their awards and honors system for both academic and non-academic accomplishments. The medals, trophies, and school letters awarded in interscholastic athletics are a powerful motivator of achievement on the playing field. Academic pursuits need a similar system of reinforcement. Public school systems in Tulsa and a number of other cities have started awarding school letters for academic achievements. Awards and honors systems should be designed so that almost every student can receive at least one award or honor before graduation if he or she makes the effort.

Outstanding academic performance (e.g., high grades or high test scores) would not have to be the only way of defining excellence. Awards could be given for significant improvements in academic performance since the previous year or since the beginning of the school year, for public service in or out of school, for leadership and participation in extracurricular activities, for participation in student government, for perfect attendance records, and for student of the week (criteria could vary weekly). The standard for making an award should be criterion-referenced: If greater numbers achieve the standard of excellence, more awards should be given.

A prominent place in the school should be reserved for bulletin boards where pictures of the most recent winners and reasons for their receiving recognition could be posted. Another form of recognition could be displays of student work; art, science, social studies, vocational education projects, and so forth. Periodically, the parents of the most recent award winners and sponsoring teachers should be invited to an evening assembly, where the principal would award the students the certificate or plaque recognizing their accomplishments.

Although the primary purpose of this system would be to improve the school's educational climate, a secondary effect would be the creation of a tool to help the student obtain a good job. The potential of these awards as an aid to improving employability should be made clear to students and parents.

Allow Employers to Use Scores on Achievement Tests in Selecting New Hires

There is now a great deal of evidence that scores on tests measuring competence in mathematical reasoning, language arts, science, and technical knowledge are good predictors of job performance in a great variety of jobs and do not discriminate against minorities or women (Hunter & Hunter, 1984, Bishop, 1988). Despite this, Equal Employment Opportunity Commission (EEOC) regulations and case law have in the past required that a very expensive validation study be conducted before a firm can use any test to help select employees. The result has been to diminish greatly the use of tests for employee selection and to reduce the rewards for learning. There is a strong public interest in strengthening the incentives to learn; government regulations should not prevent the use of tests and should encourage the use of broad-spectrum achievement tests covering the high school curriculum, rather than so-called aptitude tests. Adverse impacts on minority groups can be avoided by race-norming the test (as the General Aptitude Test Battery [GATB] currently does) and through affirmative action. Because other instruments are available for achieving societal goals for integration on the job, decisions about employment testing should be based on the effects of these tests on incentives to learn and efficient sorting of workers across jobs.

Helping Students Obtain Good Jobs

Schools can help their graduates avoid unemployment and get better jobs by improving the quality and facilitating the flow of employment-related information to students and their potential employers. Improving the information available to all parties in the job search/hiring system will have the following consequences:

- A greater share of school graduates will find employment.
- The jobs they obtain will pay better and offer more training and job security.
- The better jobs will be distributed more in accordance with the objective merit of the candidate.

- Students will commit a greater amount of time and effort to their studies as they perceive the greater payoffs for doing so.

Policies that facilitate information flow make the connection between effort in school and later labor market success more visible. Such policies include the following.

Offering Courses in Job Search Skills

Schools have an important role to play in preparing youth to navigate in the labor market. Career guidance and career counselling have been viewed as important school functions for many decades. Realizing that a career choice cannot be implemented unless a job can be obtained in the chosen field, many schools are now teaching youths how to search for work (Wegmann, 1979). Students need practice in writing a resume, in interviewing, and in using the more effective informal methods of searching for a job.

Acting as a Source of Informal Contacts

School personnel can be a reference and a source of job contacts for their students. Some students may feel that they do not have and cannot develop good employment contacts. School personnel can help them by building and maintaining trusting relationships with local employers and then helping to match employer and student needs. Students from disadvantaged backgrounds have a special need for this kind of help because their relatives and neighbors typically lack the employment contacts of middle-class families.

Many schools provide job placement and referral services for their students and graduates. Three and a half million people found their current job through a referral by a teacher, school, or college (Rosenfeld, 1975). This function of schools is much more important than is generally thought.

Whenever possible, there should be a one-to-one relationship between a specific teacher or administrator and an employer. A study by McKinney, Franchak, Halasz-Salster, Morrison, and McElwain (1982) found that *when schools formalize this relationship by creating a placement office, the number of jobs found for vocational students tended to decrease*. The best example of an informal contact system is the one that exists for many vocational students. Vocational teachers often know local employers in related fields; they also know students well enough to recommend them. This kind of informal system could be expanded to include all students not planning to attend college.

Guiding Students in Assessing Jobs and Employers

Students need help in assessing jobs, and schools can give them the information necessary to make these assessments. Career guidance tends to focus on the individual's choice of occupation, but attention also needs to be given to selecting an employer and matching employer and employee needs. Young people who find good, high-paying jobs with promotion opportunities will end up changing jobs less often. Students need to learn how to assess such dimensions of a firm as training opportunities, promotion opportunities, job security provisions, maternity leave rules, vacation policies, policies regarding tardiness, friendliness of co-workers, effectiveness of supervision, medical insurance, educational leave, and tuition reimbursement.

Releasing Student Records

The school can help students provide employers with information by developing an equitable and efficient policy for releasing student records. While developing this policy, school officials should keep in mind their dual responsibilities of protecting the student's right to privacy and helping students find good, suitable jobs. The student and his or her parents should receive certified copies of the transcript and other records that might be released.

Schools can develop a form that would explain to parents and students their rights, as well as the pros and cons of disclosing information. The Buckley Amendment requires that the form specify the purpose of disclosure, which records are to be released, and who is to receive the records. The law allows the student to specify a "class of parties." The class specified could be "all potential employers contacted by the student," which would cut down on the necessary paperwork. Once the student has filed a request, the school is required by law to comply. Schools can best serve students by handling all inquiries expeditiously and without charge.

Developing a Job Search Portfolio

Schools should consider providing students with a job search portfolio or competency profile that records all their accomplishments in one place. Students attempting to market themselves to employers will have greater success if all their school achievements are summarized in one compact, standardized document. Compactness and standardization make it easier for employers to use information in their hiring decisions, and this facilitate information flow.

The coverage and format of the document are probably best worked out cooperatively by a committee that includes school administrators, employers, and other interested parties. Developing and using such a document might be a part of a campaign to enlist commitments from major local employers to hire the school's graduates. Developing the information system cooperatively is a good way to ensure that the finished form will be beneficial to schools, employers, and students.

Students have many talents and skills that can be highlighted in such a document. The job search portfolio should emphasize accomplishments and performance indicators that are most useful in identifying a good match between a job and a youth. Students and parents receive copies of it, and students should be encouraged to bring copies with them when they apply for jobs. Employers should be encouraged to ask to see the portfolio and keep a copy when a job application is filed.

SUMMARY

Institutional arrangements of schools and the labor market have profound effects on the incentives faced by students, teachers, parents, and school administrators. When educational credentials are awarded for time served rather than for learning achievements, the incentive to devote time and energy to learning is significantly weakened. The passivity and inattention of students, the low morale of teachers, the defeat of so many school levies, and low U.S rankings on international measures of achievement are all logical outcomes of institutional arrangements that weaken student incentive to study and parental incentives to fund a high-quality education. Only with an effective of rewards within schools and in the labor market can we hope to overcome this pervasive apathy and achieve excellence.

5B8/4208/25